P9-DCI-369

"Mike Parfit is . . . a sensitive guy with a freewheeling mind and a knack for adventure. . . . Fully aware of the great white terror, Parfit yet succumbed to the strange, powerful lure of the Last Continent." —*Smithsonian Magazine*

"In *South Light* the reader too experiences the exhilaration and the exhaustion, the camaraderie and the loneliness, the energy and intrepidity, and the calm acceptance of everyday danger. It's the next best thing to being there." —*The New York Times*

"An alluring story of science and people and how they mix and mingle in the harshest, most uninhabitable spot on Earth." —*Arlington* (Virginia) *Journal*

"*South Light* blends the clarity of science writing and the adventure of exotic faraway places into a satisfying brew." —Cultural Information Services

"This is the best all-purpose book you will ever see. . . . Michael Parfit is a keen observer who writes well. He sees things clearly and describes them *con brio* as the musicians say — with spirit." —*Sunday Telegram*

"This fast-moving, entertaining account is the best of travel writing, combining exhilarating adventure with intellectual discovery." —*Library Journal*

"Parfit's ability to describe what he saw and felt and thought gives a more vivid picture than any camera could provide." —*San Diego Magazine*

"Parfit has delivered a book full of treasures. *South Light* reveals wonders from a world separate from ours." —*Wichita* (Kansas) *Eagle-Beacon*

"A fascinating portrait of a land and the remarkable men and women who heed its challenge . . . a beautiful story filled with brilliant travel writing, splendid narrative history, and epic adventure."
—Ames (Iowa) *Tribune*

"This book is something like the antarctic life it describes: fascinating, always surprising, sometimes disorienting, sometimes almost unapproachable in its strangeness, often hauntingly beautiful, in the end unforgettable."
—*The Virginian-Pilot*

"A well-written account of a part of the world few of us will ever see and few of us have even read about."
—*San Diego Union*

"*South Light* should make cool reading for hot summer."
—*American Statesman*

"Like all fine travel books, this one arouses an itch to follow the author's trail."
—*Autoweek*

"A gifted journalist's account of a full season spent on Antarctica in the company of scientists. An evocative portrait of the last wilderness."
—*Not Man Apart*

"Mr. Parfit has a poet's imagination and a journalist's eye in getting down majestic sweep and gritty detail. . . . *South Light* is an evocative reminder that among human society's material comforts and ecological vulnerabilities there still exist places of primordial vigor."
—*The Kansas City Star*

"If you cannot be there to experience that fleeting but oh-so-poignant feeling that you are doing something you will never do again, meeting extraordinary people you will never meet again, seeing a world unlike any other, Parfit's book will give you a splendid taste of it."
—Gannett News Service

SOUTH LIGHT

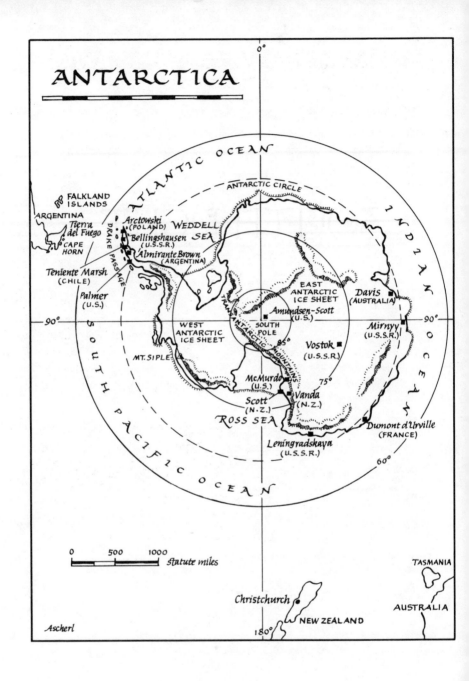

SOUTH LIGHT

A JOURNEY TO THE

LAST CONTINENT

MICHAEL PARFIT

COLLIER BOOKS

Macmillan

Publishing

Company

NEW YORK

Macmillan Publishing Company
866 Third Avenue, New York, N.Y. 10022
Collier Macmillan Canada, Inc.

Library of Congress Cataloging-in-Publication Data
Parfit, Michael.
South light.
1. Parfit, Michael.   2. Antarctic regions—
Discovery and exploration.   I. Title.
G850 1983.P36A36   1987   919.8'904   86-29886
ISBN 0-02-023620-4

First Collier Books Edition 1987

South Light is also published in a hardcover edition by
Macmillan Publishing Company.

10 9 8 7 6 5 4 3 2 1

Printed in the United States of America

To

Erica Dale Parfit

David Michael Parfit

Also by Michael Parfit

The Boys Behind the Bombs

Last Stand at Rosebud Creek

Author's Note

A warning: This is not a treatise on Antarctic politics, law, science, or history. It is an observation of many of those factors as they appear to a traveler and his circumstantial companions on and around this mysterious, cold, enthralling place. I simply wish to take the reader into the strange illumination of south light. For those who would like to learn more about the issues of Antarctica and its future, I would suggest a few other books: *A Pole Apart*, by Philip Quigg; *Antarctic Law and Politics*, by F. M. Auburn; *Antarctica: Wilderness at Risk*, by Barney Brewster; and *Let's Save Antarctica*, by James N. Barnes. In these pages I have not attempted to go over ground already covered by those books, although issues they address are raised here. In addition, I would suggest that the serious student of this fascinating place begin with the comprehensive Antarctic Bibliography published by the United States Library of Congress.

I owe a debt of gratitude to many. This book began as an assignment for *Smithsonian* magazine, and I am indebted to Constance Bond, John P. Wiley, and Don Moser, of *Smithsonian*, for conceiving of the story, pursuing the idea, thinking of me, and offering constant encouragement and assistance. Many thanks also to Barry Lippman, who believed in my ability to turn sketchy preliminary ideas into a book. I also wish to thank Dr. Edward P. Todd and the staff of the National Science Foundation's Division of Polar Programs for designing the innovative and extensive trip that this book describes. If it does not become apparent enough within these pages, I would like to say again: This is a remarkably efficient organization which I think owes its competence to the belief among its people in the value of its endeavor. This appreciation includes the combined military forces in the Antarctic that worked with the National Science Foundation in an endeavor of peace under the command of Captain Brian Shoemaker, USN; and the people of ITT Antarctic Services, Inc., the NSF's civilian contractor. I particularly want to thank Guy Guthridge, manager of the Polar Information Program, who shepherded the journalists around McMurdo and environs with enormous good humor and patience; Richard Cameron, whose wit and willingness to talk about any subject aboard the *Polar Sea* made that portion of the journey particularly enjoyable; and Pieter Lenie, skipper and aircraft pilot. I also thank every single one of the individuals whose names appear in this book, who were without exception more patient and helpful than they had to be. There are some who, by circumstances that seem to have been beyond my control, did not appear here but who also contributed mightily to my understanding of the Antarctic. I think of many of the crew members of the U.S. Coast Guard icebreaker *Polar Sea* and the research vessel *Hero* in particular, of the residents of Palmer Station and Amundsen-Scott South Pole Station, and of the staff of the Chalet in McMurdo. Among these are Erick Chaing, Larry Orr, and Joanne Heil, in the Chalet; James J. McClelland, Jr., executive officer of the *Polar Sea*; William R. Edgar, marine science officer on the *Polar Sea*, and Jay Klinck, former station leader at Siple Station. Although I have not engaged in extensive political discussions here, my understanding of Antarctic politics, as reflected in glimpses and hints in this narrative, owes much to Tucker Scully of the U.S. State Department, John Heap of the United Kingdom's Foreign and Commonwealth office, and Lee Kimball of the International Institute for Environment and Development (IIED). To all these, and to all the many others who helped, I must also offer the traditional caveat: Much of the good of this book is theirs; any errors are mine.

Finally, this book absolutely could never have been achieved without the active, painstaking help of Debra N. Parfit, my wife, research associate, accountant, and friend.

SOUTH LIGHT

Prologue

On the Hero

Like all Antarctica, the last iceberg does not seem entirely real. Out beyond the heaving gray of the storm it glows orange, the only live color in the world. Like all Antarctica, it is fanciful; it is strange. It has drawn the sun down from its hasty flight north, and has arrayed itself in beauty on the horizon. It is an old piece of glacier, rolled by the sea, seamed with years. It is a pumpkin, going down at the stern, a pyramid of glowing cold, the tomb of summer. It is a crag broken off the dying light itself, half ice, half mirage. Perhaps it is not even there. The *Hero* slides toward it, and the wind grows.

For the U.S. research vessel *Hero*, the antarctic season is ending. The ship is hastening to leave. It is April 16, deep into fall. Anytime now, the captain says, the pack ice will come blowing up out of the south, roaring in the distance like a train.

"It is getting late," Wade Church, the second mate, said two days ago. "Bad things happen to people who stay too late." That was the day of the fire.

Now, except for the *Hero*, the continent is all buttoned up and battened down for winter. The South Pole Station has been closed to the outside for six weeks, its nineteen residents already blanketed in the six-month night. McMurdo, the big city of the Antarctic, said farewell to the last of the summer tourists just a month ago and settled down, population ninety, to its winter's limited commerce with the eleven Kiwis at New Zealand's Scott Base next door. McMurdo's sun is bloody and sinking. The British Antarctic Sur-

vey ship *Bransfield* left its stores and letters for the noble two-year
men of endurance out on the rocks at Faraday Base, picked up an
airplane ski at the Chilean base, and departed for the Falklands.
The Russians don't think they'll see a ship for a year.

Captain Pieter Lenie, the famous little Dutchman, is down on
the bridge, firing machine guns from his restored World War II
trainer aircraft with his fingers, celebrating a Florida airshow of
1983. He is relieved that the crazy doctor is no longer on board,
although all the doctor stole was foot powder, and ointment for his
burns. Dave Morgan, the engineer, who spends much of his time
muffled in his green ear protectors, reading mountaineering books,
watches the captain with amusement and affection. Clamfoot, the
Indian, is in the galley, giving Spanish lessons to Carla D'Antonio,
the Italian from New York. Carla had previously been telling hid-
eous jokes on the bridge with becoming relish. The little green ship
heaves forward on the following swell, leaving Antarctica.

Tomorrow the *Hero* will enter the southern edge of the Drake
Passage, the 490-nautical-mile gap between Cape Horn and the
Antarctic Peninsula, where the tip of South America appears to be
reaching south like the hand of God, trying to touch the tip of the
continent and pass on the flame. There was contact millennia
ago, but the separation has been long. Between, the sea rages.
Marko, the cook, a man who could ballast the *Hero* all by himself,
has a cheerful expectation of what will be encountered there. "I'm
telling you," he says at any opportunity, "we're going to get our
asses kicked."

The wind is increasing. The ship leans to starboard. In the icehouse Mel Edelman sits, bracing his feet against the binnacle. He
has lived on the high, remote ice fields of the continent and on its
shores. Because of circumstances at home he will never return. He
is silent. He seems to wish to be alone. "There are two great moments in a trip to Antarctica," said Dick Cameron weeks ago—
Cameron with his huge beard and sly kindness. "When you see
your first iceberg and when you see your last iceberg." For most

this place is not so easily bracketed. This enormous, mysterious continent, whose sphere of influence covers more territory than Africa, blazes in the mind—like the last berg—in odd shapes and fragments. These pieces of memory seem unaccountably valuable, as if the assembling of them will somehow reveal why, after spending months or years being cold, uncomfortable, and lonely, so many human beings persist in thinking that their time here was a gift.

Out in the dark of the storm that is the *Hero*'s destiny, the last iceberg of Antarctica loses the sun and disappears. But the continent shines; it shines out past the moon like something young on the face of the ravaged earth.

TO THE UNPEOPLED CITY

Chapter One

Point of Safe Return

(1)

Danny East left the morning darkness of New Zealand for the antarctic winter dawn, flying the last plane out, and as the sun shone on the new world he passed the point of safe return. So when the special weather report came up the line from McMurdo, relayed back with urgency by J. J. Miller from the lead aircraft, it was already too late.

Miller expressed his anger without protocol.

"Danny," he said, "they're hosin' us."

Danny East was more formal. He knew what Miller was saying: the three Lockheed Hercules LC-130 transport aircraft flying south today were in trouble. The weather had suddenly become very bad. He said:

"Roger."

(2)

It was a few hours into Winfly—the winter flight to Antarctica. During Winfly the season's first new people and supplies for the United States Antarctic Research Program were flown to McMurdo Station to get a jump on the summer's work. Winfly occurred late in August, during the first weeks of light. Sometimes these brief days were benign, and sometimes they were not.

Lieutenant Danny East, polar transport aircraft commander, and Lieutenant Commander James John Miller, PTAC, were at the heart of Winfly. Neither looked old enough to do what they did, and even afterward they did not look old enough to have gone through all that. Maybe these things would not hit immediately, and it would only come upon them in a year or two, when people would suddenly start whispering, Where did Danny get all that white hair? How come J.J. twitches? But at the time they looked like high school candidates for the Naval Academy. They were both thirty-one.

Like all the pilots they each carried a copy of the booklet nicknamed the gouge. This was a thick little publication that contained the vital numbers, statistics, rules, and diagrams necessary to move LC-130 aircraft from one place on the earth's surface to another through the air.

In the middle of the gouge was a diagram the shape of a slice of pie. It looked like a slice of the Antarctica pie that appeared in every magazine article on antarctic politics. The map showed the enormous white continent divided up into slices according to the claims of the seven nations who maintained they owned a piece. A sliver for France's claim, for instance; a whacking great chunk for Australia. The claims for Great Britain, Argentina, and Chile were laid roughly on top of one another, and the whole arrangement looked like a dish prepared for wildly differing appetites, which was probably the case. The shape in the gouge might have been the piece of Antarctica claimed by the United States, except that the United States didn't make a claim. The United States kept hinting that it could make a claim if it really wanted to, and that it might in that case claim the whole continent, or at least a very large piece, but that at present it wished to avoid the whole issue. It did, however, partake of the pie.

The diagram in the gouge was really an outline of a safe place to put down a large airplane in the extremity known as a whiteout.

When J. J. Miller left Christchurch at 2:00 A.M. on August 29, 1983, at the very beginning of the antarctic season, in command of the first plane in a flight of three, he did not anticipate being forced to use the diagram of the slice of pie. He was in the lead, Walter

Milowic was in the middle, and Danny East was in the rear, two hours back. All was peaceful in the early hours on that morning in August. Carried by the high, smooth winds of the south, the planes flew down in long formation into the gentle spring twilight of Antarctica.

(3)

The inside of each of the three Hercules LC-130s heading south out of Christchurch was full of people and cargo. The people in the planes made an odd collection: uniformed members of the U.S. Naval Support Force, Antarctica, posted south for the season out of Port Hueneme, California; civilians employed by ITT Antarctic Services, Inc., of New Jersey, the private contractor hired by the National Science Foundation to do construction and run heavy equipment at McMurdo Station; and a few scientists, the people whose work all this effort supported, going to the ice to get an early start on their research for the season.

They shared a common purpose: an urgency to get to Antarctica and get to work, but in the plane there was little conversation. The noise of the engines and the airstream made the inside of the plane a place of isolation. It was like living in a metal building in which workmen tried to sharpen running chainsaws while dentists drilled. The noise drove the people apart, each into his or her own cocoon of sleep or introspection. The flight would take about eight hours, depending on winds. There were few portholes, and the light inside was dim. To the passengers it was a chamber more than an aircraft. It seemed to be a time machine, a spacecraft, an aluminum tube full of sound so strong you could feel it in your fingers—within which something happened to you that you might spend years trying to comprehend. You stepped out and were dazzled for life. You emerged in Antarctica.

Sometimes the thing that was done to you in the chamber didn't quite work, and to your surprise you got out and the wet runway and the poplar trees of Christchurch were still there. This almost happened during the evolution of Winfly. There were many people during and afterward who wished it had.

One by one the three aircraft headed down to McMurdo reached the invisible moving point in the air known as PSR—the place where wind and fuel and weather require a decision to continue or go back: the point of safe return. One by one each checked the quantities and the forecast and made the decision to continue.

At twenty-four thousand feet the sun shone and the air was at peace. Up in the cockpit, a place of elevation and light compared to the dim cabin behind, the pilots and copilots of the planes were relaxed. It was like every other flight, the tension sublimated and the airborne office untroubled by disturbances in the undemanding routine of cruise flight. At least once an hour the navigator rose from his seat behind the pilots, unfolded a little stool, pulled the mechanism of a periscope sextant down from the ceiling, and spent a few minutes bracketing a little green sun in his eyepiece with a grid and numbers, verifying position. The crew chief came up the ladder from aft and below with coffee. The engineer, who sat directly behind the two pilots on a sliding chair and whose activity during takeoff and landing resembled that of a man trying to play the organ and conduct the orchestra at the same time, flipped a switch in the overhead with a gesture of boredom. Winfly was evolving according to orders; in a small matter of hours the pilots would be on their way home.

In the noise-enforced individual silence of the plane the passengers, who were going to Antarctica for the season, read, stared at the floor or walls, or climbed up on top of the cargo to sleep. The planes carried everything from eggs to dynamite; the Navy men slept up there anyway. They slept on the cargo, and they slept on the big hatch in the back near the metal toilet (curtained off because there were women on board), and they slept in the stretchers that hung overhead. Everyone in uniform seemed to find it easy to sleep, normal to wait. The civilian United States Antarctic Research Program workers in their red USARP-issue parkas were more restless. Most read—Dorothy Sayers, Alistair MacLean, William Styron, William F. Buckley, James Michener.

The walls of this limbo were gray-green fabric, covering insulation, buttoned in like a quilt, with pipes and hoses running fore and aft. In the ceiling were ventilation and heating vents that blew hot breath at intervals always too frequent or too seldom. The floors were rollers for cargo. The seats were red nylon webbing. When people tired of their books or woke they read the signs around the cabin: A red stripe marked Danger, Propeller. Crates stamped Select Quality Nelson Tomatoes. Forks in the lunch box stamped with military specification numbers. A little door marked Instructions for Manual Emergency Override Operation, which a crew member opened and peered into regularly as if seeking reassurance. On the huge flat aluminum pallets—as wide as the airplane—to which the cargo was strapped were stenciled the words "Property of the United States Air Force. Return to the nearest Air Force Base." The military approach to life included a grand notion of what one might find under a bench at the park.

For at least the first five hours of these three flights of Winfly, the mood within these dim interiors was not fear. Not many people went to Antarctica afraid. In the steady, ordinary, unemotional process that prepared them for the journey there was a shucking and a girding that left them clean and relaxed against the acknowledged increase of hazard in their lives:

We're off! Like prisoners, like troops, like the condemned, we have abandoned our civilian clothes, we have put on the same things as everyone else: long underwear, black pants, parka, white boots, gloves, sunglasses. We have stood in line, bought lunch, and let Damon of Damel, a large, expensive Labrador retriever otherwise known as Joe, snuffle around our gear for drugs. Joe, we have all noted, is a happy dog. He bounces around: "Yeah-yeah-yeah, oh boy oh boy oh boy, everything smells so good." We all have stood there, feeling guilty in spite of genuine innocence, thinking that when Joe finds what he is looking for he'll bring gloom and shackles into someone's life with ebullience: "Oh boy! Oh boy! Oh boy! *Dope dope dope dope!*"

Here in this airplane we have left all the encumbrances of our identities behind, checked into the clothing-issue building with our suitcases. Now all that is important about who and what I am is in two orange bags I can carry by myself, and is here in the aircraft with me. Most of it is just warm clothes. I have become lighter, freer, less burdened in life, and if my life itself ceases somewhere off on this unknown trajectory on which I have launched myself, it will perhaps not make as much smoke going out as I had thought. I have thrown my dreams into a sack over my shoulder and headed out. The place I am going is the greatest unknown in the world.

(4)

The passengers in the three aircraft sat as relaxed as sacks of grain and considered the destination. The leap they were undertaking was profound. There was a crack in the world between Antarctica and everywhere else. Antarctica was like a piece of a puzzle that was cut wrong or came out of a different picture. There was a ragged space between civilization and that continent that had to be vaulted. The distance between Antarctica and other continents that reach toward it like unfinished bridges was so great that on some maps that attempted to show both, the gap between the worlds was drawn right there in ink, like the wavy lines draftsmen used to indicate that a line was longer than it appeared.

The route south arched high, like the trail of a rocket. Just past the top of the trajectory was a long fall of weightlessness, as the craft left the pull of civilization and entered the region of the attraction of Antarctica. It happened after Christchurch had gone a long way down around the curve of the earth and at least two hours before McMurdo Station came up. It happened before the southbound aircraft's magnetic compasses swung around to lie by saying that the plane was going north; before the strangeness had completely taken over. It came somewhere just after the point of safe return, when the pilots were required to put on their long johns and their bunny boots, when, like monks vowing themselves into silence, they committed themselves to Antarctica.

Because of the confusion of the compass, pilots flew by a grid. The grid was a cross-hatching laid across the continent, lined up with the Greenwich meridian. The grid was maintained by gyroscopes; it escaped the bewildered wandering of the iron. So Danny East flew south on a grid heading of 345 degrees; almost due north.

He was twenty minutes past the point of safe return, in the heart of the weightlessness, when J. J. Miller relayed the weather special. It was not a happy conversation.

Weather reports came regularly to airborne planes at some time during the last fifteen minutes of every hour; a Special was an interruption of the routine, giving information that could not wait. A Special, therefore, was almost always bad news.

"When you hear, 'This is Mac Center with a special weather advisory,' right away you *know*," Miller said later. "It's like right through the heart—*awwgg.*"

At the point of safe return the weather at McMurdo had been fine—a high overcast and forty miles visibility. The Special announced a change.

"Sky obscured, visibility one-eighth of a mile in blowing snow." The news was very bad.

"Whiteouts occur when light reflects and refracts from both the snow surface and from a thick cloud ceiling," reported *Survival in Antarctica*, a booklet given to all visitors. "Depth perception is lost and disorientation occurs; a discarded cigarette pack a short distance away may appear to be a distant vehicle." If it was snowing, weather people said, it was not a whiteout—it was a blizzard. But pilots used the term more generally: a whiteout was any time, blizzard or not, that the view out the window had lost all definition in a blank brightness. Under the broader view, McMurdo had suddenly gone to whiteout conditions.

Anywhere else in the world, the planes would have been diverted to a safer airport. Here there was no choice.

Miller called Danny East.

"Danny, have you passed PSR?"

"*Roger.*"

"Danny, they're hosin' us."

Miller read him the Special. He remembered later, "I thought, Oh, shit, because I knew we all had to do it now."

Christchurch was gone. Christchurch—where the first green of spring glowed in the fields, where the smell of turned earth filled the breeze with promise, where the Kiwi girls were warm to American boys—was in the past. Christchurch was history, that town that, with Punta Arenas in Tierra del Fuego, was most intimately connected to the ice continent by distance and remembrance. In Christchurch, a statue of Robert Falcon Scott stands by the Avon River. On its base the famous sentence from his last diary, written in the tent on the Ross Barrier ice soon before he died, is recorded twice, once in steel, once in stone: "I do not regret this journey, which has shown that Englishmen can endure hardships, help one another and meet death with as great a fortitude as ever in the past." Above the Southern ocean fifteen hundred miles south of the blind stone eyes of Robert Scott, the men and women in three orange-and-silver aircraft began to summon the fortitude to meet the future.

Christchurch was as inaccessible as the moon. The three aircraft, alone in the sky south of the crack in the earth, droned on in the high sunlight. No urgency or hope could draw Christchurch back. Their destiny, one way or another, was the ice.

Each pilot reduced power and slowed up. The three planes were like children dragging their feet; but it was not reluctance to advance. It was a maneuver to save fuel. Airspeed indicators dropped: 190 knots, 180, 165. The wash of air across the cockpit windows diminished, giving the illusion of approaching peace. And soon, in the lead, a new level of activity developed in J. J. Miller's plane. The navigator closed up his sextant for the last time and drew a small curtain between his radar screen and the glare of the window. The engineer moved his seat forward on the rails and began to play the airplane's drone on the panel above his head. The pilots got rid of their coffee cups and strapped themselves in. The copilot wrote numbers in grease pencil on a plastic-covered diagram of the approach. With hardly a change in sound or attitude the big plane began to descend. Shortly it seemed that the great cloud of Antarctica rose in a single long breath and gathered it in.

Chapter Two

On the Ice

(1)

Brian Matter was a passenger in J. J. Miller's aircraft on August 29. He was a heavy-equipment operator going down to operate Kathy, Suzie, and other assorted forklifts, bulldozers, and front-end loaders; to move junk, lift buildings, and sculpture snow for scientists. It was likely he would remember the first day of the season longer than any other:

"What was really incredible was you had all this time to think. There is this drone and you're lost in this whole sensual input. Being lost in your own thoughts, it could just as well be quiet."

Miller's plane entered the clouds at about eleven thousand feet. The storm awaited it. On the land of Antarctica and on the sea of its influence, storms moved fast. "They scream around the continent," a Navy weatherman once said. On satellite charts the continent looked as if it was surrounded by whirling pinwheels. "You can see the birth, life, and death of a front in twenty-four hours." Antarctica was larger than the United States; there were about thirty weather-reporting stations on the surface. Estimating future weather at McMurdo was like getting reports from Dallas, Minneapolis, Calgary, Nome, and San Francisco and trying to forecast Phoenix. "The one thing I want a new forecaster to develop down here," the Navy man said, "is a good imagination. You can never get confused here by too much information."

On August 29, the weather office at McMurdo had seen the storm coming; it just came more quickly than expected. It was a

16

full-grown Herbie, bearing down upon the little town and its ice runways with whirling arms of flat light, snow hard and biting as sand, implacable wind. The storm, far fiercer than its diminutive nickname, came down Herbie Alley: down the wall of Minna Bluff and on between White Island and Black Island, heading true north toward McMurdo. It was a familiar pattern. "When Minna Bluff starts to disappear," a pilot said, "when they can see the clouds just bubbling, rolling, and the snow just starts to roll off Minna, they start stringin' the ropes. They start stringin' the ropes between the buildings, because otherwise you just walk outside and you lose everything; you're dead."

On August 29, he said, "The Herbie god was mad; it hadn't been fed lately."

J. J. Miller's aircraft slipped lower into the whiteness: ten thousand feet; nine thousand feet; eight thousand feet.

At six thousand feet the antarctic sky tried to take the plane apart. The wind, roaring down over the ridges of White and Black islands, was tumbling like water in a falls. The aircraft was caught and flung.

"Severe turbulence," J. J. Miller remembered later, sounding briefly almost as formal as his colleague Danny East, "is when you are floating in the straps, and if you were not strapped down you would be a part of the overheads. It was that way continuously."

"Theyaw was incredible," Matter said. "Looking aft in the plane, you could see it swing back and forth. The cots hanging from the ceiling would swing out and slap against the sides."

"This was an added variable that made it a little bit more difficult during the evolution," said Danny East.

It was as if Antarctica raged, slapping around anything it encountered. The plane had come down out of the familiar high blue of the atmosphere into this stark whiteness to be confronted with violence beyond experience. The pounding seemed endless—a rolling, jolting tumble, slamming the passengers down in the seats, against the walls, lifting them, slamming them down again, over and over. The movements of the aircraft became confused, and the sensations of control and certainty that you feel in the steady turns of an airliner disappeared. The plane could have been going end over end, falling right off the earth. The power of the engines seemed to grow and fade without reason, while outside the few portholes nothing ever changed. It was white, endlessly and frighteningly white. The plane was wrapped in Antarctica, wrapped in Antarctica's eternal flag.

"Everyone at one point or another focused their attention on the air crew to see how they were handling it." Matter. "I'm going to say they weren't handling it much better than we were. We got the impression they felt it was very serious. That just reaffirmed what we already thought. No one believed that we would get out of the sky without some sort of damage to the plane."

McMurdo had as good an approach system as most major airports in the United States. J. J. Miller took the LC-130, skis down, right to the minimum: 100 feet above the ground. He saw nothing. He went around the pattern and tried again. The turbulence grabbed at his right hand on the throttles. It slapped and shoved on his left hand, tightening his gentle touch on the wheel. Out there in the murk, so close that the aircraft noise could be clearly heard from them, were buildings roped together in the wind like rescuers wading into surf. The buildings were full of men and women who yearned to see the plane as passionately as those aloft yearned for the clatter of hard snow on skis. But the connection could not be made, and in the rush of the wind the rumble and whine of the container that held all that pent-up hope slipped away from the listeners like an image of happiness they could not quite grasp.

Again Miller brought the plane down to a hundred feet, the skis reaching for touchdown. The plane and the surface were like blind lovers inches from a kiss. But a pilot did not let longing bend the rules lest it break the airplane. Again the whiteness prevailed. Again the reach for safety failed. Miller pulled the plane away from the proximity to the earth that could kill them all as quickly as it could save them, back up into the maelstrom to turn for another try. By now the turbulence had taken victims.

"My roommate got sick first," Matter said later. "Once that happened it snowballed." The only airsick bags were large greenish trash bags. "The loadmaster said, 'If you need an airbag, raise your hand and we'll get one to you pronto.'" Since no one could get out of a seat without being flung the length or height of the cabin, the bags were balled up and thrown across the aisles. Brian Matter turned to the woman sitting next to him.

"I hope you don't lose it," he said. "Because if you do I will." She grinned. She didn't lose it. Nor, fundamentally, did anyone else. Like Wally Fletcher, a construction worker who was in the plane behind them, they had their priorities in order: "Puke washes off. Death is forever."

In this extremity they became even more self-contained. They pulled the blanket of contemplation closer around them. There was something resolved in those who went to Antarctica, a determination to handle what came. Hardship was in the bargain, and even if you had to look into the muzzle of death the cost still seemed less than the gift you came here to find. Antarctica might hurt you, might bring you to your knees, might obliterate you; it remained precious.

"Once in a while you might say something to the person next to you," Matter later said. "But pretty much everyone kept to themselves. I myself had said my prayers and had made my amends. I can't say I'm terribly religious, but it seemed most appropriate at the time. It was time to start thinking about final matters."

Miller came around for a fourth time. The sky slammed him around. The altimeter unwound in jerks. The voices of the copilot, the engineer, the navigator, and the ground controllers murmured in his headphones, telling their stories of altitude, speed, and position. It was like a blind climber feeling for a foothold with the end of a string. At minimums. Missed approach point. TACAN passage. Nothing to be seen in the white wilderness. Advance throttles. Pull back. Climb.

"Mr. Miller is very articulate when it comes to this evolution," Danny East said.

"Well, I thought, we still have about two hours of fuel." Miller still had options. He could sit around in the sky for a while, and wait for a change. However— On the other hand—

The pilot in command had ultimate responsibility. Those on the ground could only advise; they could not offer decisions. Miller had to make up his own mind; and what he decided to do would inevitably have at least some effect on the decisions made by the men behind him. Shall we hang our dwindling hook of fuel in the sky and wait for the weather to go away?

Into this internal debate came a small human factor. It was the loadmaster, on the intercom. He was aft, still playing quarterback, launching garbage bags at needy receivers.

"Sir," he said. "I've got at least sixteen people throwing up back here and two of them are in the same bag."

There are limits to the human misery a sane man will allow. For J. J. Miller it was the two in one bag.

Miller knew what airsickness was like. "When I first started flying I was so ill I considered jumping out of the plane. So I felt sorry for them. And we weren't doing any good. I talked to a forecaster on the radio and he said it's gonna be like this for eight hours, and it may get worse."

"Okay," Miller said on the intercom to the other crew members. "We're wasting time here. Let's get this over with, and get it on the ground."

He turned the pages of the gouge to the diagram of the whiteout pie. They would go ahead and land blind. Formal radio protocol was, here at least, unnecessary. "Hey, Danny," he said, casting the word of his fateful leadership across the sky to the last plane, which was still up there out of Antarctica's reach. "I'm going in for this."

The whiteout approach began like any other. The controllers on the ground brought the plane down to the minimums just like before. But when the aircraft passed the runway it did not climb away. It rose to five hundred feet—this big, blind, lumbering creature—crossed the navigational equipment, and the controllers turned it loose. It escaped from their safety net of radio headings and advice, and ventured out alone.

"Mark."

The navigational fix was passed. Miller turned the aircraft into the narrow end of the wedge. The wedge was all his now, a great expanse of snow across which the wind blew so hard that the space between the surface and the sky was smudged. The pie was not aligned with today's wind. He turned to make the only possible compromise between wind and wedge, and began to bring the plane down.

COPILOT: 120, down 2. (Airspeed; rate of descent in hundreds.)

ENGINEER: 400 feet. (Radar altitude.)

NAVIGATOR: Drift 5. (Degrees of difference between course and heading, read by an inertial or Doppler shift system.)

If the drift is too high the plane will land sideways and cartwheel, end over end, throwing aluminum across the snow. But you do not think of these possibilities. You attend to the job.

J. J. Miller:

"You have to pretend to be calm. But I don't care who you are, if you say that you weren't nervous or scared at any point during something like this you're full of shit."

COPILOT: 120, down 3.

ENGINEER: 350 feet.

NAVIGATOR: Drift 8.

COPILOT: 115, down 5.

ENGINEER: 300 feet.

And in the back, where there is no work to occupy your thoughts, you consider your chances and your past. Brian Matter: "You get to contemplating your life and what you would have done differently. It is really amazing the things you have time to think about. The things you regret not having done, those things you wish you would have said."

COPILOT: 105, down 6.

COPILOT: 118, up 2.

COPILOT: 100, down 4.

NAVIGATOR: Drift 10.

ENGINEER: 200 feet.

On the ground, Captain Brian Shoemaker stood in the control tower. He was the commander of the U.S. support forces in Antarctica. Winfly was, ultimately, his. He had walked to the tower in the storm, flag to flag. He had heard the steady voices of his pilots as they approached, and he had given them advice and encouragement on the radio. Now he waited in the silence as they turned their attention inward to their own information, needing no help nor interference from the ground. The sound of the plane passed overhead and disappeared. He waited. The wind lashed at the angled windows and shook the building. The control tower might have been aloft itself: beyond the windows the day was translucent but utterly undefined. The only movement was the whirl of snow past the windows in gusts, invisible substance racing through a white infinity, looking for somewhere to congeal and form matter; for somewhere to become Antarctica.

ENGINEER: 150 feet.

In more comfortable environments J. J. Miller had trained other pilots in whiteout landing technique. He gave advice.

"At about sixty or seventy feet you start to experience ground effect. The sink rate, which has been established at two hundred feet, goes to hell. It levels off. Your initial reaction is to go 'Aw, shit' and pull off power. If you do that, you and the ground become one immediately, because you just lost your lift by pulling off your power. You have to *think* the power back, get your two hundred feet again, and *think* it back up again, a slight power adjustment, because if you make a major one you're going to blow it."

COPILOT: 105, down 5.
COPILOT: 115, down 2.
ENGINEER: 100 feet.
NAVIGATOR: Drift 6.
COPILOT: 105, down 3.

Back in the cabin there was no way of knowing where the plane was in the sky. It could have been at five thousand feet. "The wind would hit and you would go back and forth." Brian Matter. "There would be a lull. Then the wind would hit you again."

ENGINEER: 50 feet.
COPILOT: 110, down 2.
NAVIGATOR: Drift 10.
Sound of impact.

(2)

Miller, training neophytes in the arcane art:

"As soon as you touch down your initial reaction is to pull back on the yoke, because it comes as a surprise. You have to fight that. You have to hold the nose attitude where it is. You touch down blind and if you pull back you'll skip; or you touch down and you think, I'm on the ground! and you push the nose over: boom, you destroy the nose. You've got to hold the attitude and let the snow slow the plane down. You're still flying it on the ground, down to forty knots."

In the early afternoon of August 29, the lead aircraft of three touched down in Antarctica, with J. J. Miller at the controls.

"It was an absolute shock." Matter. "We were in a lull, and the skis touched. It came as the most complete surprise you could register."

An LC-130 landing on unprepared snow anytime sounded as a crash would in almost any other aircraft. The landing was smooth, but it was a thunderous, clattering arrival. But the plane didn't skip or cartwheel or mash its nose. Miller kept its attitude the same. The snow slowed the aircraft. Miller kept straight and level with the heading indicator and the artificial horizon, just as he had been doing when the plane was in the air.

The plane slowed quickly and came to a stop.

Back in the cabin the passengers put away the garbage bags. Death is forever. Puke washes off. There were no cheers, although Brian Matter, among others, sought out J. J. Miller much later to thank him. "There was the closest thing to a collective sigh, in silence," Matter remembered. "It was a sudden release of all the tension."

"If the season's going to be like this—" someone said, "—three attempts to get down here, and then this—it's going to be a great season."

Winfly was not over. Two more aircraft were still to land, and even with that evolution completed safely, the people in the planes still had to get to McMurdo through Antarctica's fiercest weather. Late that afternoon, with all the planes safely on the ground, the second plane ran out of fuel while taxiing one hundred invisible yards from the pumps. The people in that plane were safely down, but without fuel to warm the plane they would freeze.

But J. J. Miller's plane had refueled and could keep its cabin warm; so Miller's crew went out on ropes into the weather and passed the other plane's crew and passengers back along the rope, one by one, through the white river. The weather did not let them go until morning. Sixty-three people spent the night in the plane, sleeping on pads in their parkas and eating the fresh bananas, grapes, and lettuce shipped down to McMurdo for the crew.

But the moment after landing was the best time of Winfly. The greatest hazard of arrival had been met and overcome, and up in the cockpit of each aircraft, as it came to a stop somewhere on the ice, there was a moment for the members of the crew to relax and to wonder at what they had achieved.

So, at 11:45 A.M., for the first time since they had crossed the TACAN and entered the whiteout pie, the pilots, the engineer, and the navigator looked out the windows to see this place that had been so hard to reach.

COPILOT: Jesus.
NAVIGATOR: Wow.
ENGINEER: Yeah.
PILOT: Holy shit.
Everything was utterly white. They could not see the surface on which they had stopped. The plane still shook. Antarctica was wind. They had landed in the sky.

Chapter Three

Even I, Who Had Ambition

(1)

In waters never sounded, an icebreaker stood still in blowing snow and wind, waiting for Antarctica to let it go. The pilothouse was quiet. Silhouettes moved against the expanse of windows, against the enormous whiteness. Engines rumbled, but there was no movement in the ship, no heave of water. The ship could have been ashore, planted in January fields of North Dakota, with the fences drifted in and the cattle dying.

It was March, eight months after Winfly. It was the other end of the Antarctic season. Only a few days ago the icebreaker left Mc-Murdo Station, the place J. J. Miller, Walt Milowic, and Danny East had reached with such difficulty to begin the year's work. McMurdo was about to send all the planes away for the winter. A season of science and exploration had passed, but the two occasions were alike: each was an effort by human beings, organized against the opposition of wind and ice, to set foot on the edge of this least familiar, most forbidding, land on earth.

The ship stood motionless, enveloped in the same whiteness the pilots had seen from their windows when the planes had landed. The golden sweep of the radar, reaching out through the flat brightness, covered its round screen with sparkles, the pattern of humped ice spreading out to the invisible horizon. A young Coast Guardsman glanced at the hooded screen periodically, though it showed him nothing new. Directly ahead, 1,245 meters distant by the radar's measurement, lay a wall, which blazed on the screen and blanked off all electronic sight beyond with a widening shadow.

26

Occasionally, when the snow eased, this wall appeared to the people watching from the pilothouse: white cliffs marching across the path of the ship. It was a vast, long slab standing up out of the sea, a flat-topped wall, a barrier, a warehouse of ice. Sometimes we could see blue in it and sometimes only hard white. As the north wind blew the snow in and out, the iceberg appeared and disappeared. Once a faint horizon materialized behind it, then faded away.

"Death ice ahead!"

J.D. had come down from the aloft conn. The pilothouse stirred with his presence. J.D. had a red beard and a buoyant stride; he was responsible for the sign over the door into the pilothouse: "No QUICHE served on this bridge." He was Lieutenant James Dale, the operations officer. He came in, looked at the chart, and gazed out the window. His clear tenor rang through the room:

"Gentlemen," he said cheerfully, "we're doomed."

The big red icebreaker, the U.S. Coast Guard cutter *Polar Sea*, was stopped at 74°32′ south, 144°45′ west, in heavy ice. Beneath the ship the water was fourteen hundred meters deep. Whiteness stretched into the gray distance all around, and nothing moved. Great slabs of snow-covered ice lay on the water jammed together, the black cracks between them glazed over.

Off the starboard bow, four little Adélie penguins stood on an ice hump, snow dusting their shoulders, their heads tucked away. Two sailors went forward and threw wads of bread at them. The bread landed in the snow, strangely yellow. The birds did not move.

"There are two kinds of penguins in the Antarctic," Dick Cameron said, his grin flashing in his beard. "The white ones are always coming toward you, and the black ones are always running away."

He stood at a window in the enormous pilothouse of the *Polar Sea*, watching the storm. Cameron spent most of his days in the pilothouse, and the days were long. He would awaken in the middle of the short night and go to the pilothouse. After every meal, he would amble upstairs to the pilothouse. After a movie down in the wardroom lounge, he would climb back to the pilothouse. I, too, was often in the pilothouse. I always found him there. It seemed we rendezvoused there to laugh obliquely at each other's restlessness. He was cheerful, but he stared out the windows, as if urging the snow to lift and miraculously, in defiance of the charts, show the land we were trying to reach. Mt. Siple, ho! Just let us get the scientists ashore for one day!

Dick Cameron was ready to miss Mt. Siple. He had been talking gloom for a week, betting against sentiment. "There will be some heartrending moments when we have been on station so many days when you can't get a helicopter off the deck," he had said eight days ago. "But in Antarctica you have to be a realist." Three days ago he said, "That's the thing about Antarctica. You've got to be prepared for disappointment."

Now was the time for that hard realism. Cameron was chief scientist, appointed by the National Science Foundation to try to get the most use out of an expensive ship. Now the ship was getting nowhere. Cameron was not happy. But he concealed whatever burdens the job placed upon him behind the dark glasses he wore on bright days, and hid his rent heart behind a marvelous imitation of Peter Sellers—Peter Sellers as Inspector Jacques Clouseau wearing a preposterous fake beard.

"Does your doeg bite?"

"No," I said.

Snow blew across the windows and the ship lay still. The dog bit, as always. In this little dialogue our roles sometimes became confused.

"I thought you said your dog didn't bite," I said.

Dick Cameron said, "Thet ees not my doeg."

Cameron gave a little bark of laughter and was silent.

We were a week out of McMurdo, westbound into the unknown. Ten degrees east of where we waited lay the mountain called Mt. Siple, just off the coast of Marie Byrd Land. No human being had ever set foot on Mt. Siple. The chart said Mt. Siple was 10,200 feet high, plus or minus. The tracks of other ships, expressed on the chart as numerical footprints of their soundings, reached toward Mt. Siple from the north and west, but all stopped out in blank reaches of paper where the ice had held them off. Looking at the last soundings recorded on the charts—1,700; 1,470; 332—it was easy to see the ships stopped in this same implacable blankness, no more featured than the paper on which the numbers were printed. We saw the same thing out the windows today.

"About 265 miles north of Mount Siple a course was set for that huge landmark, but 24 hours later, on February 10, the course was reversed." It was 1948, the U.S. Navy's Operation Windmill. "They [the icebreakers *Burton Island* and *Edisto*] were still 80 miles from Mount Siple, and air reconnaissance showed nothing but impenetrable pack to the south. . . ." Another attempt: "The Task Force proceeded eastward looking for leads that would allow them to penetrate toward Mount Siple. . . . After penetrating the pack for about 100 miles, course was again reversed, due to impenetrable ice."

This time everyone hoped it would be different. Mt. Siple had been photographed from the air and seen by ship from afar, and this time it would join the world. Or so Dick Cameron most fervently hoped. But now the *Polar Sea*, too, was facing impenetrable ice.

Out on the ice a fifth penguin came waddling out from behind a hill of snow that was invisible in the flat light. It seemed as if the bird had appeared—pop!—out of nowhere. To the penguin the same phenomenon probably occurred with the ship, surely a stunning apparition: the sudden appearance of 399 feet of red-orange hull topped with layers of superstructure, stacks, towers, and rows of eyes.

The penguin slid to its belly and stopped, then turned deliberately and vanished back behind its hill, no doubt warped for life. The other four just stood there, little gray-and-black pillars, each occasionally sprouting a head out of hunched shoulders. The head would move cautiously around as if checking to see if the bad dream had gone away, then plunge back into feathers.

Bill McIntosh and Twitty Conway came blasting in from an outside door, snow swirling around them like a cape. They were talking about pitons and carabiners. Conway was a quiet New Zealander whose real first name was Howard. He had been given his nickname by Americans and professed not to know its origin. Sometimes Conway seemed almost tentative. That was illusion.

Conway, a new antarctic legend had it, once suggested to his employer, George Denton, a noted glaciologist, that it might be a good idea if Denton, who had just disembarked from a helicopter, crouched down behind a boulder as the helicopter took off. Just a little precaution. Instead of taking off, the helicopter tipped over, hit the ground with a rotor, and disintegrated, throwing pieces of blade and engine in all directions like shrapnel.

"We were sitting down behind the rocks and there was a lot of metal in the air," Conway said once. "We said, 'This isn't the usual way they take off.' The blade went through our gear. The transmission went quite a ways. Half a mile or so." Conway's gentleness was now seen as psychic.

McIntosh had no such reticence. He was so brash he was always getting into arguments with the geologist Wes LeMasurier, for whom he worked, about the shape of lava flows or the nature of rock samples. "Well, yes," LeMasurier would say gently. "That's possible." McIntosh had been graduated from Princeton and gone into business as an automobile mechanic. That hadn't worked out, so he came to Antarctica. "It was a different sort of place."

Conway and McIntosh were both young antarctic adventurers, each with half a decade of experience there, all wrapped up in science and cold weather. They passed through the pilothouse as if stifled by its comfort, and soon they reappeared up on the bow, Conway in his stocking cap and McIntosh in his patchwork parka that, no doubt to McIntosh's pleasure, appeared to have come down to Antarctica with Ernest Shackleton and been patched by hand by Admiral Richard Byrd. They stood out there in the biting wind, their natural habitat.

From the warm interior of the pilothouse, Dick Cameron looked down at them with fondness. He had been like that too. He quoted a friend, Carl Eklund: "Hardship," he said, "is for the young." It wasn't enough for hardship to come blasting into their lives, as it frequently did in Antarctica even for the relatively aged; Conway and McIntosh had to go out and meet it. Conway and McIntosh wanted to climb Mt. Siple. They did not speak about it much, both because they still hoped to do so and because they knew that hope was forlorn.

On the bow today they were joined by Dick Viet, the Bird Man. Viet had ridden the *Polar Sea* all the way down from Valparaiso, recording every bird he saw. He was a Ph.D. student at the University of California at Irvine. He had written an exhaustive study of Massachusetts birds. He had a voice that rasped, as if the wind had parched his larynx, and he had an enormous, steady patience. His job was to stand in the bow when the weather was reasonable —or in the pilothouse when it wasn't—and count birds. He recorded the species and number of birds he saw on a clipboard in ten-minute segments, and compiled these with the record of the ship's speed, and eventually would come up with an idea not of population, necessarily, but of distribution. He did not seem as flagrantly hardy as McIntosh and Conway, but he was out there, day after day, squinting into the blowing snow.

Ed Zeller came up to the pilothouse to check the radioactivity of camera lenses. Crewmen brought him their treasured instruments shyly, gifts to the wizard, poisoned glass to the physicist, and he would wave the wand, the radiation counter, and buzzing would bring distress. "We found that some of the lenses were made with unusually high levels of thorium oxide," he said. He was tall, slender, and distinguished, with his blue gray turtleneck and his swept-back gray hair, but his gaze, too, wandered to the windows, to the motionless ice.

The equipment Zeller brought with him would seek out the radioactive uranium, thorium, and potassium in the rock of Mt. Siple, if the *Polar Sea* ever came close enough. Right now that chance appeared remote.

"Well," Zeller said, preparing himself, like Cameron, for disappointment, "a perfect season would send us home feeling that something was missing."

Zeller, in the eyes of the sailors at least, was the most fortunate man on the vessel: his partner in this venture was Dr. Gisela Dreschhoff. She was a stunning blond German physicist, whose presence on the ship, always attended by a delicate breath of Chanel No. 19, seemed so unlikely that it contributed to the general impression that the whole journey was fiction. The hot-blooded young explorers, the wise and humorous older man who had already been to the ends of the earth, the hard-bitten journalist, the elegant physicist, and the beautiful, brilliant, enigmatic young German woman scientist. Now all we needed was a plot.

Wes LeMasurier came happily up the stairs, getting ready for adventure.

"We've stumbled on a hidden Russian submarine base," he said. "They're going to take the ship hostage."

LeMasurier's beard was half an inch long now. He looked scruffy. He brought cheer to the pilothouse. He was a volcanologist, a good-natured hot spring of a man, unhurriedly eager, reliably warming. When the weather was at all hospitable he jogged around and around the deck, one-seventh of a mile per lap; Dick Cameron and I stood up in the warm pilothouse looking down on the foredeck timing his laps. Wes went around in an average of 1:25 per lap. Wes liked J.D.'s style. He looked around at the solid ice. "We're doomed," he said.

Wes was prepared to sink or be kidnapped, but not to miss Mt. Siple. What he wanted was rocks. "We would really like to know if the volcano is composed partly, entirely, or not at all of the glass chips that are formed by eruptions underneath the sea," Wes had told an attentive crowd of sailors at a lecture held between the two parked helicopters in the ship's hangar. "Mount Siple stands three thousand meters above the sea. If it were all composed of these glassy chips, it would mean that the ice was stupendously higher then than it is today."

The scene did not change. The ship did not move. We stayed at the windows. We stared out at this strange world, endlessly compelled to watch the white swirl. We waited—to get under way, to see unknown land, to comprehend this place. For that we could wait a long time.

"Is this beautiful or fearsome?" Dick Cameron asked. I grinned, my own answer. He answered the question himself. "I guess when you're in a ship like this it's beautiful. If you were out on the floe, listening to the ship leaving you, it would be fearsome."

The *Polar Sea* waited. The captain came through, a bulky man with a knowing smile. It was the smile that you remembered about the captain. It appeared in the pilothouse briefly at intervals, then disappeared back downstairs, revealing little. In this, it seemed, the captain resembled his most notable predecessor, the British captain James Cook, the first circumnavigator of Antarctica, who, when his crew hinted about dwindling stores and the need to find a port, "only smiled and said nothing, for he was close and secret in his intentions at all times. . . ."

The satellite-navigation television screen, hung up in a corner to present its readout to all, communicated intimately with the passing metal stars and told an odd story: in spite of the stillness, the ship moved. It drifted with the ice in which it was embedded. The little triangles the seamen put on the chart each hour took ghostly steps south across the paper toward a coastline marked with uncertainties: "Probable island," the chart said. "Estimated position of island." "Ice front, 1962." "Ice front, 1947." "Extent and shape of bay unknown." Motionless, the ship moved slowly toward the distant, invisible land, and the landscape moved with it, all wind, whiteness, and blue shadow.

As the pale twilight faded and the day's whiteness turned gray-blue, the *Polar Sea* was still adrift, locked in ice. The berg ahead appeared, an ominous shadow, and was again erased. One of the four penguins waddled away. It was evening. "Where does an iceberg go?" Dick Cameron asked. "Anywhere it wants." Where does the *Polar Sea* spend the long winter—at home in Seattle or at 74° south? The ice decides.

The ship was restless. People moved up and down the ladders in the red night-lights. Sunset, 2245; sunrise, 0230. It was still early enough in the fall so that night did not yet descend completely, but in the pilothouse at midnight it was dark enough for lights in the instruments. The warm red glow outlined the faces of the men of the watch. The faces were young, clean-shaven. Outside, the world was a dim blue. Huge, indistinct shapes filled the windows: the wall of ice, a snow squall. The shapes seemed to move in the stillness, growing and shifting, gathering around.

Down in the wardroom lounge officers sat in front of the television. First they saw *S.O.S. Titanic*. Then they saw a tape of a TV movie about nuclear war: *The Day After*. They were having a good time. Ships sank. The world blew up. That was reality.

In the pilothouse it was the God watch.

"What's the sixth book in the Bible?"

The young officer who held Bible study regularly in the chart room just off the pilothouse quizzed one of the seamen.

"How many chapters does it have?"

Both men were turned from the windows, toward the reassurance of the charts, the compasses, the coffee machine, the red electricity, the Lord. The antarctic wind whined in the Clear Screen windows, and the blue twilight cast a chill like a steel gauze net across the ship. But as long as they did not look, they were safe. On the other side of the pilothouse a seaman spoke into the public address system: "Now popcorn will be served on the after-crew's mess deck." There was more than one way to put a hand across the light of Antarctica.

"How many chapters in Revelation?"

(2)

I ran on the treadmill until it hurt. Wes LeMasurier pedalled cheerfully away on the stationary bicycle. The executive officer rowed solemnly, with great long reaching strokes, kilometer after kilometer passing by on the machine's odometer, phantom miles of still water, children fishing, and ducks. The treadmill had wood rollers; my steps roared. In the forward compartment in which the treadmill leaned against a couple of dozen empty oxygen bottles that I stared at as I ran, the sound of ice hitting steel came through the hull. It was a muffled booming, a sonorous mushing sound, as if the ice was softer than it seemed, but when the boom came the whole ship began a slow lurch, and I staggered in my stride. The *Polar Sea* was moving at last.

I ran on; the treadmill roared; the ice thundered; the exec rowed; slowly we drew nearer to the unknown mountain, acting out, for one of the last times on earth, the ancient story of exploration.

"An air of impending drama foreshadowed every mile of progress," Admiral Richard E. Byrd wrote in 1929. "North, east, south and west—everything that was there was unseen and untrodden and unknown." In this little pocket of unexplored earth, hitherto shielded by cold from humankind's urgent search of the globe, our miles too were foreshadowed by awe.

As a rare form of life here—human beings in Antarctica—we seemed haunted by our own history. The voices of people long gone were part of the present wind. Maybe it was because the exploration of places where humans had not been seemed archaic itself, a pursuit common to previous centuries but strange in our own. Or maybe it was just because here it was still the same wind: except for a scattering of buildings on a few outcrops and a few bodies lost in the ice, nothing had changed here since Byrd first saw this part of Antarctica, a land of glaciers and mountains he named for his wife—Marie Byrd Land. Nothing had changed since 1774, when James Cook pursued civilization's last dreams of a green southern continent to their death in the pack.

What dreams!

"The latitude in which it lies promises all the crops of the Mother Country," wrote Yves-Joseph de Kerguelen-Trémarec in 1772. Here was another New World, grander and more mysterious still than Columbus's. Kerguelen had seen it on his own expedition: headlands in fog, shrouded and inviting. He had been unable to stay, but what promise lay behind those mists! The wisdom of the ancients held truth—all the way back to Aristotle, geographers and philosophers had speculated about an enormous southern continent, the missing piece of the earth's great puzzle. Kerguelen had found it:

"No doubt wood, minerals, diamonds, rubies and precious stones and marble will be found. . . . If men of a different species are not discovered at least there will be people living in a state of nature, knowing nothing of the artifices of civilized society. In short South France will furnish marvelous physical and moral spectacles."

Why not? At about the same time, Thomas Jefferson and others in the place called the New World were learning some of the details of democracy from the Iroquois. Why shouldn't this newer world, more remote even than upper New York State, yield as great a gift?

Outside the *Polar Sea* the antarctic wind blew cold, forever blowing the words of James Cook across the landscape, a scour of reality, rubbing Kerguelen's optimism from the face of the land. Cook was in the same sea that the icebreaker sailed 210 years later; in this timeless white waste he was with us now.

December 15, 1773:
The Ice begins to increase fast . . . so fast upon us that at 6 o'Clock we were obliged to alter the Course more to the East, having to the South an extensive field of loose ice. . . . We therefore hauled to the NE on which course we had stretched but a little way before we found our selves quite imbayed by the ice . . . soon got clear of all the loose ice but had yet many huge [ice] islands to encounter . . . one of these masses was very near proving fatal to us. . . . According

to the old proverb a miss is as good as a mile, but our situation requires more misses than we can expect. This field or loose ice is not such as is usually formed in Bays or Rivers, but like such as is broke off from large Islands, round ill-shaped pieces from the size of a small Ship's Hull downwards, whilst we were amongst it we frequently, notwithstanding all our care, ran against some of the large pieces, the shocks which the Ship received thereby was very considerable. . . .

Like others who came south later, Cook and his expedition were rooted in war and politics. Cook originally rose to prominence because his surveying talents led directly to the British capture of Quebec during the French and Indian War. The expedition was liberally financed partly because the British didn't want anyone else—particularly the French—establishing an empire where wood, minerals, diamonds, rubies, precious stones, and moral spectacles might be found: "[Y]ou are to discover and take possession in the name of King George of convenient situations in the South Land."

There were no convenient situations.

Christmas Eve, 1773:
[A]s we were standing to the SE, fell in with such a vast quantity of field or loose ice as covered the whole Sea from South to East and was so thick and close as to obstruct our passage. . . . [W]ith the wind northerly a strong gale attended with a thick fog Sleet and Snow which froze to the Rigging as it fell and decorated the whole with icicles . . . the cold so intense as hardly to be endured, the whole Sea in a manner covered with ice. . . .

A "right-headed unaffected man," James Cook. He found some of the loveliest places on the earth and some of the most harsh. His tremendous journey around the world at its base led to a bitter conclusion: Antarctica would offer human beings nothing at all.

January 30, 1774:
At 4 o'Clock . . . we perceived the Clouds over the Horizon in the South to be of an unusual Snow-white brightness, which we knew

denounced our approach to field Ice; . . . It extended east and west far beyond the reach of our sight, while the southern half of the horizon was illuminated by rays of light which were reflected from the Ice to a considerable height. . . . It was indeed my opinion, as well as the opinion of most on board, that this Ice extends quite to the Pole, or perhaps joins to some land to which it has been fixed since the creation.

He was stopped at latitude 71°10′ south, longitude 106°54′ west —not far, in Antarctic distances, from the mountain later to be named Siple. He would spend another whole season trying to find the mystery continent, but he would never get any farther south, nor would he see any part of the ice-smothered land he thought might be there. He saw a few of the sub-Antarctic islands, but they did not impress him with their gentleness. It seemed likely to him that anything he might have found buried deeper in the ice would have been worse.

Thick foggs, Snow storms, Intense Cold and every other thing that can render Navigation dangerous one has to encounter, and these difficulties are heightened by the inexpressable horrid aspects of the Country, a Country doomed by Nature to lie buried under everlasting ice and snow. . . . It would have been rashness in me to have risked all which had been done . . . in finding and exploring a Coast which, when done, would have answer'd no end whatsoever.

The place was useless. He turned away with relief.

Even I who had Ambition not only to go farther than any one had done before but as far as it was possible for man to go, was not sorry. . . .

I ran on the treadmill, and the *Polar Sea* steamed on: 73°50′ south, 135° west. Dick Cameron was up in the pilothouse, watching. Wes LeMasurier prepared his equipment. Conway and Mc-

Intosh stood in the wind. For some reason they all thought James Cook was wrong.

The clouds over the horizon were of an unusual snow-white brightness: there was ice blink shining in the direction of Mt. Siple.

Chapter Four

Looking for a Virgin

(1)

The hours moved slowly. The position recorded on the monitor of the navsat seemed to change even more gradually, the longitude numbers shrinking one deliberate second at a time, the latitude rising and falling imperceptibly, like the barometer. We waited. We exercised. We ate too much at short intervals: 7:30, 11:30, 4:30. Popcorn. Cookies from the ship's store. "Do you realize," Ed Zeller said after loping up to the pilothouse one morning soon after breakfast, "that we have to eat lunch in five minutes? This is the most strenuous part of the entire cruise."

The triangles of the ship's position hopped around on the Defense Mapping Agency chart, drawing vaguely closer to the outline of Mt. Siple with its plus or minus peak. The only progress we seemed to make was against time itself; almost every day the clock was advanced an hour as we crossed the narrow time zones jammed together at the bottom of the earth. This floating clock was bewildering. Soon the midnight hours of deepening twilight were filled with insomniacs roaming the ship. The time was always changed after breakfast, bringing lunch gruesomely closer. We stuffed and slept. But we always came back up to the pilothouse to look again at the ice and at the story on the screen of the navsat.

Latitude 73°58' south; longitude 143°55' west

The *Polar Sea* glided like a ghost ship on the still water. The water was as dark and clear as an antarctic night, on which icebergs floated motionless like stone clouds. "A stillness, weird and uncanny, seemed to have fallen upon everything when we entered the silent water streets of this vast unpeopled white city." Ernest Shackleton, 1908. There was no wind, no swell, no motion upon the whole earth but for the ship and the birds. Snow petrels flitted around us like white bats, invisible against the ice but dazzling against the black of the water, so that they seemed to appear and disappear at will. They were eerie birds, suited to this strange continent: the first ones we saw flew up off the initial floe we hit sailing out of McMurdo—they seemed born in that instant, the spirit of the broken ice. Even the Defense Mapping Agency's sailing directions for Antarctica, which we examined to help pass the time, found the snow petrel almost supernatural: "Some expeditions have not seen this bird until the edge of the pack was reached," it said, "after which they became abundant as if by magic."

Penguins stood on flat, thin floes that looked like trapezoids cut from poster card. When the ship hit, the trapezoids split and the birds ran like windup dolls, with their wing arms jerking and their little stiff legs slipping around on the snow. Eyes round and aghast, they were full of absurd terror. Crew and scientists laughed and laughed, heartlessly. Shackleton: "Marston, our artist, whose sense of the ludicrous is very fully developed, was in ecstasies at their solemn astonishment and profound concern."

From the top of the flying bridge, out in the breeze, the ship seemed to cross the water with an effortless soar, bow wave and wake invisible and the sound of the huge engines almost mute in the vessel's depths. The ship seemed to be held up less by the skin of the sea than by its own lightness in the light world.

Latitude 73°54' south; longitude 143°55' west

"I guess I've always liked going places where people haven't been," said Dick Cameron. He was happier today; in the night the ice had cast the *Polar Sea* out into the black space of open water, and now the ship slid deeper and deeper into that diminishing artifact of history he found so precious—the unknown. He had come down here first on the icebreaker *Northwind* in the fall of 1956, leaving his wife pregnant. The ice squeezed one of the ships in the group and buckled plates, and he finished the journey in the icebreaker *Glacier*. His son was born on March 11, 1957, the day Admiral Richard E. Byrd died—a day when Dick Cameron was still on the ice. When he returned, his son was a year old, and perhaps the foundations of separation that later broke his marriage had already been formed. His more permanent attachment was to Antarctica.

"When I remarried this past year I told my wife I'm going to have to do these things," Cameron said with a grin. "She said she knows that."

The ship glided across a sheet of ice and split it with hardly a jar. The ice was four feet thick. Two Adélie penguins on the far side ran around on the edge for a while and then appeared to abandon all hope. With little flapping gestures of despair they dove for their lives.

"There is something about the Antarctic, the isolation of it all," Cameron said. "It's a beautiful place. It's like being in another world."

Latitude 73° 24′ south; longitude 140° 39′ west

On their way to the pilothouse or the wardroom from their staterooms below, the guests aboard the *Polar Sea* paused at the porthole in a door on the first deck. It was their first glimpse at what had been happening while they were below. It got to be a habit, a little genuflection to Antarctica. Most of us just glanced—Aha! Ice! Blizzard! Stuck again!—then continued on up the sairs. I came up one morning with Bill McIntosh, but he, naturally, didn't just peer at the ice; he opened the door and went out on deck. It was a return to his natural element—in his patched coat he slipped out there as easily as a mottled leopard seal sliding off a floe. For me it was more like stepping unclad into space: the wind and cold hit so hard that Antarctica might have been vacuum. It drove my breath away.

I came back inside. The door dogged shut; it sealed like an airlock. The ship was a strange warm enclave in which we ate fried chicken and pizza, watched movies on TV, quizzed each other about the Bible, thought about mail and summer sun on little lawns, while the creatures of the ice planet stood out in the snow like native sentinels distracting us with antics as the great coldness closed in.

Latitude 73°24′ south; longitude 140°38′ west

In the pilothouse Wes LeMasurier raised volcanoes and glaciers with his hands.

"As a gross simplification you start twenty-five million years ago and all the land here was probably above sea level," he said. He waved his hands around. The earth's crust pulled apart. Great slabs of continent thinned and subsided. "The material beneath it rises up and melts. It forms volcanoes." His hands brought forth lava. Steam and smoke boiled up out of ice. "The ice level changes rapidly, and all these volcanoes are building themselves up by repeated eruptions. When the ice sheet is down you get volcanoes made of lava. When the ice sheet is high you get volcanoes made of chips of glass." Antarctica lay white and heaving in his palm. It was history he was after, the magnificent history of heat, stone, and ice. Glass chips—volcanic tuff—would tell him a story of ice; lava would speak of open air. He glanced out the window. The sun that had appeared briefly was going down into a fog of blowing snow, trailing light. It looked like a drop of syrup sliding down the glass.

"Nobody's visited Mount Siple before," LeMasurier said. Was there wistfulness behind his good cheer? "So there's no telling what we'll find there."

Latitude 73°26′ south; longitude 139°46′ west

It was a late twilight. Snow fell. The *Polar Sea* worked through heavy ice. The floes were ten or fifteen feet thick, with narrow streaks of black water between. Speed was two knots. As the ship encountered each floe its bow rose up on the ice and slid to port or starboard, and for a few moments the whole vast mechanism seemed stopped, while the propellers thundered, breaking huge blocks of ice and sending shudders through the ship. In the pilot-house the enclosed air quaked. Then a crack ran slowly through the floe, opening a black space into which loose snow blew like dust, and the ship slid off into the crack and surged ahead. The ice pushed the ship around; the wake wound tortuously through the ice fields, as if following a river. Up in the pilothouse a quiet litany of steering instructions hummed between the officer of the deck and the steersman. Behind it was a faint rhythm, the constant *tink, tink, tink* of the directional gyroscopes swinging back and forth through the degrees of the wandering heading.

In the snowfall a lead opened out ahead, a crack just the width of the ship, leading into the white gloom. No one had ever been here before, but it looked to us, reaching in vain for normal things, as if someone were out there just ahead, a smoky old man running the Siple County Highway Department snowplow, plowing out a black macadam road. The ship lurched along, banking itself off the roadside drifts, and coasted down the dotted yellow line.

Tink, tink, tink.

"Rudder five degrees port."

"Rudder five degrees port aye."

Tink, tink, tink.

Two hooded joggers crossed the foredeck. A minute and a half later they trotted past again, stepping nimbly among bollards, coiled lines, and hatch covers. Beyond them the moon, golden but faint in the falling snow, hung above the road to Mt. Siple. For a while it seemed reassuringly familiar. It reminded us that we were still on earth. But the snowfall slowly squeezed it oblong, the phantom snowplow went back to the yard in the black deep, the road dwindled down to a deer trail and then nothing, and the *Polar Sea* once again heaved itself across frozen prairie. In the whiteness all shape and definition faded, and as the ship weaved and the directional gyros plinked, the moon became a lamp carried before us, a lamp on a chain, swinging in the wind.

Latitude 73°24′ south; longitude 139°10′ west

Out of thin air the captain appeared in the pilothouse. He was smiling. Everyone within sight watched him surreptitiously. Would he abandon hope for Mt. Siple and turn north for open water?

He kept smiling. He had to. The atmosphere charged whenever he appeared. The scientists were overfed, but they hungered for Mt. Siple. He held their only hope of nourishment. If they starved on this journey they would let him know. Yet only weeks before, the old icebreaker *Westwind*, working its way through the ice in the Weddell Sea, had been pushed against the Larsen Ice Shelf and split like an orange. The eighty-three-foot gash had been patched at King George Island and the *Westwind* had limped home, possibly never to return south. A shipload of frustrated scientists was a small price to pay to avoid something like that.

James Cook, who had his own inscrutable smile, had suffered most at the hands of science, right at the beginning. His antarctic naturalist was a snob named John Reinhold Forster, who believed his own presence at Cook's table raised the captain's self-esteem above his station.

"It can only be said that Forster's demands on other people were very great, his ideas of his own rights extreme, his ability to compromise little; and his opinion of his own virtues permanent," wrote J. C. Beaglehole, editor of Cook's journals. Cook suffered at length from Forster's pomposity, and eventually, freed from the burden, expressed himself briefly. When a lieutenant recently appointed to the *Resolution* for Cook's third expedition said to his new captain that it was too bad no scientist would be on board this time,

Cook replied, "Curse the scientists, and all science into the bargain."

Scientists and the people who supported science had grown more amicable later. But the captain of the *Polar Sea* kept to himself as he could, out of reach of the tension his presence made.

Now he looked happily out at the smothered sea. He put his coffee cup in a holder, picked up a pair of binoculars, stared out the window for a few minutes, put the binoculars back, picked up the coffee cup, and smiled. He may have been thinking about sacrifices to the Herbie god, or perhaps of the *Resolution*'s more pleasant encounters among South Sea isles. He said:

"If we don't get good weather tomorrow we'll have to start looking for a virgin."

He smiled. He disappeared.

Latitude 73° 47′ south; longitude 134° 17′ west

Ice blink blazed on the horizon. The snow had stopped. The overcast was bright ahead, to starboard and aft, telling its reflective story of ice going on and on over the world's curve. Out to port, ninety degrees off the course, was a cave of water sky where open sea absorbed the light and the clouds were dark.

"What you're looking at out the window right now is absolutely critical for global weather," said Ed Zeller. He and Gisela Dreschhoff stood in the pilothouse. The crew was particularly alert this morning, pleased to be living in charmed air: Dreschhoff was wearing perfume. "We believe Antarctica has a grossly out-of-proportion influence on world climate," Zeller continued. "You have what amounts to a pulse beat: Antarctica goes from about fourteen million square kilometers of ice for the continent alone in the middle of summer to over thirty million square kilometers in winter including the pack. Because of the reflectivity—the albedo—the amount of energy the earth actually gets is critical.

"Our contention is that when you have an extensive ice cover you reflect more heat back into space, and more importantly, you effectively shut off fourteen to eighteen million square kilometers of water that could be evaporating into the atmosphere but does not. You actually influence the global water budget."

The *Polar Sea* slid across the snow and into a little polynya—an area of open water—which was scuffed by the wind. The clouds were dissolving, letting in sun. Zeller and Dreschhoff were here to fly in helicopters close to rock outcrops with a radioactivity counter, reading for signs of uranium, thorium, potassium. But their interest in the continent seemed more encompassing. They had a restrained, elegant curiosity about the whole place. Wes LeMasurier, for all his kindly sardonic eye, was hot as a lava rock about the long bubble and crunch of the antarctic crust; Zeller and Dreschhoff were cool, detached, and entangled in the continent the way a mathematician is linked to an elegant equation. "Wes is very intense about these volcanoes," Dick Cameron said. "Zeller's tendency is to pick out interesting little things." Antarctica offered a wealth of these curiosities, some more curious than others.

Zeller and Dreschhoff lived in Kansas; during the previous year a grain company, looking for an edge, asked them to speculate formally on the season's grain yield based on the extent of the antarctic ice. It was an oddly specific bit of information to pry from theories that are not only largely speculative but are based on a relationship of Antarctica to the world that is still poorly understood. And at first it looked as if the Zeller-Dreschhoff report would prove that the stretch was too long. On the spring day the grain company representative came to Lawrence to get the report it was pouring rain.

"We said, well, you know, ah, there may be a mistake this year," Zeller said. "But our numbers say it's going to be a lousy year. Of course you look outside, it's low clouds and rain—people had gotten out their crops and the crops had sprouted—and we say it's going to be a lousy year." Zeller laughed. "We didn't believe our own forecast, for God's sake!

"So along about July we were having hundred-degree temperatures. We hadn't had a drop of rain in Kansas—the crops were going to pot everywhere—but the prices on grain were still very low, and about a week before the prices went up the company decided these idiots at the university were probably not quite such idiots after all."

Zeller paused. As the strength of the sun grew, making shadows, the flat world of the morning turned into a scene, like a sheet of photographic paper in the tray taking on shapes and shadows and, at last, color. Far off in the distance, under the remains of the racing overcast, an iceberg glowed briefly—a perfect golden pyramid—then vanished. "I wish I had believed myself," Zeller said, with no regret whatsoever. "Damn fool!"

Latitude 73° 10′ south; longitude 133° 29′ west

In the wardroom the officers watched Gregory Peck straighten out a combat squadron in *Twelve O'Clock High*. In the wardroom lounge Adolf Hitler preached peace through strength in *The Winds of War*. The ship moved through the land of ice and peace. On an afternoon when the *Polar Sea* was parked in a floe again, waiting for better weather, a small group gathered for a rare occasion: a film about Antarctica. It was a video-tape of an old 16-mm documentary about Ernest Shackleton's magnificent journey from 1914 to 1916.

Up on the screen that hung from the ceiling above the tables, the frayed black-and-white pictures flickered with the famous story. There were Shackleton and his men setting forth in their ship, the *Endurance*, planning to blaze a path across the continent. There they were mugging for the camera, hugging the sled dogs they would later have to kill for food. There they were penetrating the pack at the edge of the Weddell Sea, through weather and ice that could have been photographed that same day off the bow of the *Polar Sea*. There was the ice trap, the ship beset for the winter. There

was the shifting light, the deceptions of Antarctica, that Shackleton, searching endlessly for release from this deadly bondage, described in his diary:

> The weather is foggy and unseasonably cold. Mirages are continually
> giving us false alarms. Icebergs hang upside down in the sky; the
> land appears as layers of silvery or golden cloud; cloud-banks look
> like land; icebergs masquerade as islands, and the distant barrier to
> the south is thrown into view, although it is really outside our range
> of vision. Worst of all is the deceptive appearance of open water,
> caused by refraction or by the sun shining at an angle on fields of
> snow.

On the small screen the pictures flickered, the ice moved, and
in October and November the *Endurance* was crushed, masts falling into kindling. In the wardroom we sat back in our big chairs
while the wind beat at the small windows, and watched as Shackleton's hopes for exploration were ground to despair by the ice. On
the screen the masts fell, the men hauled their whaleboats away
from the wreck, and finally they reached Elephant Island at the
end of the Antarctic Peninsula. The quality of the film was poor,
but we saw right through it to the drama as, on April 24, 1916,
with winter again closing in, Shackleton and four others set off in
the twenty-two-foot whaleboat *James Caird* on their attempt to
fetch rescue that must have seemed a sorry end to all the hopes of
glory.

There were no photos of the crossing of the tumultuous Drake
Passage in the whaleboat, the same passage the passengers aboard
the huge *Polar Sea* looked forward to with dread, but the film
showed paintings of the arrival at the forbidding cliffs of South
Georgia, 870 miles north. By sketch and narration we crossed the
mountains with Shackleton as he and two others glissaded down
an ice slope and climbed through a waterfall to tumble, bruised,
disheveled, unrecognizable, triumphant, at the edge of a Nor-
wegian whaling camp. The film, as if its producer had worried that

his story of incredible hardship and adventure was not enough, drifted off into natural history sequences and shameless anthropomorphizing of penguins and Cape pigeons before it got back to Shackleton's return to the Antarctic for the rest of his men; but Shackleton stayed with us. As he walked the last yards to make contact with the world again, he knew that his journey of adventure was triumphant.

"We had flung down the adze from the top of the fall," he wrote later, "and also the logbook and the cooker wrapped in one of our blouses. That was all, except our wet clothes, that we brought out of the Antarctic, which we had entered a year and a half before with well-found ship, full equipment, and high hopes. That was all of tangible things; but in memories we were rich. We had 'suffered, starved and triumphed, grovelled down yet grasped at glory, grown bigger in the bigness of the whole.' We had seen God in His splendours, heard the text that Nature renders. We had reached the naked soul of man."

There were no photos in the movie of Shackleton's arrival at the whaling station, although it was enough of a legend to need none. Three men, drawn down to hair and sinew and bone by the cold, walked up out of the eternal southern wind, out of the embrace of death, to confront others who had known them and had already spent the passing grief of their loss. They were specters; they had the faces of those who had looked the wind in the eye; they had seen what few see and live, and they were different. Antarctica changed people. In 1911, when Douglas Mawson dragged himself home from his terrible walk through the Kingdom of Blizzards, with the bodies of his two companions left behind in the ice, the first member of the base-camp party to reach him looked hard at that ravaged face and said, "Which one are you?"

"Everybody knew Shackleton well," wrote a whaler who was at the station when the three men walked in. "And we very sorry he is lost in ice with all hands. We not know three terrible-looking bearded men who walk into office off the mountainside. Manager say 'Who the hell are you?' and terrible bearded man in the centre of the three say very quietly 'my name is Shackleton.' Me—I turn away and weep. I think Manager weep too."

It was May 10, 1916. Shackleton had sailed back from the moon. The men on the ice had received no letters, listened to no radios. In the months of terrible cold, in which all on the expedition had spent their whole store of life fighting the slow violence of the ice and the rage of the sea, they had not known what happened in the world of human beings. Now, like all those who came after him, Shackleton reached to renew that contact. What he got was the first spark of the horror of the twentieth century, the kind of news that later became familiar.

Shackleton wrote in the book *South!*:

> Mr. Sorlle [the manager] came out to the door and said, "Well?"
> "Don't you know me?" I said.
> "I know your voice," he replied doubtfully. "You're the mate of the Daisy."
> "My name is Shackleton," I said.
> Immediately he put out his hand and said, "Come in. Come in."
> "Tell me, when was the war over?" I asked.
> "The war is not over," he answered. "Millions are being killed. Europe is mad. The world is mad."

On January 5, 1922, Shackleton died of a heart attack in the cabin of his ship *Quest*, trying to get south again. He was buried on South Georgia Island.

Latitude 73° 48′ south; longitude 132° 33′ west

Every lump of snow in the fields in which the *Polar Sea* was parked blazed white and cast a shadow. All the whipped-cream peaks of broken ice, all the swirls of drift, every frost goose bump on the surface, every distant iceberg, every little windblown contour line of snow, lay sharp-edged, defined to the horizon. At last the sun shone. A whole landscape, whose features could be utterly erased in a moment by a cloud or windblown snow, had appeared out of the blankness in which we had traveled for days. Even the surface of the snow itself had grain, as if the wind were a whisk of hair.

"At my present position it's ten-tenths," said a voice on the radio. "There's an area around it of nine-tenths."

The *Polar Sea* was parked again in the ice. The white sheet appeared solid in all directions: ten-tenths. The ship had sent its helicopters—the long-range modern substitute for reading ice blink and water sky—out to find a lead. The reports were not encouraging. J.D., muttering to himself about death ice and doom, yelled at the pilots over the microphone in his amiable tenor, and offered gloomy predictions to the pilothouse in general: "Looks like a red light, gentlemen."

The helos ranged farther out: twenty-five nautical miles, thirty-five nautical miles.

"Massive floes. Consolidated ice." Helicopter 13.

Forty nautical miles.

"We're sitting right over a polynya right now. It's not very big, but it's all the open water we can see."

Forty-five nautical miles.

"Solid floes, fifteen acres in size, surrounded by nine-tenths."

J.D. made notes. The helos were down over the horizon, bringing the whine of engine noise to places that had only heard wind and penguins since the first penguins popped up out of the sea. The scene was all black and white, but when you looked long it resolved itself into a loveliness of subtle color. Hidden in the glare and in the hard shadows were bright shades of gold and white on the crests of ice, the many blues of shaded snow, the ethereal blue of iceberg cliffs, the gleaming black of the water in the few cracks between floes, the green-blue depths of ice reaching into the black, and the faint brown tone at the deepest edges of the ice footings: the algae growth that, with its prodigious feat of turning chilly water and muted sunlight into life everywhere beneath the ice, nourished the whole pyramid of antarctic beings—plankton to penguins to seals to whales—and made these forbidding waters among the most productive on earth.

"Zero four two degrees at forty-six miles DME." Helicopter 13. "Essentially no difference. We're going to change heading."

Fifty miles. Helicopter 13.

"Seven-tenths. Fairly small floes. It's the best we've seen, but it's not too good."

"Yellow light, gentlemen." J.D.

"At zero zero zero, fifty-four DME." Helo 12. "It's down to five-tenths. It appears to be proceeding 330 magnetic."

"Fairly open area now." Helo 13. "Fifty-seven miles DME."

J.D. smiled a fanatical grin.

"Holy shit," he said. "Green light flickering!"

The captain materialized, smiling a broad, knowing smile. He used the binoculars. He examined the satellite ice charts sent by radio from Washington. He said:

"Mount Siple, here we come."

J.D. began to move around the pilothouse, preparing the ship to receive its scouts, preparing it to move. He exhorted the troops: "No prisoners!"

Dick Cameron was grinning too, in his beard.

Someone quoted Sir Francis Drake: "So shall we not doubt victory," he said. "For our cause is good."

The *Polar Sea* moved, the brief night came, and at approximately 2:00 A.M., in the twilight of dawn about thirty miles by the chart southwest of Mt. Siple, land appeared about ten miles away on the horizon, in a place where there was supposed to be only sea.

(2)

During the previous evening the *Polar Sea* moved out of an area of five-tenths ice into what seemed to be nearly open water, where the water-sky clouds hung in gloomy dark masses over blackness. The blackness was still, but wind howled at the superstructure and whistled in the Clear Screen windows. For those just arriving in the pilothouse it took a couple of moments to realize that the strangely flat and undisturbed surface was frozen.

The fresh ice was just a skin on the water. In the early evening a minke whale, the small baleen whale most common in Antarctica, rose to breathe. It broke the thin ice in a chain of sudden pools. The wind tore into the exposed water as if it felt deprived. It made pocket storms; mean black flusters and threads of spume. Cameron was in the pilothouse watching the whale. He could not resist. "Does your minke bite?" he said.

"Is that a vast floe or a giant floe?" Cameron said a little later, grinning in his beard. This was a continuing discussion. Cameron and I argued whether a floe the ship bounced off earlier, a chunk perhaps fifteen acres in extent whose edges were rounded and humped by a season's collisions with its neighbors, would be called vast or giant in formal ice terminology. We finally looked it up in the executive officer's ice glossary. Giant, it turned out, would have been a gross exaggeration: it only applied to floes ten kilometers or more across. The floe, which certainly seemed vast enough, probably only deserved the mild adjective big.

This happened all the time. The scientists, none of them students of sea ice and all of them in love with precision, tried to sort what they saw into their own growing polar vocabulary. Soon they became conversant with terms that, in addition to giant, vast, big, medium, and small floes, included other items such as bergy bits (small chunks of floating glacial ice), growlers (smaller chunks), frazil ice (fine spicules), and grease ice (a soupy layer on the surface). The present thin cover was probably dark nilas.

The matter of the floe partially settled, quiet descended on the pilothouse again, and in the insulated peace of the big room there came a ringing ceramic clatter as a seaman carried a fistful of cups up the ladder inside the mast just aft of the pilothouse. He was going up to the aloft conn, a cozy lookout high above the pilothouse, where J.D. was directing the ship. Stitching his wake through the floes across a straight line on the chart, J.D. was aiming at a destination marked on the chart beside Mt. Siple with a small pencilled square, the words "Be here," and the estimated time of arrival: 0600. In a matter of hours a universal human desire, so impossible to feed in the twentieth-century world, would be momentarily satisfied for 160 people: the longing to be somewhere utterly new.

The door to Mt. Siple was open. There was contentment in the pilothouse. Arrival was no longer in doubt. Now the sound of the distribution of coffee reminded us that although others had to stay awake, we were not so constrained. The glorious morning would demand all attention; it was only fair to ourselves to be prepared. So as the short night fell, the pilothouse emptied of all but the watch, and Mt. Siple came upon us in our dreams.

(3)

Soon after early light, at about 0200, land emerged gently and unexpectedly from the pale distance. A seaman named Larry James, the lookout, saw it first. It was just two fuzzy marks against the indefinite sky, standing slightly above the horizon, gray spots growing slowly darker as if the flowing dust of space were clotting into stone right there in the swirl. It was not imposing. One of those who first saw the land later described it eloquently as "a little point sticking up there." But it was rock where no rock should be.

The quartermaster hurried to the chart drawers and pulled out more charts. They indicated with only a hint of self-doubt that what was out there was not land. In other circumstances, perhaps, it could have been a mirage, the *fata morgana* of the cold that could stretch penguins to six feet tall and pull mountains up from three hundred miles over the horizon. But radar was not vulnerable to *fata morgana*, and whatever was out there marched brightly into the golden screen.

"We're used to looking at the chart and things are there," said one of the men on watch when those who were asleep at the time arrived in the pilothouse at 3:00 A.M. "That's what we're used to as sailors. This *wasn't* there. It wasn't *supposed* to be there. It was just an odd feeling."

The motion of the ship stopped. The passengers awoke in the unexpected stillness. On up the stairs! Look out the porthole! Parked again. Snow all around. Then when we reached the pilothouse we saw it: the indistinct shapes had become two little towers of black rock, standing out there in the whiteness exactly 14,300 meters by the radar from the ship. Now it was agreed: this land was part of Mt. Siple. The charts were wrong. The Be Here box was fifteen miles ashore.

Mt. Siple had been seen before, of course, although because of its vast distance from anywhere definitively charted its location was not precise. It had first appeared not to the human eye but to the camera lens, when a faint conical shape developed on photographs taken from a plane in 1940. The observers had missed it, but the emulsion caught its glow. It had been seen from the air other times—the scientists were prepared for their venture with aerial photographs taken from a C-130. And it had been observed at least once by a ship passing to the north. One of the outcrops we saw now even had a name, Lovill Bluff. The other outcrop, an abrupt black tower like a thumb sticking up out of snow, surrounded by a moat dug by wind and by the faint warmth collected by the dark rock from the sun, soon also gained a name, at least for the duration of the *Polar Sea*'s visit. J.D. studied it at length through the binoculars and finally made his decision.

"That," he said, "is Death Rock."

(4)

"Go ahead and say we'll probably have flight quarters shortly after twelve-thirty," the captain said, smiling, to the lieutenant j.g. beside him.

The lieutenant turned to the seaman beside him.

"Announce that we'll have flight quarters at approximately twelve-thirty," the lieutenant said.

The seaman flipped on the public address system.

"Now," he said, and the voice boomed through the ship. "Flight quarters will be called at twelve-thirty."

The mountain lay there now at our mercy, or so it seemed: ice and rock within reach at last of the mechanized, acquisitive grasp of human beings, the long reach for knowledge. Ashore! Ashore to the new land!

"A boat was lowered and we piled into it eagerly." The year was 1898, and the words were written on the ship *Belgica*, during the first truly scientific expedition to Antarctica, in the diary of Dr. Frederick Cook. "It was a curious evening. Everything about us had an other-world appearance. The scenery, the light, the clouds, the atmosphere, the curious luminous grey of the water—everything wore an air of mystery."

Eighty-six years later, a helicopter was rolled out on deck of the *Polar Sea* and Wes LeMasurier and his crew put on big orange flotation suits and piled into it eagerly. But Antarctica was still mysterious.

The ship was jammed into an ice floe. Perhaps it was a vast floe. Its boundaries were far off in the distance, little broken ridges that might have been hummocks or might have been edge. The ship's stern was turned to the mountain, as if the *Polar Sea* refused to look at the thing it had found lying on the sea. Between it and the rock lay an ice-locked lagoon of black water, cold as obsidian. Past that a great flat tabular berg stood close to shore, listing slightly to the north, a dying guardian of the mountain's secrets. The berg's shadowed ice cliffs looked as solid as land. But the real land showed only as those two dark ruined teeth against the white of the mountain behind them, faults in the rising ice.

The mountain gave just a hint of its existence. It was a discomforting hint. It would have been easier to grasp if it had been invisible and we didn't have to deal with this glimpse. After we looked at Lovill Bluff and Death Rock for a few minutes, the shape of what was behind became apparent: a single huge curve in the swirl of gray and white. It changed all perspective. It was like looking at a big black spot on a painting and suddenly realizing the spot was just the pupil of an eye and the face was all over the wall. The slope of Mt. Siple began far to the north of the outcrops and rose from the plain of ice in a gentle curve up to the base of the cloud, where it disappeared. Just a single lower slope of the mountain was visible, but it was too much. It was too large, out of scale. This soft lift of ice must rise inexorably beyond our sight into a vast, smooth outline of an enormous mass, towering above us in the cloud.

Hidden, the mountain had its own ice blink: the muffling damp that concealed this weight of rock and ice glowed with reflected light. Invisible, Mt. Siple shone, its cloaked radiance white, flat, and chilling.

"It doesn't make a lot of difference to me that nobody has been there before," LeMasurier said. "That's interesting, but what I really think about is the anticipation of finally getting this material. At last you're going to be able to get some information about it. It will be only a small idea; some hint, and some hint of the age of it, so it isn't just a big blank sitting up there."

Mt. Siple was like all of Antarctica: unlike everywhere else in the world, this place's pioneers were not followed by the scientists—the pioneers *were* the scientists. When the helo landed on the beach below Lovill Bluff, the first to set foot on the new land would be a crew member. The next four out would be scientists, carrying their hammers, their sample bags, and their burden of representing the human race in a place where men and women had never breathed the air. They would not make us ashamed; they came at the urging of humankind's most generous drive, the pursuit of knowledge.

"I'm finally going to get a little idea of what the composition of the volcano is," Wes LeMasurier said before he left. "That's really more exciting to me than being the first."

Helicopter 13 rose from the ship in a flurry of powder snow and an arrogant roar, but as it swept away toward the rocks it dwindled down to an orange speck and a fading smoke trail, shrinking in front of the mountain as if the rock grew larger in defense of secrets that had seemed eternal. But long after the helo's sound vanished we could see the speck that bore the shield of science advancing on the mountain's loom.

Chapter Five

Death Rock

(1)

Mt. Siple was made of penguin guano and feathers. Ah, the smell!

The helicopter landed on a rubble beach below the cliff of Lovill Bluff. The pilot had difficulty finding a level place among boulders. The boulders and all the stones that protruded from the primordial ooze of which Mt. Siple was made were dark rock. The rocks were splattered with the ooze, and it filled all the spaces between them. The ooze was grayish orange, and mixed with millions of small feathers. It was like an unset mortar mixture made of terribly wrong ingredients.

"If it's lava," Wes LeMasurier had said earlier, referring to the rock, "we'll only need to spend an hour there. If it's tuff, we could spend half a day." After a quick look around he spoke to the pilot. The pilot called the *Polar Sea* pilothouse: "The people on the ground at the beach want to be there three hours."

The four first people on Mt. Siple moved away from the helicopter. The helicopter lifted off and turned back for the ship. "It was with something of a pang," Ernest Shackleton wrote in 1908, about being left on Ross Island for a year, "that we severed our last connection with the world of men." The volcano party, out for the day, felt no pangs. Abandoned by the thundering beast that brought them, the four scientists advanced across the slope.

They were not alone. The makers of the ooze, the ludicrous sentries of Antarctica, surrounded them. The penguins were scruffy —they were molting. They did not look pleased. They squawked,

60

bobbed their heads, and renewed the slime. They were everywhere. They kept the volcano party under surveillance from all sides and from far above.

Lovill Bluff was a cliff just under a thousand feet high. Behind it, toward the mountain itself, the white slope curved out from the cliff in a sharp-edged ridge of ice and snow where the wind, hugging the rock as over the curve of a wing, swept a moat around the stone castle. The ridge above the moat curved around to the upper ridge of rock. On a guano-painted pathway up the beach to the ice, and all the way up the long curve of ice to the hilltop, penguins marched. "They went all the way to the top?" someone would later ask Wes. "Yeah. You could see little bands of them walking along up there." Out on the sea ice, penguins always found the high points. They climbed hummocks and broken chunks of ice, either for the view or to put as much distance as possible between themselves and the leopard seals. Lovill Bluff was the ultimate high point. Their shoulders hunched with the effort, the solemn, upright birds lurched up and up, to stand solemnly in the wind and survey their teeming empire.

Down near the water a single elephant seal, a thousand-pound brown slug with a lugubrious face, lay brooding in its own sludge. The volcano party—Wes and Bill McIntosh, with Dave Johnson and Pam Ellerman, two other geologists—began moving across the slope in the first steps of its meticulous journey to knowledge. They cracked and collected rock samples; they recorded dates, times, locations; they took photographs. Mt. Siple rose above them, immaculate, into cloud: virgin, austere, and unattainable. But below, in infinitesimal steps, the four scientists attained it.

"Like some wild Wagnerian scene," wrote Roland Huntford in *Scott and Amundsen*, "the air rang with the clink of the geologist's hammer and the massed cries of agitated penguins." He was describing the *Belgica* expedition of 1898. The importance of science in itself was one of the strongest currents of tradition in the human culture of Antarctica. What Frederick Cook wrote on the *Belgica* in 1898 also described this day on Mt. Siple: "Thus far we have not unfurled a flag, nor have we made any other effort to take formal possession. . . . [T]he staff of the *Belgica* went ashore to gather, not financial returns, or titles to unclaimed lands, but links of truth to add to the disconnected chain which is to bind the growing annals of terrestrial knowledge."

The three men and one woman, looking at the flecks of color in the broken rock and the texture of grains that fell in their gloved hands, began to explore the great questions that their arrival here on the perimeter of the unknown had only begun to answer. How was this mountain born? What was then on the face of the young world?

(2)

On the *Polar Sea* the helos thundered in and out. J.D. directed their assaults on the mountain from the pilothouse. "Confirming your reservation, sir. You will be on Copter Thirteen at 1300, to go to Point Bravo. And would you like a rental vehicle?"

One of the pilots came up to the pilothouse after a sortie. He arrived in his orange flight suit, bringing with him a breath of burned oil and cold, the whiff of adventure. Cameron and I, who remained on the ship against our yearning because we weren't needed on the mountain, questioned him:

What did the rock look like?

"Rock looks like rock to me."

What did Wes say about it?

"They looked pleased."

When we were done, one of the young sailors took over:

"Any women on that beach over there? Were they bathing?"

The captain came in, smiling, and ordered a ladder put over the side so I could take pictures of the ship and the mountain. I climbed down out of the ship onto the ice and walked away in a foot of snow, poking ahead with the point of an ice ax. Sailors on icebreakers who were allowed to get off on giant floes to play football or photograph penguins called it "ice liberty." This was indeed freedom. A lieutenant who came along as chaperon, to protect me from seduction by the enchanted ice landscape, grinned as we stepped down from the ladder. We would both yield willingly to the spell.

The white world stretched off in all directions. We walked out into an expanse of hard air and white light. The sound of the generators faded. In the ice the big red ship looked like a flat-bottomed plastic model resting on a vast table. It became remote, diminished by the enormous whiteness. The smell of heated air and stack smoke was gone. The smell of food was gone. The smell of Gisela Dreschhoff's perfume was gone. The wind swept across us. It chilled our faces. Tiny bright flakes of snow touched cheek and forehead. They felt like glitter. The wind came from the land, sweeping down off the mysterious highlands of ice. It had a scentless taste of purity.

"We were now revelling in the indescribable freshness of the Antarctic that seems to permeate one's being," Shackleton wrote, "and which must be responsible for that longing to go again which assails each returned explorer from polar regions." Would we be captured too, now that we had taken the fateful breath? Shackleton went again and again. He was rewarded with pain, desperation, endless hardship, and, on his last trip south, death.

We returned to the ship. We watched from the pilothouse. The shape of Lovill Bluff changed. It slowly narrowed. Its little peak where invisible penguins stood guard became more prominent. The floe in which the ship was parked was drifting south. The glacier party went ashore. The survey party went ashore. The Zeller-Dreschhoff party flew over the shore, but had technical difficulties with its equipment. The volcano party was divided: Dave and Bill climbed Lovill Bluff with the penguins, and Wes and Pam were airlifted to Point Charlie, an outcrop of lava. Dick Cameron and I watched from the pilothouse, and slowly the gauze of white drew back from Mt. Siple.

All day clouds had drifted across the sky, smothering all feature. Now, in their withdrawal, as the light from the sun became more strong, they developed shapes: long streaks of mist, stretched out against the mountain in tapering layers. At the surface the wind was less than twenty knots, but the high lines of cloud showed a rush of air aloft. A pale sunlight appeared and cast faint shadows. I climbed up to the flying bridge, and the sun fell warmly on the back of my neck as I watched the mountain.

The clouds took more distinct form. The long slope we had seen in the beginning extended upward now, past one layer of cloud. Slowly another layer of cloud dwindled down to a sheet, and the slope appeared at another level, still rising. On the ship there was a stir. The mountain was coming out of the weather for us.

All that could be seen of Mt. Siple, even almost revealed, was that sloping edge, a very faint but sharp line between the different whites of the ice and the distance. The rising slope and the ice blink of the morning had made the mountain an oppressive mass; now it was entirely insubstantial, a great stone ghost.

At last both sides of the cone appeared, tapering vastly upward to a summit smothered by a windswept hump of lenticular cloud, above which rose more lenses of vapor, gray upon white, like a tower of sculptured smoke. Then the last cap was blown thin, even as more clouds gathered around the base, and for a moment we could see what appeared to be the summit above the indistinct shape of the mountain below. The top of Mt. Siple was not a sweep of crater or a ridge of crags. It was a little bump, a windblown knob. The huge sweep of rock and ice culminated at 10,200 feet above us in a pimple.

The wind blew. Clouds moved against the ice. The sunlight on my neck grew stronger. It seemed that at any moment the intervening shreds of mist would blow away, the whole mountain would shine, and we would know it completely. But even as the distant clouds dissolved, seeming at any moment to give us the entire scene, a flat layer of stratus near the ship moved across the sky like a hand close to the face and shut off the distant view.

"As we say in Antarctica," said Dick Cameron, "*C'est la* goddamn *vie.*"

(3)

Death Rock erupted. Off in the distance a cloud of smoke rose from the pillar of black rock. Within the smoke a red light glowed, on and off, on and off. The smoke faded away and dispersed in the wind of evening, then another white cloud rose from the rock. It became a whirl, then disappeared. The flashing light remained. It was Copter 12, blowing snow, landing next to its burned-out smoke bomb to pick up two scientists and bring them home.

The day of discovery was over, over too soon. The *Polar Sea* was hauling in the science. Twilight came so softly that its first announcement was the appearance of the red lights on the helicopters against the mountain's gray, and then J.D.'s arrangement of return trips. The helicopters came home, two little powerful red bubbles rising off the rock in the white twilight, trailing their thin gray vapor, flashing red lights. They were the only color in the evening, the most brazen presence of technology in the scene all day—in this whole immense solitude of fading light where day and darkness had been the only rhythms of light forever. The red flicker of their lights rose against the vast pattern of black and white, against a picture too rich and subtle for my senses in only two colors: the wonderful gentleness of the northern slope rising up into the clouds; the authority of Lovill Bluff, of Death Rock; the multiple, horizontal layers of black water and white brash ice and floes; the shades of gray-and-white cloud over open water and ice; and the flat white of the fast ice. The red light flashed again on top of Death Rock. It was a radio tower, a lighthouse, an ambulance. Warning: *Flash! Civilization! Flash! Civilization! Flash!*

On the flying bridge I stood transfixed by this ending to a day that saw one of the last unseen places on earth pinned down and examined, watching these messengers of humankind, with their big orange feet, their bulbous noses, their big blank eyes, and their smoke, flying away from their handiwork—another place whose domain was no longer secret. I wished to stun my mind with the sight so its memory would never come out.

The deed was done. Satellites were even now looking down into the machine the United States Geological Survey party had left on Lovill Bluff with the penguins, narrowing Mt. Siple's position down to fewer and fewer meters each hour as the night went on. The scientists had done the deed and now would move on, to find islands and more coastline, to surround the north edge of this island with the net of knowledge, to use that to capture more. It was a good thing, this hunger to know more. For these men the first footsteps on this land meant almost nothing in themselves; what mattered was adding another detail to the grander puzzle, advancing one step farther into the more lasting frontier that they had been pushing back all their lives: the eternal mystery of their own piece of nature's whirl.

The first helicopter thundered back to the deck. On the pad at the ship the scientists came tumbling out of the doors in their fluorescent orange suits, happy as clowns. Like the pilot of the command module circling the moon while others made news, Cameron, who so cherished the unknown, had not sent himself ashore. Now he met the returning explorers, grinning and curious. If he felt envy it did not show.

"Gold!" said Wes LeMasurier. "It's made of solid gold. No, you may not quote me on that."

They came striding back into the hangar, tired, elated. Outside the doors the rotors whistled on Copter 13 as it waited to take off for another run. Wes struggled out of his enormous floppy flight suit, grinning.

"If I smell like penguin shit," he said, "please excuse me."

"It's not that," said Dick Cameron. "It's the way you were walking."

"As long as he doesn't get down on his belly," said someone else, "we'll be all right."

Wes and Cameron lugged his rock box over to the side of the

hangar. Wes was slightly breathless. He waved his hands around and talked rapidly. He talked above the shouts of men, the clatter of equipment, the blast of the public address system. He could not wait.

"It was interesting because it might be that we've got some of the oldest stuff and some of the youngest stuff," he said. "Or it might all be some of the oldest stuff. What we found is basaltic, and it—"

"*Now set flight con two, set flight con two,*" said the hangar loudspeaker.

"—it sort of fits the kind of structure we found elsewhere in Marie Byrd Land. The last thing we were on was a succession of horizontal basalt flows. The other thing was a tuff cone of sorts that might have been submerged when it was erupted." There was consistency to Mt. Siple now, if only from a glimpse: layers of basalt—lava—that had flowed on the side of the mountain some time when it was above the sea; a cone of tuff, the lighter, broken material that lava became when it erupted in contact with water or ice.

"*Now anticipate setting flight con one at 2055.*"

"Now," said Wes, "where's the guy that wanted a rock?"

Sailors gathered around. Wes opened a bag of samples he didn't need and, like a Santa Claus giving candy, handed out little bubbly black rocks. The men took them back down below decks to the berthing areas. There, after all the scientists returned with their gummy boots, the halls would smell of Mt. Siple's penguin guano for two days. In their rooms the men hid the rocks away, saving for their children the pieces of the mountain's shattered unknown.

Chapter Six

An Appearance of Mountains

(1)

The *Polar Sea* heaved mightily, leaned to port ten degrees, and didn't come back.

I was down in my stateroom. Below, the sound and motion of breaking ice was always strange: there were noises of grinding and thumping, and the ship lurched unexpectedly. The sounds did not belong in a seagoing vessel, except as proof of distress. There were booms, hisses, and occasional gushes that sounded like a waterspout opening in a nearby part of the hull. There was thunder, and brushing on cymbals. At night I wore earplugs to prevent being startled awake by some strange new noise.

Now the *Polar Sea* listed, and hung in the list forever, while all forward motion stopped. Everything seemed to hold its breath, to stand on tiptoe, to wait, and wait, and wait.

The icebreaker was traveling again, stealing away from Mt. Siple. It was the last part of this year's Coast Guard antarctic mission, for which the National Science Foundation paid 15 million dollars, for this and other ships, about a hundred thousand a day of it for the *Polar Sea*. At Christmas it carried scientists across the Drake Passage to Palmer Station; in January it broke open the harbor at McMurdo so Captain Brian Shoemaker could get his food and fuel for another season, and it carried scientists up and down the northern Victoria Land coast and along the perimeter of the Ross Ice Shelf, the famous Barrier of history. In February it reached Mt. Siple. Now, with another nod or two in the direction of science on its agenda, it was heading back to the Peninsula to stop at Palmer Station again and then leave the south. Within a month it would be in Montevideo. I would not be with it then; I was going to get off at Palmer.

The hanging list seemed to become permanent, until at last with a long shudder the ship moved forward, the list fell off, and there was another boom and rumble.

When I went below, the *Polar Sea* had been gliding through black water and thin floes under a dark overcast, the clouds reflecting the color of the open sea; the sailors called it water sky. Since then something had happened.

I climbed upstairs. Outside the porthole by the stairs a huge, thick plate of ice, tilted by the ship, was passing slowly aft. No water was visible at all. The sea was white again. The clouds were white; the water sky had gone; the ice blink was back. I plunged outside and walked forward. Up on the bow were Conway, McIntosh, and Dick Viet. Viet was watching petrels. Conway and McIntosh were watching six-foot-thick slabs of ice heave and roll right beside the rail. There was a great splashing and grinding, and a hunk of ice about fifteen feet square and eight feet thick rose ponderously to the surface, its underside pale brown, heaving aside water and broken ice. The wind blew hard snow against our faces. Antarctica had changed its face again.

Viet stared calmly out into the wind. A fleck of living white moved against the pale gray. He recorded a snow petrel on his clipboard. "The Bird Man's a typical biologist," Dick Cameron had said from his geologist's perspective. "They're hardworking people." To Viet nothing was new; nothing was boring. Mt. Siple, exploration, drama, ice—they were all part of the larger world of Antarctica that he alone among the passengers had seen. Many of the scientists on board knew Antarctica as bits and pieces tied together by vast unknown spaces; to Viet the continent and its waters were a whole. He knew the shape, the dimensions. The rest of them were like the first explorers, pushing down through the ice to touch one protrusion of an invisible mass; the continent spread out beyond comprehension. Viet was modern. He had embraced the expanse. Antarctica was circumscribed in his memory: sixty days steaming around the bottom of the world.

Viet had seen a perimeter—the long, unrolled white edge that Antarctica appeared to be on all maps of the world. He had been aboard the *Polar Star*, sister ship to the *Polar Sea*. Last year the *Star* had circumnavigated Antarctica, and for all those days, except for the few the icebreaker had spent at McMurdo Station, Viet had stood staring out into snow, wind, and dazzling sunshine, turning the slow time of the ship's passage into ten-minute slices on his clipboard, recording birds, and watching the profile of the strange land as the ship, steaming counterclockwise, ticked away the degrees of the world. Now, standing in the same position in which he had stood those two months around Antarctica, he recalled the journey.

Steaming northeast out of McMurdo, in a direction opposite that taken this year by the *Polar Sea*, the *Star* made its first important landfall at 170° east, due south of the green hills of Dunedin, New Zealand. The ship passed within sight of Cape Hallett and Cape Adare. "Hallett's a very steep bluff. It rises up about four thousand feet directly from the ocean, too steep to be snow-covered, even. Adare is sort of like that but not quite as high. There's a long ridge of mountains that extends up to a point."

Black rock and gray sky. The Defense Mapping Agency sailing directions contained a photo of Cape Adare—sea, a floe, an iceberg, a sloping, snow-seamed promontory—taken just after the turn of the century. Elsewhere in the world the latter part of the twentieth century seemed distinct from the first years because the old photos lacked color. In them the past was a drab world, foreign to the chrome present. But in Antarctica time dissolved in the permanent gray. Cape Adare would be black and white forever, and the distinctions between the human past and present faded. The birds wheeled and cried above the strangers' ships, the ships moved in the ice and went away. The colorless cold remained.

Antarctica's continental shelf was deep and narrow. As the *Star* moved east it crossed it often, weaving through the ice that usually extended past the edge of the shelf, and Viet recorded the changes in life at the front, where the depth plunged. "At the shelf break here, there's a concentration. You get more penguins and snow petrels and skuas here; and you get into deep water beyond the continental slope and there is a change in species, like mantled sooty albatrosses and mottled petrels and birds from New Zealand."

After turning the corner at Adare, the ship moved east off the coast through ice and icebergs, gaining hours on the world just as the *Polar Sea* lost them going east. At 162° east, due south of the Tasman Sea—south of the greatest north-south reach of the Pacific, where a torpedo fired north along the meridian would, if it missed the net of the Solomon Islands, reach the Aleutians—the *Star* parked in ice offshore and sent helicopters over the horizon to visit the Russians at Leningradskaya base. Among those going ashore was a four-person team of U.S. inspectors. They were a function of the operation of the Antarctic Treaty, that remarkable document signed in 1961 by twelve nations, including the United States and the Soviet Union, that demilitarized the continent, established the preeminence of science, and provided that, among other things, all bases would be open to inspection. The United States, which liked the idea of inspection in general, particularly when it thought about what it would like to see at Soviet nuclear bases elsewhere in the world, sent the *Star* on its mission to remind everyone that it took the free-inspection clause seriously.

At Leningradskaya, Viet stayed on board, watching birds; the inspectors climbed into the helicopters and went thundering ashore. There the team leader, Albert S. Chapman, who had not been in Antarctica before, found that the people of Leningradskaya, like those of all other stations he visited on the continent, seemed overjoyed to see the strangers.

"We were welcomed everywhere with enthusiasm," he wrote later, "because frequently our hosts had not seen a new face for many months. After the serious business of the inspection . . . was over, our visit was often the cause for celebration. We exchanged souvenirs and toasts and shared the wish that such cooperation and friendship could prevail elsewhere in the world."

On the long reaches between the outposts the *Star* was alone in wind and ice. It was an austere place. Wilkes Land, the sailing directions instructed the captain, "lies roughly along the Antarctic circle, and presents high ice cliffs which rise to the interior plateau with bare rock visible only in isolated places. The coast is fronted by glacier tongues and shelf ice which, with dense pack-ice, have defeated efforts by vessels to traverse the coast line in its entirety." Pleasant sailing. Due south of Adelaide, Australia, at 142° east, the *Star*, undefeated, came upon another human refuge, this time occupied by French. "The first place I remember seeing the coast was at Dumont d'Urville Station," Viet said. "That's the place where there are a series of small islands right off the beach where the French are putting in an airstrip."

In January 1840, the French explorer Jules Dumont d'Urville, sailing south in search of the elusive continent, saw land far sooner than he expected from a position of only 66° south. "A distinct appearance of mountains," he wrote—a manner of phrasing that suggested he didn't believe his eyes. His skepticism was warranted. He had already had enough of the *fata morgana*, of phantom shimmering hills. Antarctica so dazzled its explorers with dreams and ghosts that a prudent man did not believe what he saw.

The harsh land welcomed him gently. On the morning that followed the appearance of mountains the weather was clear and at peace, and the land was broadly revealed: ice cliffs and rising snow. The mountains were true. The scene did not, however, give him illusions of a land resembling France. The continent he saw, he wrote, "appears to consist of a formidable layer of ice, rather like an envelope, which forms the crust over a base of rock." And yet it was a place of such beauty that Dumont d'Urville, who had discovered the Venus de Milo earlier in his career, later described Antarctica at passionate length in ten volumes.

After showing him its beauty, Antarctica tried to prevent him from carrying that message away. The benign weather turned wicked in late January and Dumont d'Urville barely escaped. That, it turned out, was to be the common experience. Seventy years later this landscape killed two of the three men who traversed it, and the survivor, Douglas Mawson, called it the Kingdom of Blizzards, "an accursed land." The cheerful sailing directions described one of the bays not far from the French station as "probably the windiest region in the world."

"There were four or five places around here that were supposed to have the worst weather in Antarctica," Dick Viet said laconically, tapping the map at the coast. "We did have a big storm here." The French station was not immune to the storm of controversy, either; because the airstrip construction had displaced penguins, it had been criticized by a group of environmentalists, who thought Antarctica's best role in the world would be as an international reserve or park.

Pushing east, sometimes forced as far as a hundred miles off-shore by the pack, the *Star* passed rivers of ice that flowed ponderously out from the continent. On satellite photos these rivers looked like flares leaping from a frozen sun. They were ice tongues, the great outlapping of the interior glaciers, where the moving ice poured down to the coast and out to sea. Ice tongues, like the enormous shelves that filled most antarctic bays, were unique to the south. The crew of the icebreaker, who served alternate years in the north, saw nothing of their scale in the Arctic. Ice tongues reached far out into the pack ice or the wind-cleared open water, and sometimes gave birth to icebergs as large as nations.

The *Star* skirted the ice tongues and drove through the pack, through the longitudes south of Perth, south of Burma, south of Bombay. Oates Coast, George V Coast, Adélie Coast, the Banzare Coast, Sabrina Coast—everywhere grounded icebergs and heavy pack; and then one morning at dawn the ship entered a region of magic.

It was off Cape Ann, south of Madagascar. Here the British captain John Biscoe, sailing through pack ice in late February 1831, had emerged from a night of aurora, of whirled curtains of light, to see another appearance of mountains rising darkly in morning skies. But this was a different kind of beauty.

"It happened to be a very clear morning," Viet remembered. "It was right at sunrise. We picked up a shadow on the ship's sonar that probably was an enormous krill swarm. Then we went through a flock of what we estimated to be about one million Antarctic petrels, all actively feeding." The main purpose of the trip might be political, but to Viet the sight of this magnificent abundance was worth all the money, all the cold.

The snow petrels that occasionally passed the ship were dazzling white, the free spirit of the white antarctic light itself, but the Antarctic petrel was more subtle, a union of land, water, and ice. Its lean wings were dark brown at the leading edge, blending back to white; so that when it was over the water all watchers noticed at first was the thin band of white; and when it was over the light gray sky all they saw was the black. So always the Antarctic petrel seemed less than it was, a fine light life soaring past on knife blades that had been whetted down to the rib, slim and sharp. The Antarctic petrel, the sailing directions said, "follows leads of open water in the pack and this characteristic may be of value to the navigator." But on that early morning in February halfway around the continent from McMurdo, the navigator and all aboard were suddenly hopelessly rich. The whole world was filled with Antarctic petrels.

As far as Viet could see in every direction, the water was alive with birds. They flew, they dipped to the water, they plucked krill from the surface, they flew again, their swift, sharp wings quick above the glitter of the waves. From the bridge the birds were almost all below eye level, so it seemed that the ship was riding on the fizzing waters of antarctic life.

For two hours the *Star* steamed through this magical throng, lifted on the wings of Antarctica's abundance. Viet recorded two to five thousand birds each ten minutes. Then, as if the krill swarm had vanished, the great flock dissolved into the cold air, and the ship steamed on around the world.

Antarctica was ice, wind, glimpses of hills and rock, loneliness. Prince Olav Coast; Princess Astrid Coast; New Schwabenland; ice cliffs and nunataks; shadows of rocks in the snow. Fourteen times the inspection team helicoptered ashore; fourteen times the villages of Antarctica greeted them with joy. "For us team members the trip had some of the feeling of a royal progress," Chapman wrote later. The little communities, with their miles of antenna wire, their snow-smothered huts, and their bearded men, broke out the wine, the beer, the vodka. Dumont d'Urville, France; Casey, Australia; Mirnyy, the Soviet Union; Davis, Australia; Mawson, Australia; Molodezhnaya, the Soviet Union; Syowa, Japan; SANAE III, South Africa; Georg von Neumayer, West Germany; General Belgrano, Argentina; Halley, Great Britain. The crew traded *Playboy* magazines and blue jeans for Russian fur caps or German beer; they shook hands and clapped shoulders and looked around at the austere villages with awe.

"Some are perched on rocky outcrops surrounded by ice or glaciers and a few are on bare islands just off the coast," Chapman wrote. "Others are situated at the coast in areas miraculously free of ice. Several sit on (or in) ice shelves with little to be seen of them except ventilator shafts and antennas projecting above the surface. All seem to have a rather tenuous toehold in this inherently hostile environment."

All around the continent they clung, in the face of the windy sky, the desolation of ice, and the bitterness of isolation, wrestling the implacable angel of cold, all doing the same thing the *Polar Sea* had done at Mt. Siple: fighting to reveal what was hidden in the white mantle—the gift of Antarctica.

(2)

I heard a woman laugh. In my little metal room the sound hit me like a thrown knife. Was it the sound of a movie, floating out of the first class officer's lounge across the hall? No. It was too real. It was Pam Ellerman or Gisela Dreschhoff, conversing with someone next door in the science workroom. But it did not sound like either. It sounded like every woman anyone ever cared about or desired. It seemed a tease to all the longing on this ship, whetting it, leaving it shining, unseen.

I had received a telegram from my wife, in which she wrote of Girl Scout cookies and kindergarten field trips. I did not pore over it long, although communication with the outside was so rare that just her choice of words seemed so personal and intimate that the block text was as precious as handwriting. I could not give my loneliness rein. It was all right to think about the little things I missed from the other world: green fields, warm wind, a fifteen-minute shower, a drive in city traffic. But thinking about my wife and my children seemed dangerous, as if that longing, sought too deeply, could ruin me, could withdraw me from this amazing world that required so much attention to comprehend, and could force me into a life dominated by the pressure of waiting. I had months yet to spend here; I could not wish for home. The petty things seemed all right to consider, but I had to beware of touching the core nerve. I knew from all the others here now and in the past that Antarctica was worth the loneliness. So I left the room and the laughter and went to the bridge, where there was a crowd.

The *Polar Sea* wandered in deteriorating weather off the coast of Siple Island, on which Mt. Siple stood, still trying to get away. In the morning the sun shone through breaks in a thin white cloud; the day seemed promising and pleasant. But the sea was invisible —nine-tenths ice cover; the few patches of open water glittered thinly, as insubstantial as puddles. The ship slipped across them briefly, then wallowed in ice for hours. Behind it the wake was squeezed into a trickle. Bergs were everywhere: tablelands as level as Iowa; ice mountains tilted to the sky; enormous flat-topped white ships, foundered and sinking; ice in decay. The spotlight of the sun roved across the ice world, following the racing clouds. The mixed light picked out berg after berg, putting one set of ice cliffs in blazing sunlight and dousing others with shadow. The bergs shifted position as the sun hit them, moving abruptly closer as they shone, like soloists stepping forward out of the crowd to sing their blue silence.

But the pleasant morning was swept away by wind. The helicopters could not fly in twenty knots or more, so the ship stood impotently off the north shore of the island while the scientists looked out through twenty-eight knots of wind at the outcrops and islands they wanted so anxiously to reach, with nothing to do but to wait until the snow came down and hid them from view. The ship worked its way around a couple of islands north of Siple Island, and LeMasurier and McIntosh argued about their formation, but they were frustrated at having to infer major structures from shape when they could almost reach out and pluck samples from the beach.

The sun rolled around the horizon and slid, red and weary with the lateness of its season, behind the heavy slope of Mt. Siple, sinking beneath a weight of cloud. Then two spots on Siple Island's edge showed up unexpectedly as the ship prowled through the ice looking for a way out. On his aerial photos LeMasurier had labeled these outcrops locations J and M, and had hoped to land there. Now McIntosh and LeMasurier stood in the pilothouse with binoculars, arguing about what the flow lines in the rock might reveal of its composition. Then the wind died. There was a scurrying on the ship. The scientists began to hope the helicopters might get away to actually find out. But the wind increased again, and LeMasurier and McIntosh stared sadly at the fading view of the precious outcrops on the mountainside. The chance that either of them would ever be back here was remote.

The ship turned away. The wind blew. Sites J and M grew distant. The two men watched them as they disappeared. Well, perhaps it had not been such a loss after all. Nobody could have landed up there anyway. Probably.

"I don't know if we could have gotten onto that," McIntosh said at last.

LeMasurier grinned ruefully. "I know," he said. "Looks repulsive, doesn't it?"

They were silent for a long time. The ship lurched in the ice.

"Tantalizing," said Wes.

"Damn close," said McIntosh.

The *Polar Sea* halted in the twilight. As darkness came I went upstairs. In the hall a seaman sat in the red light, wearing a T-shirt and boxer shorts, smoking a cigarette and dropping ashes into a can. I climbed the stairs and went out onto the weather deck. The shock of the cold hit me again. If the helicopter hit the sea and turned over, the pilots said in the flight briefing, the water would be so cold that you would not be able to hold your breath more than five seconds. Yet they also said you had to wait for the machine to fill with water before you tried to get out.

I got out of the warmth of the ship and closed the door behind me. Once outside, breath came more easily; the transition was the hard part. Now the world was eerie, coldly alive. Fore and aft lights made a glow against the moving air, which was full of blowing snow. Close ahead was a gray, tall shape, the shadow of a berg. There was a dark void between the ship and the edge of the ice about fifteen feet away. It was a lee clearing in the ice, the same sort of semicircular, ice-free space I saw in the lee of an iceberg the day before. It was perfectly black. I felt for a coin in my pocket to toss into it, to be reassured by the glint of a splash that there was surface there. But I had no money.

Someone walked the deck above. I saw a figure with a halo, lit from behind. It was a seaman in a parka. The fur of the hood shone. He was carrying a hand gauge for wind direction and speed. He walked back from the flight deck. A door opened, throwing a warm wind of light down toward me, but before it arrived it was shut off. I grew cold. The lights fore and aft made a horizon out in the blowing snow; the floes faded out from it into uniform darkness. You could walk on this water, if you could get across that little lee space there. You could walk all the way to Siple Island. You could not walk home.

I went up to the pilothouse and watched the night. On the bow twin spotlights pointed out into the storm. They made the blizzard a maelstrom of tiny lights streaming at the ship out of the dark. I went below and slept, and in my sleep I heard a woman laugh.

(3)

The *Polar Sea* was stuck in the ice for twenty-four hours. On the morning that the storm cleared, the flat-topped icebergs all appeared to have built domes in the blizzard. That morning Dick Cameron discovered an island—a black window of rock staring out from under its cap of ice. After consulting aerial photographs and the navsat at length, the U.S. Geological Survey declared the island genuinely new. "Cameron Island," someone said. "No," Dick said lightly. "There already is one." His presence was so blithe and undemanding that we forgot that his place among explorers was earned.

The little island, the tiny brave outcrop so heaped over with crushing white frost, made the power of Antarctica's cold more personal. The ice on the mountains and the great flowing glaciers were geological, so grand they seemed as natural as the cliff strata and alluvial plains of the temperate world. But this poor little hump of lava out in the white sea was so piled upon by the weight of cold that the burden seemed suddenly malevolent. The little island was familiar—its modest size was common to a world of vacation homes and fishing skiffs.

A few acres of trees; a cliff off which the children leaped when the bay was mild; an old wooden cottage with rusting chairs on a porch that sagged amiably. In a foot or two of snow it was lovely, and photographers came out on calm days to capture the serenity. But one year, after the summer people had gone, the snow came in September and stayed. It piled layer upon layer. January was harsh and silent. The layers of snow rose higher. They compacted together on the bottom and turned hard. In the spring a fierce wind blew, sculpting the snow. Summer was watery sun and sleet. Layer piled upon bitter layer, season upon season, years recorded now in the subtle shades of the ice. And now the ice was a hundred feet deep, curling over the ends of the island with its own weight. The land was just a glimpse of bare cold rock.

J.D. considered the island. It was too inviting. He vacillated. "That's the Island of the Damned," he said. He looked at it some more. "It's the Island Made in Hell."

Wes LeMasurier looked out at a decaying berg on the horizon. It was tilted, eroded, castellated. It reminded him of a mountain in Chile: the Torres de Payne. He had the right attitude. "Looks like the Tower of Pain to me," he said.

"In its own special way Antarctica is a pretty free place," McIntosh had said earlier, thinking about traveling in snowmobiles across ice. Now, looking out at the white sea, LeMasurier mused about the intellectual freedom here: the room it gave a scientist to explore all the questions that came to his mind.

"In a lot of places you're going into a place and there's been no geology done there before at all. It isn't that you are refining or honing in on a problem that somebody else might have outlined in the first stages. From the very beginning the first thing you have to ask yourself is 'What am I working on?' It's interesting, because you can develop the project in whatever way it leads you.

"If you're trying to figure out why one volcano is different from another one, for instance, you are almost driven to look into some things about glacial history, and a volcanic geologist usually doesn't think about working with problems of glacial history. Then it leads you off into all sorts of different things that you're free to pursue because nobody else has ever done anything else with it."

Out the windows of the pilothouse the surface and the sky were dazzling white. For a few miles the ship followed a lead hardly wider than itself, while its headings pinged from 240 to 30 the long way around. Finally the lead tapered off into heavy ice. The ship stopped. Again it was parked in ice, waiting. But now it could not wait long. The season was advancing. The scientists needed to reach land for more research; the ship needed to deliver cargo to Palmer Station: the crew needed the beaches and grass skirts of Montevideo. It was time to leave the region of Siple Island and continue north. So a moment came that the passengers had been looking forward to the whole trip.

" 'Loft conn to bridge." J.D.'s voice came down on the intercom. "Call the captain and say we recommend using the turbine on the center shaft."

"We'll get the port turbine up," J.D. said after he came down. "If that doesn't work we'll wait awhile. Not to worry." He put his hand over his mouth, opened his eyes wide, and stifled a scream.

"A successful icebreaker must have a powerful main propulsion plant," read the brochure passengers had been handed as they came aboard the *Polar Sea*. "The diesel-electric plant can produce 18,000 shaft horsepower and the gas turbine plant 60,000 shaft horsepower, making her and the *Star* the world's most powerful conventionally-propelled icebreakers." The passengers had been speculating the whole voyage about watching the turbines work. Their power was legendary. Last year, the Coast Guardsmen liked to remind anyone willing to listen, the *Polar Sea* had cracked a pressure ridge 120 feet deep. But the ship had enough fuel to steam a year on its diesels and it could run its turbines a grand total of only ten days. So they were used sparingly; as seldom, at least, as the captain ceased to smile.

Now the time had come. After hours of preparation, a whine developed in the bowels of the ship. A blast of pale brown smoke poured from the stack. Two turbines were engaged, with the diesels on the third shaft. The ship was using 56,000 horsepower.

The ship moved slowly ahead. The speed did not seem increased, and the breaking ice still pushed the *Polar Sea* around. But progress, it seemed at first, was inexorable. If the ice did not yield, the ship would slide up on the ice, and right on up the slopes of the mountain.

Behind the ship there had suddenly been created a white-water river. Foam and blue-green waves roared aft. A man in a kayak would go shouting joyfully off into oblivion. J.D. was happy.

"Gentlemen," he said, "this is a beautiful experience."

Hunks of ice clanged against the hull. The ship surged and caromed. The sun came out on the ship for a moment, calling the *Polar Sea* to the center of the stage, making the ship the singer. Mt. Siple, visible one last time to the south, showed a creamy shoulder out of a froth of lace. But the big ship was trying with all its strength to get away.

"We're on our way," J.D. said. "Montevideo! I can taste that *cervesa* now."

Latitude 73°8′ south; longitude 125°41′ west. The ship moved against a medium floe. It was a very thick medium floe. The floe did not give way. The ship backed and advanced. Its power was marshaled. Now the floe would be crushed beneath an iron foot. The sea churned. The river tumbled aft over invisible boulders, waterfalls crashing horizontally. The power controls were advanced. Fifty percent power on the port shaft; 50 percent power on the starboard. Seventy-five percent on the center. The needles rose. The ship advanced. It hit the floe.

Slabs of ice were sucked into the props. The props chopped chunks the size of automobiles out of the slabs. The cars tumbled end over end down the river. The floe did not yield.

The *Polar Sea* backed and rammed. The floe did not allow passage. It did not crack. The ice landscape around the ship seemed to move slightly, the floes like vast meshed gears turning imperceptibly against each other in response to an enormous hidden power.

Dave Johnson was standing beside one of the power consoles, watching the dials. "We're maxed on all of them," he said. "And we aren't going anywhere."

The air in the pilothouse shuddered. The lights in the long room shook. The turbines swigged oil and roared. The ship rattled like a can with a pebble in it blown down the street. The entire force of the U.S. government, of human technology itself, was applied to the resistance of Antarctica. The United States would prevail!

A voice said:

"Steering casualty."

Another voice said, "Come back down on all of them."

Stillness returned to the bridge. The shuddering subsided into uneasy quiet, as if all that racket had been a fit. The wild river aft went calm. An officer: "The wheel shows stuck forty degrees left."

The ice closed back in. J.D. said nothing amusing at all. The *Polar Sea* lay dead in the water, what water there was. Suddenly it was just a large red fish in the world's last puddle, a big eye up and cloudy, waiting for the puddle to freeze.

Chapter Seven

"On the Verge of Being Bizarre"

(1)

It was summer on the Big Lost River in a high valley of Idaho. The air was warm. It smelled of hay and sagebrush. Trout lay dozing in the tea-colored river. On the dark water cotton drifted: little flecks of white, the fluffed seeds of the cottonwood trees. In the heart of summer the cotton flew and floated on the languid air, and floated down the river. I had fished in the morning and had caught enough; now, drowsy, sitting in the long grass in the shade, I watched the cotton whirl slowly past on the current and listened to the gurgle of the water in the willows by the shore.

An Adélie penguin rose among the cotton. It shot into the air like a small, stout torpedo, plunged, and flew away beneath the surface. It blasted the Big Lost River into drops of glittering memory. It was summertime indeed, this day in early March, but the wind was chilling. The cotton was bits of brash ice, splintered off an iceberg. The dark water was —1 °C. The penguin went porpoising off toward a hunk of blue-and-white ice on which six other Adélies stood like a squad of butlers on bivouac. It was strange to wake up, even from a daydream, and be in Antarctica.

The sun was going down on the Gerlache Strait, the stretch of water named for the man who led the *Belgica* expedition. We were a week away from Mt. Siple. Freed at last from the ice by its turbines (the captain's smile had remained inscrutably intact), the *Polar Sea* had escaped the advance of winter, dashing north away from Mt. Siple.

It had been an eerie voyage. The ship traveled in snow and fog, slipping among the icebergs like a spy. Technology had advanced in the days since James Cook. Early mariners, poking gingerly into seas mined with ice, had watched for the blink of bergs, tested the water temperature with microthermometers to detect the slight rise caused by the fresh water of a berg's melt, watched for the trail of brash ice, or stationed seamen to listen for the roar of surf or of calving; "a noise like breakers or distant gunfire." But the *Polar Sea* glided swiftly among the bergs, protected by the sweep of the magic golden wand of the radar, and the passengers watched the deadly monsters pass, unafraid. In the fog the bergs were glow instead of substance, blue mist sifting through the gray.

On the way north, the *Polar Sea* had tried to reach Pine Island Bay, in which another icebreaker had left an automatic weather station on an island ten years before. No one had been there before or since, so all this time the strange machine had rested there on the shore, recording cryptic messages for its alien masters. The *Polar Sea* tried both to retrieve it and to take the scientists to the mouth of a nearby glacier to seek clues to the stability of the great interior ice sheet, but again it was stopped.

While the captain was deciding whether to push in against the pack to Pine Island Bay, the *Polar Sea* spent a dark night parked in nine-tenths ice. It was a curious night. Drifts of brash ice brushed on the hull with the sound of blowing dry leaves. The ship was surrounded in the distance by massive bergs that stood like monuments on the horizon. They were tilted, they were creased, weathered, washed into pinnacles, rotting away to water. They were monuments to time, to decay. Sailors threw boxes, old oil, and trash out onto the ice; the memory of our visit would be a stain. Around the ship the ice was still as rock, a slab of the continent itself, but beneath it ran the force of a distant storm; the *Polar Sea* rose and fell softly upon the invisible swell as if it breathed in its sleep.

In the pilothouse Dick Cameron looked out at the white landscape, where the spotlights on the bow shone out on a penguin trail, a line of small footprints meandering off across the snow into the darkness.

"You have a whole continent here that's virtually untouched," he said. "So much is under cloud you can't even see it from a satellite. From the point of view of geography the moon is better known."

Two days later the ship had entered the islands of the Peninsula near Deception Island, near such charted landmarks as Desolation Island, Cape Danger, and Devil Point. "Love those names," said J.D. The ship temporarily lost control of its passengers when a snowstorm grounded the helicopters and stranded the scientists on Deception and Livingston islands, to the consternation of the officers and the delight of the field parties. While the *Polar Sea* paced anxiously back and forth in the strait between the islands on a rectangular course J.D. called the "box of death," Wes and his crew ate freeze-dried lasagna and watched penguins and fur seals. "It was wildlife city," Pam Ellerman said later. When night fell the volcano party discovered that their survival gear, painstakingly chosen to protect against the bitter cold of the antarctic summer, contained tents, sleeping bags, an abundance of dry food and cooking equipment, and even reading material—*Turok, Son of Stone* comic books—but made no provision for darkness: there was not one flashlight or candle in the gear.

Now it was almost autumn. When the sun set it would be gone for hours. The dark would be complete. Tonight, two hours before sunset, the ship glided before the wind, coasting down into Antarctica's strange night. "This place," one person had told me long before, "is on the verge of being bizarre." I climbed to the flying bridge as the sun rolled lower in the sky ahead, a dazzling spot behind thin white cloud. Ahead of the ship it made a long silver road.

It was utter calm on the bridge. The ship's speed was just under ten knots. The breeze from astern was just under ten knots. The only cloud was a long scarf flying across the sun. All around rose the crags of the Antarctic Peninsula: black cliffs seamed with snow and capped with heavy white brows of ice. Between the cliffs, glaciers tumbled to the shores in huge broken blocks of cream and blue ice. Woodbury Glacier, the chart recorded. Hippocrates Glacier. The Downfall. Glaciers and icefalls surrounded the ship; they looked like avalanches of snow blocks arrested in the middle of their tumbling by the hot-blooded human presence. We brought our hasty time into the midst of this roaring geological enterprise, and suspended it with our mortal lack of patience. When we left it would resume: the ice would thunder, the rocks would split, in a few short millennia spring would return.

"Our position at this time was in the centre of a wide waste of water about twelve miles from the nearest land," Frederick Cook wrote on the *Belgica* not far from here. "We were too far from the rocks to see birds, and except for an occasional spout of a whale there was nothing to mar the dead silence. A strange pang of loneliness came over us as we paced the deck. There were indications of channels to the south and west, but from the distance at which we reviewed the lands every projection seemed a continuous mass of impenetrable crystal solitude. Could there be a place more desperately silent or more hopelessly deserted?"

Out in the long silver reflection ahead of the *Polar Sea*, the waters became disturbed. A small group watching in the bow—McIntosh, LeMasurier, Conway, Pam Ellerman, Dave Johnson, and a few others—began pointing at it urgently. Out where they were looking, four hundred yards ahead, the sun's reflection was darkened in a pool of agitation. The sea was mightily stirred. Within the dark place there was churning and thrashing. Then, from out of the whirlpool, a huge arm arose, a monstrous long shape silhouetted in the path of light, raising a giant fist, brandishing spray.

Spontaneously, the group on the bow cheered. The sound of their voices was both muffled and enhanced by the stillness. They sounded like a crowd in a distant stadium: two hundred billion fans out in the faraway bleachers of earth, cheering life.

The whale fell back and threw a glittering wave. The scientists cheered again. "You just about get bored with the Antarctic," said a Coast Guardsman who was standing on the flying bridge, "and then it springs something like this on you."

The whale ceased to breach. The ship moved on. The sun rolled toward the horizon, reaching for the rim of the Arctowski Peninsula. The mountains grew ahead—a ridge like saw teeth, a vast ice dome, a broad smooth glacier. Astern, clouds massed in the distance, a shapeless advancing grayness against which sunlit icebergs shone. The coming of night was still unfamiliar enough to seem odd. As darkness grew, the sky seemed to lift on the world, opening into space. Ahead of us flew a long wing of cloud, its tip dipped into the last sunlight, its plumage shading from tawny to deep gray. Higher and beyond, a feather of pink floated on the high wind.

As the sunlight dimmed, the blue of the bergs ahead grew more luminous. The *Polar Sea* had slowed in the twilight hours, as had the breeze, and as the ship coasted in the stillness it seemed as if the whole vessel were hushed, tiptoeing through the beauty.

(2)

The sun disappeared. Darkness overtook us from astern. In the pilothouse the red lights in the instruments began to have authority. In the room's dusk a sailor sharpened a knife on a stone. The noise seemed loud. *Whisk-whisk. Whisk-whisk. Whisk-whisk.* The darkness grew.

"At about eight o'clock a speck of fire was seen above the purple ice northward, but neither the ice nor the sky showed any signs of a reflected light." Frederick Cook, 1898. "The sky was a dark purple blue. All was still and dead; there was not a breath of air stirring. The dull flame slowly increased in size and changed its form with marvelous rapidity. Above it there was a little blackness suggestive of smoke, and under it was a cone-like image of a mountain peak from which the fire and smoke seemed to ooze. . . . As it rose slowly higher it seemed to pull the mountain up with it; presently we noticed that the weird object had not only an upward movement but also a lateral progress. Then the fire separated from the mountain and later the smoke separated from the fire, and then both smoke and mountain vanished, leaving only a cone of rayless flame."

In the pilothouse the religious officer made the Sign against the Threat of Antarctica, raising rhetorical crossed fingers at the strangeness human beings have encountered here since the beginning. Preaching quietly to a sailor, he attacked the science that brought the ship here, the science that looked all strangeness in the eye in its search for those links of truth. As night cloaked the poised glaciers around us, he told the sailor that the notion of great depths of time out of which life had emerged was faulty; that the dating of the history of life based on the ticking decay of radioactivity was false. "It is all based on assumptions." He held up to the light of strangeness an opaque wall of superstition. But the strangeness did not go away.

"Every few seconds for fifteen minutes this extraordinary object underwent a remarkable transfiguration," Frederick Cook wrote. "[N]ow it was oblong with its greatest diameter parallel to the line of the horizon, again it formed an inverted cone. At other times it became semi-circular, and, most curious of all, it was a globe divided by a line. There was at no time any sign of luminosity about the spot. It remained a dull red, fading into orange, and when it had ascended about five degrees it assumed the form of a ragged ball of old gold. . . . [I]t was the moon."

Ahead of the *Polar Sea* the last clouds melted into the cold darkness, and the sky filled with stars. The Milky Way became an arch over the ship, horizon to horizon. There was no moon this night in Gerlache Strait. The horizon was jagged; the mountains were faintly illuminated by starlight, their dark gray shapes marked with black patches of rock. A light on the mast shone down on the water beside the ship and caught the bow wave oddly, so it looked squirming and alive—something long and slimy, plunging beside us in a spurt of foam.

"This is the cleanest air in the world," said a seaman, a dark silhouette in the red light.

"Yeah," his companion said. "I can't stand it. Somebody light up, would you?"

It was 10:00 P.M. A seaman spoke into the public address system: "Now, taps."

The voices of the men on the bridge became more quiet, as if not to awake the sleepers. The ship moved slowly now. Four knots showed on the navsat screen. A giant petrel flew past the light, showing a sudden swift shape of unbent tapered wings. It looked prehistoric, as if it had web wings and a cold heart: a pterodactyl flitting out of the past.

"After we had stood on the snow-decked bridge for ten minutes, shivering and kicking about to keep our blood from freezing, we saw on a floe some distance westward a light like that of a torch." Frederick Cook. "It flickered, rose and fell, as if carried by some moving object. . . . We could only explain the thing by imagining a man carrying a lantern. . . . Is it a human being? Is it perhaps some one from an unknown south polar race of people? For some minutes no one ventured out on the pack to meet the strange messenger. . . . Amundsen, who was the biggest, the strongest, the bravest . . . slipped into his *anorak*, jumped on his ski and skated rapidly over the gloomy blackness of the pack to the light. . . . It proved to be a mass of phosphorescent snow. . . ."

On the *Polar Sea*'s radio, static sounded like waves breaking on gravel. Within this surf faceless voices swam: a Russian, a Chilean. Whalers? Fishermen? Antarcticans? The night before, this background of faint communications had been abruptly penetrated by the booming voice of the Coast Guard communications station on Kodiak Island, Alaska, almost 120 degrees of latitude around the earth to the north. The ComSta was organizing a search-and-rescue effort in the windswept Pacific on the other side of the world. The *Polar Sea*'s officer of the watch couldn't resist reaching for contact. On Kodiak Island you could go to a supermarket; you could play baseball in the park beneath the trees; you could send out for pizza.

It was like coming around the back side of the moon and hearing the welcome voice of earth.

"ComSta Kodiak, this is the *Polar Sea*. Radio check."

"Loud and clear," Kodiak said.

Earth was still there. The officer hung up the mike.

"Now *that's* good coms," he said.

Tonight the static in the radio washed back and forth without casting up anything familiar. Below in the wardroom lounge, the officers escaped from Antarctica with a night full of hard, violent films: *Sharkey's Machine*; *The Mechanic*. Death and betrayal. In the pilothouse two sailors practiced using a night vision scope, peering through it at green, ghostly shapes of icebergs in the distance.

"Torpedoes ready to fire, sir," said the lookout.

"Fire one."

The pilothouse became quiet.

"I saw again, in the southeast, touching the horizon, a star so bright as to be startling." Admiral Richard E. Byrd, 1934. "The first time I saw it several weeks ago I yielded for an instant to the fantastic notion that somebody was trying to signal me; that thought came to me again this afternoon. It's a queer sort of star, which appears and disappears irregularly, like the winking of a light."

I stood at a window on the port side of the pilothouse, looking out into the luminous night. At 10:55 P.M., just up from the horizon, almost directly ahead, there appeared a flashing light.

"I have an aircraft," said the lookout, giving its heading off the bow. "Three forty-five."

There was no question: it was an aircraft's strobe lights, flashing rhythmically, a familiar sight everywhere else in the world.

"Good work," the dark form of an officer said to the lookout, as all eyes turned to the sky.

"No coms or nothing," someone else said. "Must be an airstrip out there."

But there was no airstrip out there. The ship was heading south.

No airlines cross Antarctica. Ahead of us there was nowhere on the face of the earth on which an aircraft could land at night for three thousand miles. It was, in fact, impossible for there to be an aircraft in this night sky.

No one said anything. They watched the light.

The flashing changed its pace. From a regular on-off beat it changed to a quick double flash separated by a full second's pause. It still looked like an airplane ten or fifteen miles away. Then it began to fall out of the sky. The flashing became ragged, without rhythm, and the light dropped swiftly down toward the horizon, its intensity fading. In a few seconds it disappeared.

We stood watching the clear night sky. In the field of stars nothing else moved. The stars were sharp and steady. Slowly, each of us began to fit what we had seen into an acceptable niche of our experience. The flashing light had been a satellite swinging past layers of atmosphere. It had been a flickering mirage of a star thrown up from far beyond the horizon. It had been some signal we did not understand. But it was now gone, and it left behind a dark spot of uncertainty, an afterimage on the eyes of those who had seen it.

"It just vanished right where it was," said one sailor.

"No, it didn't," said another. "It went down to the horizon."

The lookout slowly lowered his binoculars and turned to the officer of the watch. He said:

"That was weird, sir."

The *Polar Sea* slipped farther into the antarctic night, embraced by ice and starlight.

PART TWO

THE EGG OF
THE PENGUIN

Chapter Eight

Gift of the Ice Planet

(1)

At the Officers' Club, where people went to hide from Antarctica, there was no escape. In desperation, someone had stuffed a mitten into a gap in the heavy wooden shutters, but a shaft of Antarctica's summer blaze split the wood and drove in all the same. The sunlight picked out some popcorn on the floor. The popcorn looked like spilled teeth. The bar of light was straight and fierce; it drove everything else away from it into shadow, as if it were a blown flame. People sitting in its way ducked their heads or covered their eyes.

The Officers' Club was full of civilians. It was full of smoke. The civilians sat around tables drinking beer. Four men played pool in an adjoining room. Two loudspeakers on the walls played rock and roll music. Six men danced with four women in a small open space near the door. In the dim light the women were lithe and beautiful. The men sitting with other men at tables watched them, and sipped their beer slowly. The men at the bar leaned on the bar and thought about the women, but pretended not to notice. They talked to each other about mail.

Malcolm Browne, Ellen Hale, and I sat at a table while the life of Antarctica swirled around us. We were part of this year's complement of journalists, shipped to McMurdo Station by the National Science Foundation to observe the natives. We already felt at home. But only days before we had taken turns kneeling at one of the few portholes in a C-130, looking down at Antarctica. When my turn had come I had, at first, seen nothing at all.

95

(2)

Everything was light, a great white shine that hurt my eyes. I squinted and grimaced at the light out the little porthole as the C-130 descended slowly over northern Victoria Land. It was still too bright. My sunglasses were back at my seat in my coat. Finally, as my eyes adjusted as much as they could, a faint pattern emerged in the landscape: gray rock, blue crevasses, and endless dazzling snow. It was a hint, a glimpse, and seeing it I thought for a moment that we were crossing space, that we had, at last, left the earth behind. But we had not, and we had not come down here unencumbered. Although we were restricted in baggage only to what we could cram in with the extra long johns, the mittens, scarves, headgear, and boots in the two orange bags issued at the clothing warehouse, we all carried our own special cargo of longings down to the ice.

I went and sat back down in my red nylon-webbing chair and thought about the day before.

It had been a beautiful day, a lovely and curious day, a day that had been an elegy to the world we were about to leave. But what I remembered most about it was how it ended, in the dark of the car, returning to our hotel for the last night. I was driving, and Malcolm's voice came out of the darkness, calm as always.

"The last time I was in Antarctica," he said, "I had no idea that within three weeks I would be having a terrible experience in Vietnam."

There was a long silence—just the noise of the road. I didn't know what to say. I was suddenly afraid.

We were returning to Christchurch, where we had been waiting for our ride south. At McMurdo, 2,200 miles away, the weather was almost as deadly as it had been at Winfly two months before; our flight was postponed. We were given a day of our own. We rented a car and drove out into the New Zealand countryside. Spring poured in the windows. Up in the hills south of Christchurch the sheep were in the paddock. With ice on our minds we rolled through green fields, past green trees, across warm rivers. We were three men—Malcolm, of *Discover* magazine, Bob Cooke, of the *Boston Globe*, and myself, representing *Smithsonian* magazine —and one woman, Ellen, of Gannett News Service. In the gardens hydrangeas and roses bloomed. The air smelled of wet earth. In a distant, haunted way we courted Ellen, as if in this live world we must honor the affinity of life toward life before it grew cold. She charmed us, and perhaps we charmed her, and the light new air enchanted us all.

We laughed and laughed. Bob and I became eloquent at length about how we would fish a stream we passed: nothing could be used, of course, but a two-pound-test tippet and a number 16 fly. Malcolm observed from the back, "I take it you would disapprove of grenade fishing." In the daylight his war stories were fantastic, not frightening. "I have a sense of high explosives," he said. "A medically proven sense, developed to a fever pitch by cowardice." His sense of explosives, it turned out, was affection: when he was a boy he had made nitroglycerin, put a blob on an anvil, and blown himself and the hammer across the room. Later, as a war correspondent, he had ridden happily close to the armaments in the back seats of jet fighters.

"Weren't you afraid on those kinds of things?" Ellen asked.

"Well, yes," said Malcolm. "On the three times I was in airplanes that got shot down."

Ellen chose the route. She found a countryside too beautiful to be real. We drifted without time among budding leaves, deep grass, and water. The day was a gift of our future imagination. In frozen deprivation we could have dreamed no gentler landscape. We wound up into the old volcanic hills, among bleached hulks of old trees, and down toward a beach. We ate New Zealand seafood in the town of Akaroa, and we stopped on a hillside to overlook the village, where green hills edged with windblown pines swept down to the harbor.

Even Malcolm's hard edge softened. "Everywhere," he said, "the light is just right, showing the land at its most flattering." All day, it seemed, the hills were edged with the gold of late afternoon; the earth itself seemed arranged for our affection. The boats in the harbor were painted bright yellows and reds. Buoys danced among sparkles in the waves. The row of *radiata* pine on the ridge had been planted a half century before with us in mind, planted with the knowledge that it would grow to make this unblemished silhouette against the afternoon glow, the silhouette of wind and wood and time.

On another hill above the water we found a little town, with a church made of shells and pebbles and carved kauri beams. The gravestones were mossy, and the graveyard deep in fragrance. An old man came through the gate and took us into the church. He whispered about a congregation of twelve. He had watery eyes and wild white hair. I took him to be a fisherman. But when we left the church and closed the door the organ broke into music and caught us in midflight on the grass, and suddenly we were all young and without defense.

Ellen turned and ran back to the door to listen, but the rest of us stood transfixed in the grass, too young and wise at the instant to reach for more than we were given. In the heart of the sweetness was the departure and the day to come—the airplane, the noise, the hard blaze of antarctic light, the cold. We could cherish this place of peace and have none of it. Our love for the earth we knew came to us softly, like the music through the door of the stone church, but was so sufficient that none of us, caught in the moment by it, would wish to hear it more clearly.

Then we were in the dark and Malcolm remembered the Vietnam War.

"I had a lot of souvenirs from McMurdo," he said. "Stuffed toy penguins and things. I didn't even get back to the U.S. I guess they're still in Saigon. I never thought."

There was a silence in the car. Against the green beauty there was sudden death in villages, shiny weapons, empty bowls, the slow-motion tumble of words into chaos.

At last I said lamely, "Let's hope this trip augurs tranquility."

Malcolm muttered something reassuring from the back. A fire-hardened man, but infinitely kind. "Oh, yes, it will." But the answer was noncommittal. The car was very quiet until we had to worry about getting back to the hotel. Then the laughter began again as Ellen navigated and I got us lost. And in the morning we prepared to depart for Antarctica, that great white place off the edge of the mapped world that seemed so alien to the green earth we cherished, and so innocent of the raging colors of sovereignty. Like those condemned, or those honored with flight beyond earth, we had saluted the familiar in farewell. In one day we had seen the world's great loveliness and remembered what was ugly. We were ready for the future. We submitted to the affectionate scrutiny of Joe the Drug Dog and boarded the C-130. Nestled in the roar, emissaries of the beautiful, battered earth, bearing love and fear, in search of hope, we sailed off the edge of the world into the light.

(3)

And then we were engulfed in it. The point of safe return was passed. The plane was descending. Within the aluminum cocoon was a stir of excitement. Malcolm bounded from porthole to porthole, looking like a stretched silent-film comedian in his baggy U.S. Antarctic Research Program–issue black trousers and his long-john top. "We're going to have a great few days," he said exultantly. "Malcolm's just like a kid," Ellen said. She was wry and happy. She wore her USARP dog tags outside her shirt like a charm. We compared this to other momentous occasions in our journalistic careers. "Reminds me of the time I had to pose as a prostitute," she said. A young sailor who wore his cold-weather cap with the earflaps turned up so they looked like Mickey Mouse ears reveled in his nobility of experience on the ice, casting bits of advice out into the plane's noise. "When you first step out," he said, "it's like stepping onto the moon." And as the plane banked right and left on its approach, the light shone through one of the tiny portholes and made a moving bright circle on the opposite wall that wandered among the faces of the passengers like the spotlight of Antarctica searching for a star.

We landed. The door opened. A breath of cold air and diesel fumes swept into the cabin. The air rolled in fast, like something hard and violent, blowing the door aside and invading the interior. Resistance was impossible. We were filled with the bright cold. Our breath turned white. The open doorway blazed. The crewman who stepped out of it was dissolved by the light before he reached the ground. The young sailor with the Mickey Mouse flaps detached them from the top of the cap and pulled them slowly down. He fastened them around his chin. He zipped up his green coat. He carefully put on Navy sunglasses that looked like goggles and hooked them behind the flaps and around his ears. He pulled on his black leather gloves. He closed the little air valve on his big white thermal bunny boots. He turned to us. "Welcome to Antarctica," he said.

The sun was dazzling. Mt. Erebus rose in the distance, steaming. A cluster of huts on the ice nearby blew steam from stacks. The air whined with the engines of airplanes. Men hustled the passengers into a truck. Other men waved the aircraft away to the fuel pits. Lines of red and green flags on bamboo stakes stuck in the snow led off into the distance in several directions. The truck went bounding over the bladed humps of ice that made the road and followed a row of flags that led off toward the black lump of Observation Hill, beneath which lay McMurdo. Like everything else here, the truck was in a hurry. We caught the hurry like a germ; a living and demanding urgency swept into us with the first breath of that air, nurtured by this strange bright atmosphere. Antarctica was here. Antarctica awaited our attention. It demanded all of it. There were places to go, things to know. The day had twenty-four hours and the sun never set, but there was something here that had to be learned, something vital, something not to be found anywhere else on this earth or others, and even in this endless day there was not enough time, not enough time, not enough time. Make haste, or the precious gift will escape. There is not enough time. We have been swept up into the maw of the American science assault on Antarctica, into MacTown, the mad Camelot of the Round Table of knowledge, and there is not enough *time!*

(4)

McMurdo was the peopled city of the Antarctic. It stood on the slope above the little rectangular hut built by Robert Falcon Scott in 1901, in a rising clamor of streets and buildings, festooned with wires and antennas, surrounded by huge round tanks and junk. It was McMurdo Station, MacTown, the Hill. Here were dormitories, workshops, a sprawling mess hall and dormitory, a chapel, laboratories, garages, an administration building. The buildings were linked with dirt roads that were iron with frost most of the time and turned to mud and dust in the forty-degree days of summer. Sewer and water pipes ran aboveground from building to building, encased in big corrugated tin tubes filled with insulating foam.

The dormitories were named for places back home: the California Hotel; the Mammoth Mountain Inn; the Salmon River Inn. The administration building was called the Chalet. The heavy equipment was named for women: Suzie the D-9 Cat; Nancy the front-end loader. Other places were named for people who had died here: Williams Field, out on the ice shelf, for the driver whose bulldozer and body remained in the sea offshore; Berg Field Center, where you got your sleeping bags and sledges for your expeditions, for the man who died in a helicopter crash in the Dry Valleys; Thiel Earth Science Lab, for Edward C. Thiel, who was killed in 1961. This background longing and sadness was made formal by the crosses that bracketed the city on elevations just outside of town: Vince's cross on the black knoll by Scott's hut, where a sailor named

George T. Vince fell into the sea in 1902 and disappeared forever; and the cross on Observation Hill in honor of Scott himself, in which the 1911–12 expedition's survivors had carved the words from Tennyson: *"To strive, to seek, to find, and not to yield."* Down by the Chalet, where Distinguished Visitors first came up from Willie Field or the Ice Runway, was a bust of Admiral Richard Byrd, surrounded by stands in which the sixteen flags of the Antarctic Treaty nations were placed when DVs were expected. The flags were not left out long or the wind would tear them to shreds.

The sound of summer in MacTown was the thunder of helicopters. The C-130s (not ski-equipped) and LC-130s that brought people down from New Zealand landed five miles away, but the helicopters landed on a pad just down the hill from the Chalet, next to the blue Quonset hut that was the gym. They were red U.S. Navy UH-1N twin-engine turbine-powered machines. The pilots called them helos, with a long *e*—"heelos"—so everyone else did too. The helos were a part of life; they were the only way to get anywhere more than a few miles out from McMurdo. They were also a part of breathing in the city: you could feel the beat of their coming and going in your chest. They shook the California Hotel like an earthquake.

MacTown lay in its jumbled splendor against a black-and-white landscape of volcanic rock and snow. Hills rose abruptly behind the buildings, bearing on their lower slopes the fuel tanks that ringed the city. The slopes were rutted in long vertical parallel lines. As McMurdo had been built over the years since 1957, bulldozers had quarried the hills for gravel, scraping the slopes over and over for the few inches of loose rock released from their ice bondage by the brief warmth of summer. When the wind blew the snow around and uncovered the rock, it left drifts along the ruts and the hills looked striped.

On the ridges antennas stood like sentinels. Beyond them, invisible from town, lay the rising glaciers and ice fields of Mt. Erebus, the mountain that had drawn James Ross toward this icebound island with its beacon of flame in 1840. On a clear day, Sunday climbers going to the top of Observation Hill could see the mountain rise up behind MacTown, heaving upward like a thunderstorm on its billows of heat, and could watch the plume stream west in the wind. Sitting up on the rocks beside the cross erected to Scott, the climbers could see the whole panoply of the Antarctica they had come so far to see: Erebus; the black slopes of Ross Island; the white sheet of McMurdo Sound reaching away to a sliver of blue sea in the distance; the low ridges of Black Island and White Island, where the Herbies blew down over Minna Bluff beyond; and, across the sound, the ramparts of the Royal Society Range—peaks, ridges, canyons, all mantled in snow and floating on the *fata morgana* mirage. The Royal Society Range, Katherine Bouton had written in *The New Yorker*, was like a cathedral in a medieval village, to which eyes turned from the squalor of the town for reassurance. When the wind blew raw pain, the food was boring, the water system broke down and you had to walk out in the cold to the mess hall building just to go to the bathroom, and MacTown seemed to be just another primitive camp frozen in a puddle of desolation, you could look up and there it was, fifty miles across the sound, a wall of folded light, so bright it seemed translucent, like quartz with the sun behind it. Antarctica was still there.

In the night the sun swung around the world, casting the shadows of the buildings across the streets like a host of synchronized clocks, changing the shadows and shape of the Royal Society Range. In the evening the sun looked as bright and fresh as if it had just risen.

The air was clean with cold as we walked to the bar. The wind blew. Mt. Discovery shone faintly golden across the ice of McMurdo Sound. It was an extinct volcano. It looked like a bell. It seemed to have filled right to bursting before it turned cold. The streets in McMurdo were frozen ruts and puddles after the summer day's brief thaw. The frost was in control again. The enormous ice cube the men building the new salt-water intake had trucked over to the yard outside the galley just for the hell of it stood unmelting on the little gully that Lieutenant Doug Hocking, the public information officer who talked like a chaplain, called the Bean River. Hocking liked to talk about Bean River fishing tournaments and sunbathing in the park, a strip of artificial turf beside the Bean River. When the weather warmed up to thirty-eight or forty degrees, Hocking issued Bean River flood alerts. The Bean River was at present the Frozen Bean Slough.

Two scientists—Dr. Jay Zwally of the National Aeronautics and Space Administration and Dr. Ian Whillans of Ohio State University—stood beside the ice cube, looking at it. It was about as tall as they were.

"Where are the brine channels?" Whillans asked.

"There are no brine channels," said Zwally.

A short truck pulled to a stop near the ice cube. The truck said Scott Base on its side. Scott Base, a New Zealand station, was two miles away over a small hill.

"The real question," said Whillans, "is how many Kiwis can you get in a Land-Rover?"

Twelve New Zealanders climbed out and went inside. Whillans and Zwally knew they were Kiwis because they wore yellow parkas. U.S. civilians wore red parkas; the military were clad in green.

Whillans and Zwally walked away.

Malcolm and I roomed in the California Hotel. Ellen stayed in the Mammoth Mountain Inn, next door. Before we went to the Officers' Club we had taken showers, a rare luxury. I had figured that since we were restricted to two two-minute showers a week, I could have one thirty-eight-second shower a day. Malcolm and Ellen expressed the thought that this was unnecessary. Malcolm adhered strictly to the rule; Ellen cheated.

Over the main door of the California Hotel were stenciled the words from the song after which the hotel had been named. "You can check out any time you like," it said on one side of the door, and on the other side it said, "but you can never leave."

(5)

We sat in the bar and listened to the rock and roll. The women changed partners, laughing. The pool room became suddenly loud, then subsided. The long bar of antarctic light moved across the room.

Suddenly the rock and roll music stopped. The music feed paused for a second, and then a new song came on. It was "Oh, What a Beautiful Mornin'," from the musical *Oklahoma!* For just a moment it rang strangely into the room, a simple, old-fashioned tune after the rock and roll. Then a few of the men in the Officers' Club began to sing. The women stopped dancing. They picked up their beers. They began to sing. Everyone sang, holding up their cans of beer, standing at the tables. It was a booming deep chorus; a wild, strong, single voice. They were in Antarctica! They could sing! The people in the crowd looked at each other, clanged their beers together, and roared together at the blazing Antarctic night:

> *"Oh, what a beautiful mornin',*
> *Oh, what a beautiful day.*
> *I got a beautiful feelin'*
> *Ev'rythin's goin' my way!"*

The song ended. The men at the bar put their elbows back down and talked about mail. The rock and roll resumed. The women danced. Antarctica shone through the crack in the shutter, but everyone pretended not to notice.

Chapter Nine

Natives

(1)

The minutes ticked past, and still Max did not return. Wind swirled around the little red hut. Outside the window snow blew along the sea ice like smoke, and the flags leading back to McMurdo disappeared into it two hundred yards away. Inside, five people stood on plywood staring down into a big blue hole in the ice. The minutes ticked past, and all that rose in the hole was a chip of clear ice that, floating slowly upward into the light, looked like a flake of mica. Surely Max was gone.

Warren Zapol, a small, gentle, black-bearded man with disheveled hair who squatted beside the hole, did not seem worried. He was an anesthesiologist, and intensive care physician at Massachusetts General Hospital; perhaps he had been in enough critical situations not to be concerned now. Instead, he smiled kindly at a question asked partly to fill the worrisome quiet of waiting. Within the question, posed artfully by Malcolm Browne, who had experience in these matters, was hidden the big *why*. This was a common weakness of journalists in Antarctica, who always wanted to know: Why are you doing this? What *good* is this restless quest? We could not seem to imagine why people pursued a goal with such passion and patience unless it was to yield glory.

"Honestly," Zapol said a bit sadly—as if, recognizing the question for what it was, he knew the message would not get through —"we study him just to find out how he works."

Max, whose full name was Maximilian, was a Weddell seal, a male captured by Zapol and his colleagues at a break in the ice several miles away and trucked to this drilled hole. He was captive, in a way. Zapol had surveyed the ice by helicopter for about five kilometers around this hole, and had found no other places for a seal to break through the ice to breathe. So Max, who was not tethered, had to return to this hut to get air.

When we arrived at the hole the seal was there, a great, sleek, dark, 300-kilogram brown form hanging suspended in the cold water, with his eyes and nose just out, looking up from the hole with an expression of soulful yearning. Ellen blamed this on his mateless condition. Zapol blamed it on our anthropomorphism. "In many species," he said, "cuteness is related to the size of the eyes." Max had huge, dark eyes. Zapol called him "a little warm man in a fat shell." He tolerated our flash photography and Zapol's gentle nudges to show us the computer strapped to a neoprene pad glued to his fur. From the computer, tubes ran into Max: in a three-hour operation Zapol's group, which included several other physicians from hospitals in the United States, Denmark, West Germany, and New Zealand, had run a seventy-centimeter line clear to his aorta. The operating room was a slab of plywood floor in an adjacent hut, which was scarred in semicircles by the teeth of another patient. Weddell seals had hinged jaws that let them reach up and carve out the ice at the edges of their holes with their front teeth, with a swift back-and-forth sawing. They could not be kept in captivity because of this habit: they always tried to carve out the sides of their concrete pools. They died of dental infections.

When Max dived, the computer on his back recorded the seawater pressure and depth, his speed through the water, his heart rate, his blood temperature, and took samples of his arterial blood.

"They have sixty liters of blood in them," Zapol said, meaning members of Max's species. "Sixteen percent of their body weight is blood. They have twice as much blood for their body weight as humans. They are the deepest-, longest-diving seals. They're the world's champion diving seals."

Eventually Max had enough of this dazzling attention. We had not, after all, improved the loneliness. When he decided to leave he rose slightly in the hole, expelled breath, sank the ten feet to the bottom of the ice, turned, and swam away. It was a quiet, graceful departure and seemed wonderfully free. His massive body only ounces heavier than a bubble, he flowed away out of sight.

"Bye, Max," said Malcolm.

For a few seconds after he left, a cloud of ice flakes rose in the hole. One of the researchers scooped them out with a pool cleaner, poured clearing agent into the pool, and settled down to wait.

Beneath the ice, light from the single hole shone down into the clear depths like the distant light of home, the only one in Max's reach. He must return or die.

(2)

The world beneath the antarctic ice was cold and beautiful. We had been there. On a bright, breezy day we had gone out in a vehicle called a Spryte, which thumped along on tracks at a top speed of less than ten miles an hour, to another hut out on the ice near McMurdo. There another group studying seals—this one from the University of Minnesota—had put a glass chamber through a hole in the ice. The chamber hung on the end of an access tube just below the bottom of the ice and contained a folding steel chair, a tape recorder connected to hydrophones out in the water, and the end of a pipe that brought warmed air from the hut. The hole that contained the diving bell was surrounded by several other holes, foster homes for a group of Weddell seals trucked over from a distant colony. The four seals that shared these holes under the scrutiny of the Minnesota group's behavioral scientists were named Don Juan, Trudy, Priscilla, and Alice. Two others had managed to break away from the constraints of the isolated holes by swimming long distances; they were Clarice and another female who no doubt had fled to escape the terrible pun of her name: Luseal.

The shaft down to the diving bell was a narrow corrugated drainpipe containing a ladder and the hot-air hose; it was so cramped it was notorious for trapping Distinguished Visitors, who had no difficulty going down it, but always had trouble getting out. When we visited, the current story was of a stout DV, a civilian representative of the United States Armed Forces, who had to be yanked out with a rope. We soon provided our own story. Malcolm, who was tall and lean, proved conclusively that he was the most distinguished among us by getting wedged in the pipe by his long legs on his attempt to climb out, and suffered the same fate as the military man.

But when I climbed down the tube myself, I discovered that their troubles were subterfuge: they could not bear to leave.

The inside of the pipe was narrow, chilly, and claustrophobic. A ladder led down into a cramped darkness. Going down was like descending into a mine. The hard antarctic sunlight blazed down into the pipe and made the depths black. As I descended, one of the students of the seals stood ready to cover the pipe with a piece of plywood to shut out the sun. It was the final closing of a hatch, or of the mouth of a trap.

Then the space below opened out, the hatch slid over the sunlight, and I emerged into a spacious, blue-green-silver, softly bright world. Just outside the heavy plate glass of the little chamber, fronds of the platelet ice that grew down from the bottom of the sea ice curled delicately across the top of the view. Beyond this silver lace, the sky of this cool sea glowed. Through ten feet of ice the sun came muted but strong, illuminating the sea with a gentle, diffuse light. The bottom of the ice was colored by diatoms, so the light was white and green and golden brown. These few colors were rich enough, endowing the clear water with a wonderful subtlety of shade. It was like being inside one band of a rainbow, at the edge where the colors changed.

Directly in front of the window by the steel chair was one of the seals' breathing holes. The sun shone down through this in a broadening shaft that plunged at an angle deep through the sea toward the invisible bottom. Beyond it the ceiling, or the sky, was not flat: the ice undulated, and its outline was everywhere softened by the fringe of platelets. Glowing, it rolled away into a luminous green distance.

In that depth I could see nothing; the bottom was several hundred meters down. But I had an idea what it was like. I had watched a diver, Gregg Stanton, of Florida State University, on a dive near McMurdo. He went down in about eighty feet of water, close to the shore. Even though he was clad in what was euphemistically called a dry suit (it had a slow leak) and wore two layers of underwear beneath it, the first five minutes of the dive had been pure pain. "After that," he said, "you have just a sort of creeping cold that starts in the head area, with a pretty bad headache, and sort of moves down you. After forty or fifty minutes you can feel that cold."

But Stanton, a big, happy man, didn't let the cold chill his enjoyment of being underwater in Antarctica. While I stood beside the hole during one of his dives, bubbles and ice and laughter rose from the bottom.

"Look at this spicule mat!" Stanton chortled through the intercom. "The herbivores are *enormous*." A bloom of bubbles roiled the surface. "Okay," the voice from below said, as Stanton talked to the creatures he was picking off the bottom to put in his sample bucket, "who else wants to be famous?"

"The bottom is sort of bathed in dusk," Stanton said after his first dive. "The holes are like beacons. We swam between one and another. On the bottom it is sort of black and white. Starfish all over the bottom. *All* over the bottom. That's the first thing that catches your eye. Then as you come closer, as your head starts to level out a bit, you begin to recognize that the bottom at seventy feet has a bit of profile to it. There's sponge communities, and there's a lot of worms. Very few fish. It's sort of siliceous, almost glassy, on the bottom.

"This must have been what the Pleistocene sea was like. Huge isopods; big jellyfish. Really silent. There was no crackling of shrimp or humming or busying of anything. Everything was set. Little moved. It was like diving into the past."

From out of the past below the diving bell rose the seals. I heard them before they appeared. They approached with a noise that Katherine Bouton had described as the sound of a jet airliner passing overhead: a long, descending, whistling roar. A green shape, lean and fluid in the water, rose from out of the limpid depths and soared effortlessly to the hole. It was one of the females, Priscilla perhaps. Because the ice was so thick Priscilla disappeared up into the shaft completely. Then a second seal arrived—Trudy?—and, finding the hole occupied, hung in the water a few meters below.

I began to feel the need to breathe, in empathy, but Trudy did not seem disturbed. A few minutes passed. Whistles came through the hydrophones. Then Trudy opened her mouth, humped her neck, and uttered a series of noises. They were like barks, but harder. They sounded more as if someone were whacking on a hollow door with a crowbar. That, of course, may have been the sense of urgency Trudy tried to convey. Whack! Whack! Time's up! During this whole performance, not a single bubble arose from the barking seal.

Priscilla, who now seemed to be indulging frivolously—arrogantly—in the luxury of air, did not respond. My lungs were ready to burst. Finally Trudy ran out of patience. She turned and disappeared behind me, where she knew there was another hole.

I lingered in the chamber, enraptured by the cool light. I could always claim to be stuck. No wonder Max stayed down so long.

(3)

"We're all seals," Warren Zapol said gently, "once in our lives."

Max had now been gone a full half hour. The journalists were worried. Max was not, after all, any more of a fetus than we were.

Surely he would have to breathe soon. We were beginning to get quietly desperate, asking Zapol more and more questions, trying to ignore the possibility that our unwanted attention—all that curiosity and strobe-popping right into those big eyes—had driven Max to a desperate hunt for an alternative hole, taking all that equipment and research effort away with him. Zapol remained unflustered, making a kind gesture toward our need to know why. "Anesthesiologists are interested in patients holding their breath," he said. "And in the idea of binding a lot of oxygen on the red blood cells."

But mostly he celebrated the animal itself.

"Their arteries are beautiful," he said. "All that polyunsaturated fish." The seals were beautiful, strong, talented. "Given twenty million years they've designed the submarine very well." He poured some clearing agent in the hole. "They're too smart to be sprinters," he said. "They're marathoners. It seems relatively clear from what we're doing that their heart rate is modulated by their swimming speed. He'll use his reflex and modulate it with his mind. He knows what he's doing."

He paused. Everyone looked hopefully at the hole. In the bright light in the hut the water was dark and bitterly cold. A few pieces of platelet ice had accumulated. Zapol swept the hole out with the pool scoop.

"The reason they're the deepest divers is that the water is so much deeper here," he said. "This is the deepest continental shelf. The fish they eat are within fifty meters of the bottom, fifteen hundred feet down. You put a man under that kind of pressure and he'd suffer the frankest epileptic seizure. They don't do that. Weddells have the largest plasma concentration of adrenal steroids, which may be involved in the ability to tolerate tremendous pressure." He grinned. "He's full of tips on how to go to five hundred meters for twenty minutes."

Max returned.

He came back with no fanfare. The hole was empty and then

it was full of seal. The water surged. Max rose, puffed once, and rejoined the company, breathing slightly harder than he had been before he left. He appeared nonchalant, but still lonely. He looked around with those big eyes as if hoping that while he had been gone the scene had changed. Nope. The photographers started taking pictures again, popping away with relief. A strange species, bearing pulsing stars in the middle of their heads. Max looked around and sighed. He had been underwater thirty-two minutes and twenty seconds. He had not found another place to live.

Zapol and his colleagues attached a tube to the computer and began taking blood samples. As Max replaced the oxygen he had used, binding those molecules of his life's sustenance back into the matrix of his blood, the blood changed color. The samples taken five minutes after his return were brighter red than those taken first.

"His heart rate is eighty," Zapol said, reading data. "During the dive it was twenty to thirty. It takes him under thirty seconds to get the heart rate to go down. He was only down to eighty meters, which means it was a snoop dive—he was looking around."

The wind whistled around the little red hut. Zapol took the blood samples into the next hut—the one with the tooth marks on the floor—where another colleague would sort the gas components, looking for the pressure of nitrogen in Max's blood. On the door of the hut was a sign: You Slamma My Door, I Slamma Your Face.

Closing the door carefully, we went back out into the cold, leaving the doctors at work. We drove away. The Spryte clattered along the humped road, jerking on its tracks like a tank. The blowing snow had lifted off the surface into a light gray ice-blink sky. The ice stretched out in all directions. Max had been out here, ranging through the glowing green world of the icebound sea, modulating his heart with his mind to the slow beat of the deep, searching for the beacon of freedom. Native of Antarctica, attuned to the light, he would find it soon.

(4)

"We are probably the only scientists," said Anna Palmisano softly, her big eyes luminous in the muted light of the Biolab, "who use bulldozers in our work."

Anna Palmisano had big, thoughtful dark eyes and an obscure interest. She wanted to know what was going on on the bottom of the ice. This was more significant than it at first appeared.

Once, on board the *Polar Sea* somewhere south of Mt. Siple, Dick Cameron stood watching the ship break up a small floe. The ice cracked into several pieces and turned over, and the place where the ice had been bright white became a churned mass of chunks of overturned ice, all pale greenish brown. Cameron ruminated on the sight and then found the perfect metaphor. "I hate to say it," he said, "but that looks just like someone flushed the john and it didn't work."

Thaddeus von Bellingshausen, the Russian captain who came south in 1820, had roughly the same idea. "Many of the small pieces of ice were covered with a yellowish substance from the droppings of sea birds which sit in great number on them."

The yellowish-brown substance was a whole complex community of life, which grew like corrosion on and in the bottom layers of ice everywhere the ice grew. It was made up of bacteria and algae; dominated by diatoms, and Anna Palmisano wanted to find out what affected its growth. The title of the study was "Factors Which Influence the Growth and Development of Sea Ice Microbial Communities." The project, which was led by Cornelius W. Sullivan of the University of Southern California, was Sierra 039.

Like a little whirlpool sucking up information indiscriminately from all directions, our band of journalists rushed around McMurdo and its environs talking to the knights of the science quest. Our own search for the meaning of all this was directed, but not curtailed in any way, by a representative of the National Science

Foundation, Guy Guthridge. Guthridge was eternally patient and enormously energetic in a peaceful kind of way, but he watched quizzically, as if no matter how much time he spent with journalists he could never quite get rid of the feeling, nestled deep in his geologist's gut, that we were strange. It was Guthridge who shepherded us into the Biolab to talk to Palmisano.

The Biolab at McMurdo was a collection of prefabricated huts, started in 1958 with a twenty-by-forty-eight-foot building and added to in four-foot-wide modular increments called T-5s. It looked like an ice cave; shafts led off into distances glittering with glass. In a small lobby, near a blackboard bearing the names and current locations of biology projects on the ice, named by S number, were display cases in which the skulls of leopard, crab-eater, and elephant seals shared space with scallop shells, skua remains, dried sponges, and bottles containing the pale, pulpy remains of sea creatures. In one small jar in a corner was a little array of white knobs on a stem, labeled *Spini bilobota* in Coffee 10%. The specimen was plastic.

The diatoms Palmisano and her colleagues studied grew everywhere beneath the vast fluctuating sea ice of the continent. It was a farm of about 22 million square kilometers. Each season 75 percent of this ice melted into the cool sea, and the algae community that had grown within it was released into the water, where it could be eaten by anything that browsed on greens. During the algae bloom the water, which was so clear in the early spring that divers could see six hundred feet through it, became murky and dense with this enormous cloud of food. Krill gorged on it; penguins gorged on krill; leopard seals gorged on penguins and krill; killer whales gorged on anything alive; skuas gorged on anything dead or alive; baleen whales gorged on krill; and so the life that teemed in these cold waters was nourished another year.

"This constitutes one of the highest standing crops in amount of biomass in the world," Palmisano said. "It's very unusual, especially when you consider that the environment is very cold and very low-light." We asked, What did the stuff look like? "It's a green slime," she said with a smile. "Really very pretty."

Palmisano's bulldozer operator was Brian Matter, the same Matter who had been on J. J. Miller's plane at Winfly. He had enjoyed the task she set him to: she needed one rectangle on the sea ice covered with exactly one meter of snow, and another rectangle covered with only four centimeters. "I did it with a D-6," Matter had said earlier. Did he get it right? "Within a centimeter and a half."

The point of this exercise was to learn how different levels of light affected the growth of the algae. This involved diving. One afternoon we went out to still another little boxy hut on the ice, where Jon Kastendiek was getting ready to dive. Under the rectangles of different levels of snow the team had stuck flags on twelve-foot-long poles under the ice, so it looked from below like a capsized portion of McMurdo road. In order to visit this place and take samples both of the ice in which the diatoms grew and of the creatures that browsed on the algae, Jon put on three layers of underwear: polypropylene first, then the standard waffle-weave long johns issued to all USARP antarctic visitors, then a thick quilted layer of Thinsulate, including a little cap. "You definitely know you're going into cold water," he said.

Within the little room a heater poured warm air over us, so we became sweaty in our parkas. Outside it was fifteen degrees. The sun blazed. A helicopter passed, thundering faintly on the sides of the building. Jon sang to himself, *"I've been free . . ."*

At last, equipped and tanked, Jon was prepared to swim. He sat down on the edge of the hole, feet in the water.

"Do you always go in feet first?" Malcolm asked. Jon was putting his regulator in his mouth. He mumbled.

One of the team members who had been assisting him translated: "They've tried half gainers, but they tend to get stuck in the hole."

Jon sank down into the bitter cold water, then hung at the

surface for a moment. He adjusted down the mask. The flesh
showing around it looked pale and vulnerable.

All for science! Jon grinned, adjusted the mask, and sank. A
froth of platelet ice rose in the hole as he disappeared. We all
drew around, peering down. Finally Malcolm spoke.

"Bye, Max," he said.

(5)

Out on the ice, skuas pecked out the eyes of *mawsoni*. They
fought over the black dead fish, dancing around in a fury of pale
feathers. They cast long bounding shadows down the ice in the
late-night sunshine. The fish hut here had a name painted on it:
Mawsonic Lodge. Inside, Art DeVries cranked up the gas engine
of the winch and hauled a cold fish up from the bottom.

Dissostichus mawsoni were very cold fish even while they were
still flopping in the rack in which DeVries weighed each one,
tagged it, plucked a scale, and injected it with tetracycline to
mark the scales for the next time he caught it. The temperature
of their blood was below 0°C. They weighed between 18 and 170
pounds, and averaged 75. The line of cold water that lay out from
the shore close to the 60° south boundary of the area covered by
the Antarctic Treaty isolated the environment of the Southern
ocean from the rest of the world, so the *mawsoni*, like most other
creatures here, were unique to the Antarctic. People called them
Antarctic cod, making an inaccurate comparison. DeVries called
them *mawsoni*. He hauled them up with a winch powered by a
gasoline engine, on a 1,000-pound test cable from which hung
hooks baited with little pale 1-pound fish called *Pagothenia
borchgrevinki*. He called the bait fish borks.

Once I had a short conversation with another scientist about
Art DeVries, who was associate professor of physiology and bio-
physics at the University of Illinois. We'd been in the mess hall
eating good navy food to the constant music of the metal trays.
"I'll bet that back in Illinois, Art is real straight," the other scientist

said. He worked on some mashed potatoes. His fork played a short backbeat to the clangor. He considered what he had said. He looked up and grinned. "But I doubt it."

DeVries wore a USARP-issue wool shirt, a wool cap, wool trousers, a woolly beard, and running shoes. Almost everyone else had a beard here too, but DeVries wore his as if he had had it since 1961, when he first came to the Antarctic; there was a little fey smile lodged in there behind it, a wary, knowing smirk. He talked very quietly. He carried a blue toothbrush in his left shirt pocket. On the wall of his space in the Biolab there was an old news clipping about discussions the treaty nations were having about mineral development: ANTARCTIC VITAL TALKS UNDERWAY. There was no escaping the pressure of the world.

In his lab freezer DeVries kept a cluster of ice crystals formed in glacial ice caves near McMurdo. DeVries was a regular stop on any DV tour of the city. When the DVs came he took the ice crystals out of the freezer and talked about how his fish used glycopeptides secreted in the liver to prevent initial ice crystals from forming in their blood.

"Fish normally freeze at minus point seven degrees Celsius," he told us, ice in hand, when we trooped in. "So if you took a temperate-water fish and put it in this water it would quickly freeze. You find these fish sitting in a water at minus two. We think they bind the glycopeptides to the surface of the ice crystals to prevent water molecules from forming a mass in their blood." The ice in his hand shone coldly in the fluorescent overhead light —feathers of ice, diamonds of ice, little blue castles of ice, grown into a clustered, glittering model of Antarctica.

DeVries had an aquarium down beside the sea, a Jamesway hut full of round fiberglass tanks in which captured *mawsoni*, their skin color transformed from dark to pale in response to the light of the room, circled endlessly in water pumped out of the sea, practicing not freezing. When we visited, DeVries tied a live ten-inch bork on a hookless monofilament line and dropped it in a tank to tempt a fifty-pound *mawsoni*. "Here, kitty, kitty, kitty," he said. The *mawsoni* circled slowly, a huge grumpy head at the end of a tapering body. The *mawsoni* looked as if it had given much thought to life in cold waters and had come to the conclusion that it was bad. It circled slowly, staring at the tank with protuberant eyes that would, in due course, nourish skuas. The *mawsoni* was doomed to give its life to research; it had a right to feel discouraged. It did not, however, feel full. With a single swift flash of its jaws it consumed the bork.

The *mawsoni*'s expression of distaste did not change, but when DeVries pulled on the line to produce action for the cameras it slashed moodily at the surface, dampened the spectators, broke the monofilament, and returned to the bottom to brood.

"You see," DeVries said. "Out on the ice, when they hit, they shake the whole hut."

We were not there when any *mawsoni* hit the cable, the night we went fishing with DeVries. We went out in a tracked vehicle like the Spryte, called a Trackmaster, which Malcolm, with his Korean War memories of tank training (he was a man of many wars), managed to commandeer for a trip to an adjacent hut. He developed a wicked grin, grabbed the twin brake handles, floored the accelerator, and raced across the humped ice at eight miles an hour. He needed practice on the turns. It was a beautiful evening on the ice. The sun dipped toward its lowest point in the sky, turning the snow golden, and shreds of the Royal Society Range floated in the distance across the sound through wispy clouds. A thin plume rose from Erebus, behind McMurdo; the caldron simmered.

In the nearby hut one of DeVries's assistants caught, measured, and released several *mawsoni* in a hole in which three beer cans floated, ideally cold. But DeVries himself only winched onc fish up out of the depths. It was a dispirited black specimen of 105 pounds that had been on the hook a long time. It lay quietly in the wooden trough when DeVries hauled it out of the hole. He laid a rag across its eyes, giving the impression that he was going to shoot it. Instead he weighed and measured it, injected the tetracycline, tagged it with three tags, removed the blindfold, and let the big fish go. The *mawsoni* sank away with no more animation than the 45-pound weight at the end of DeVries's cable.

It was unlikely, but possible, that it would see DeVries again; this year he had recaptured a *mawsoni* he had first caught seven years before. In that time the fish had grown from 49 pounds to 54.5 pounds and had put on all of fourteen centimeters of length. It was possible that the biggest ones were already living back when Douglas Mawson himself ate them in 1911.

After lowering the baited cable back into the hole, DeVries closed the windows of the little hut and did some sportfishing. In the dark the hole glowed blue, bringing the deeply muted sunlight of Antarctica into the dim room through the ice. Four of us stood around the hole like worshipers at the light, our faces blue, our hands blue, our lives ultraviolet, and dangled little spinners on monofilament twenty feet down to catch borks. DeVries lowered a chemical light stick on a rope. It emitted a wavering cool light at the bottom edge of the hole, drawing fish. The spinners glittered blue and the borks came up meekly, looking transparent, living ice in the hand. We threw them into buckets for bait and then we drank New Zealand Riesling from 150-ml beakers DeVries had brought out from the lab. (After some discussion about what they had previously contained, he had, at our request, rinsed the beakers before pouring the wine.) One of the borks was sacrificed to science and promptly became sushi, but when one or two of the fillets flipped themselves off the plate, some of us declined the delicacy.

DeVries uttered gentle homilies about living in Antarctica: "It's a good idea to have a girlfriend here. That way there's one person who cares where you are." "This is the only place where you can be a bus driver and be chic. You do that in New Jersey and you're typed, but in Antarctica . . . It's utopia; except it's not real."

We had heard that DeVries's work might lead to the use of antifreezes similar to the *mawsoni*'s glycopeptides in protecting frost-sensitive crops. In the dim light of the fish hut we cloaked the need to know a practical value in ever more transparent questions. Why? What for?

"I believe," Larry Gould, Byrd's geologist, wrote in the book *Cold*, "that to the sort of person for whom the idea of the love of knowledge for its own sake is something of a mystery, there is not much use to attempt to answer that question." But people here kept trying. Finally DeVries responded directly. He looked at us kindly, wryly, patiently. We were not, after all, like the fish, the seals, the skuas, the diatoms, and the men and women of science. We were not natives of Antarctica. Perhaps we could not comprehend the truth: understanding was important all by itself.

"This work has provided me and several students with Ph.D. dissertations," he said with a bit of that sly smile; shocking us, mocking us. The smile faded away. "I guess you know it's basic research. My overall goal . . ." He said it carefully, as if at last revealing the secret, the great *why*: "My overall goal is to explain how these fishes use this antifreeze to avoid freezing."

We drank more wine. We passed the plate of almost-dead bork to others. Riding the Trackmaster home we fell asleep in the rising light of morning, as the sun shone on the crosses on the hills.

"And I tell you," wrote Apsley Cherry-Garrard, one of the survivors of Scott's expedition, who undertook what he later called "the worst journey in the world" to recover emperor penguin eggs, which were incubated in the winter darkness: "And I tell you, if you have the desire for knowledge and the power to give it physical expression, go out and explore. . . . You will sledge nearly alone, but those with whom you sledge will not be shopkeepers: that is worth a good deal. If you march your Winter Journeys you will have your reward, so long as all you want is a penguin's egg."

Chapter Ten

On Tour

(1)

If the helo had had machine guns we would have killed them all. The aircraft went slashing over the camp at two hundred feet, rising up from behind a huge gravel ridge and thundering past on the deck, so low it seemed the wind must blow the little yellow pyramid tents into rags. "You'll have to just wave at them, Doc," the helo pilot said on the intercom to Donald Elston, the weathered, good-natured geologist who was the guide for this journalists' tour. It was his camp we crossed so rudely, flashing low and loud over the open gravel, the tents, the drilling rig. But there was no stopping now. We were getting the hell out of the Dry Valleys before the weather went bad again.

In McMurdo the civilian workers hired to maintain the city looked with longing out across the sound to where the mountains rose in ethereal ridges of light and mystery. They could not get there. On the edge of the strangest, wildest land on earth, they were trapped in a city, tied down by the net of power lines and safety rules. As visiting journalists—fresh from fishing with Art DeVries—Malcolm, Ellen, Bob, and I were more lucky. We had access to the windy red steed of the knights of science, the helicopter. In the early morning after the night's angling, we vaulted into the air, blew freezing dust on MacTown, and galloped off across the sound to the dry gulch canyons of grid east.

This was a standard Distinguished Visitor tour. Guy Guthridge was with us, peacefully delighted to be along, respectfully amused at our awe. The tour was like a wind itself, driven somehow by intention, but carrying us wildly across the landscape, dropping us at odd moments in settings so strange we did not feel our own presence to be substantial. We were taken places others found important. They did not explain why; they just let us out for a moment to look, to breathe, to pick up rocks, to express our amazement. Then they swept us away again.

The Dry Valleys were Antarctica with the skin peeled back. We crossed the ice-bound sound, crossed arms of open water that were black as chasms, crossed the long low white swell of the Wilson Piedmont past a rock of a mountain called the King Pin that the pilots used for navigation, and then the ice was gone and we roared across gold, brown, black, bare rock. No tree, no bush, no grass, no water, showed on the expanse of rubble. We were on the bones of the continent, out where the wind blew even the snow away. For fifty by fifty miles, a patch of Antarctica was swept clean of its white cloak by a quirk of climate and terrain by which the wind and the absorbent dry sweep of the air kept ahead of the accumulation of snow that smothered the land everywhere else.

Here were valleys with lakes that were frozen year-round, or with lakes so salty they never froze in the bitterest winters. Here was the Onyx, the continent's only river. It started near the coast, near the base of the Wilson Piedmont, a long waterfront glacier that lay like a barrier across the mystery of the Dry Valleys, and it flowed inland. It ran for a month a year; as we crossed it today it was still, its flow gathered in glittering motionless eddies in the elbows of its curves.

"Easy down, sir," said the crew chief over the intercom. "Three inches to your toes, sir." He leaned out of the open door and watched the strange land come up. "Easy down, sir." The machine landed gently on a lip of a pass above the Taylor Valley, and we piled out, bearing our orange survival bags, as required, to look at stone carved by wind-carried sand and ice crystals.

The engines died and the blades glided to a stop. The valley's enormous silence sucked away the noise like a vacuum. Nothing moved in the world but us. Our voices had no echo; our plastic boots made no clatter on the rock.

The pass was high and desolate. In all directions the land was broken, smoothed rock. The slope dropped down across the lip of the pass and vanished into depths. Beyond it the valley floor, brown rubble seamed with black intrusions of volcanic rock, rose again to a ridge of bare rock. Around us the rubble was of two kinds—a grainy kind of granite and a black, basaltic stone. Both were shaped not by water but by wind. River- or sea-sculptured stone has a weight and roundness to it that reflects the weight of the water; a field of alluvial stones is composed of soft edges and submission—it has been defeated by the power of the flow. But the shaping of rock by wind was more fanciful. The rocks arched against it, raised smooth little boulder pinnacles, ripples, ridges, and curls to its passage. There were holes in the rock, curving waves of rock, rocks raising arms or fingers for attention. The smallest black stones, called ventifacts, were faceted smoothly by the wind; they looked like cut obsidian tools without the glisten. Their facets were clearly defined and yet smooth; they looked like tools used by an unknown hand for centuries in a task involving sand and grain and rubbing. Their color was somber; the rock of which they were made was called dolerite.

Up close all the rocks of the hillside seemed to have a rough texture, but in the direction of the sun the wind-polished stone gleamed. A few minutes later, when I looked that way again, a cloud had come across the sun and the rocks were just dark stones on a shadowed hill.

Malcolm picked up ventifacts like a scavenger. He slipped them into his survival bag. In his apartment in Manhattan he had plastic skulls, ultraviolet light, perpetual motion models, and a collection of jeweled daggers. The ventifacts would fit right in. His survival bag became substantially heavier. He lugged it back to the helicopter, grinning. Grinning made our teeth hurt with the cold, and we had already heard of teeth cracking and fillings popping out, but we smiled anyway. Malcolm, Bob, Ellen, and I, mute in our headphones and mittens in the roaring machine as the helo warmed its engines to carry our squad on into the heart of the strange land, grinned away at each other for no reason except that we were here.

"Easy up, sir," the crew chief said, hanging out the open door. "Right side coming light. Easy up, sir." The helicopter bounded off the side of the hill and sank into the valley. Around the peaks above it the clouds gathered.

(2)

On the floor of the valley we paused to look curiously at death.

The helicopter landed on a field of gravel a hundred yards away from a small shape that lay on the stones. The gravel was divided into roughly symmetrical polygons by ruts in the surface drawn by the heavy hand of the cold. "Frost polygons," Elston said. "The permafrost is six inches below the surface. In the Taylor Valley there are six hundred feet of permafrost." In one of these outlined slabs lay a still form, a shape in a frame. We walked over to it, our feet crunching loudly on the six inches of loose gravel.

The shape was a dead seal. It was a small crabeater, the kind that frolicked among schools of krill and slept on ice floes a hundred miles out from shore. Its skin was mottled gray, yellow, and grayish green. Its body was lumpy and fallen in. Two teeth showed in its muzzle. In the lee of its body was a small drift of gravel. All around it the gravel stretched for hundreds of yards. The valley swept away from it, mile after mile of dry rock, cobbled with granite, seamed with dolerite, penetrated by no path. Miles away, across a perimeter of broken ice and moraine, lay a coastline that very briefly each year heard the sound of waves and the bark of seals. This one had come a very long way from home to die.

We immortalized it on film, juxtaposing the seal and the orange helicopter and the huge empty valley. We speculated upon the meaning of its fatal pilgrimage, or its mistake. Had the seal, like Scott, been engaged in a doomed expedition, seal hauling to the South Pole? Suffering was a resource in which the continent was rich. Had the seal, too, sought nobility in enduring anguish? It left no record; only a lip lifted from teeth by its drying skin.

"Must be something up here they're looking for," one of the pilots said. "Last year we had a penguin come walking up the Taylor Valley." Paul Siple, the Boy Scout who came south with Byrd and left his name on a coast and his wife's name on a mountain, thought the seals navigated like sailors, using ice blink and water sky. The darkness of the Dry Valleys would cast a shadow up against cloud and lead you on and upward to a mirage of open sea.

The tour went on. The helicopter raced from place to place under the accumulating cloud. There must be something up here. Between the Wright Valley and the Taylor Valley we crossed another corpse. It seemed to be the same colors as the seal: gray and green and yellow-orange. It was the ruin of the helicopter in which Thomas E. Berg, whose name was on Berg Field Center, and Jeremy Sykes, a New Zealand cameraman, died in 1969.

We soared up a cloud-free ridge where the air was so cold that the helicopter made its own cloud with its rotor blades: a long shadow followed us across the ground. The crew chief tossed a bomb of black smoke to show the direction of the wind. The helo landed on the ridge at 5,750 feet above sea level, blowing snow, and we clambered out on ice to look down into the valleys on either side. The view among the clouds was of ridges of rock and distant glaciers. From there the pilot talked to McMurdo via the South Pole. Mist gathered around and we swept down away from it to land on a pad outlined by painted orange rocks beside a Jamesway hut built next to the Meserve Glacier, one of several tongues of ice that came lapping down the dry sides of the mountains.

The tour had become a ritual: the ventifacts, the seal, the high ridge, the glacier. Those who had been here before us thought of these things as Antarctica: we had to touch them all. Nine years before, Malcolm had been initiated with practically the same tour: he was working for *The New York Times* then, and the *Times* printed a photo he had taken of two scientists dashing away from the glacier to avoid falling ice. With this memory now common property, we approached the little glacier gingerly, stepping quietly among rocks. Below the pale blue walls of the glacier were chunks of fresh ice, light as wood, full of glitter, as if the little bubbles in the snow were bits of light itself that had fallen with the snow and were trapped by the pressure. In the darkening weather the whole glacier glowed.

The Jamesway was tied down to fifty-five-gallon fuel drums filled with rocks. It was dark inside, and as somberly green as the Army. It contained a stove and emergency supplies. People who had lived there had signed names and slogans on the curving walls. "The Asgard Rangers, NZARP, 1970–71." Among the supplies were cans of "GREASE, AUTOMOBILE AND ARTILLERY." An old *Time* magazine cover was taped up to the wall. On it was the face of a famous television newsman. Written across his genial, wise countenance were the black letters: "Walter Cryokinite."

(3)

"I don't like this too well," one of the pilots said. The helicopter was up among clouds and ice, climbing at seventy knots, trying to get home in deteriorating weather. Passes were clogged with mist. Falling snow flowed through the passes on the current of the wind. Inside the machine everyone was connected to the intercom. No one interrupted to discuss geology. Around the helicopter pale shapes swirled, appearing and disappearing in the whiteness, while below fields of humped and buckled ice slid past more and more slowly. The helicopter came to a kind of junction, where two streams of ice divided around a monolith of gray brown stone. We listened in:

"What do you think?"

"I wouldn't bet on it."

"Well, we've got enough to make it out there and take a look, I guess."

"Yeah. The worst part is going to be crossing the Piedmont. I've got a feeling this stuff is laying right on the ice shelf."

The commodity about which the pilot was concerned was fuel, not daring. He was well equipped with the latter. One day at lunch in McMurdo two young sailors talked about helicopter pilots over their metal trays. Among the civilians at McMurdo the scientists were the elite; among the troops it was the pilots. "Yeah," one of the two had said, "you can be a defensive driver, but you can't be a defensive helo pilot."

"Could be worse," the other said. "Somebody could be shooting at you."

Now the weather was shooting at us. The helicopter climbed a long white heave, bounced around by bursts of wind. It crossed an ice ridge at twenty-seven hundred feet and bucked slowly down into the whitening world. Straight horizontal lines of snow, like a cloud of white tracer bullets, filled the air between us and the land below. Hillsides were ghosts on either side. The horizon was a faint gray joining of white and white. The helicopters could not fly on instruments because of the lack of navigational aids; they had to maintain contact with the ground. But the ground was losing contact with itself, dissolving into the royal white light of Antarctica.

"Back to Vanda," said the voice on the intercom. You could be aggressive in this business, but you could not be stupid. The helicopter turned away from the deadly brightness.

(4)

Vanda was a settlement with a substantial human population, for Antarctica: four. It lay among stony hills of moraine above Vanda Lake, into which the Onyx River drained. Nothing flowed out of

Vanda Lake. Vanda Lake was always frozen: in the summer a perimeter of open water appeared near the shore, but the center of the lake was a permanent block of ice. When the helicopter flew over it we could see the difference between the seasonal and the permanent ice: the ice that would never melt was murky and pale blue; the new ice was a deep cobalt, seamed with cracks. It looked like ancient tile. It did not, at the time, look cold or forbidding; premonitions never come to your aid when you need them.

Vanda Station belonged to New Zealand. It had been a brief part of the tour earlier in the day. The four Kiwi Vandals, who were living at the base from October 22 to January 29, had served us potato soup and scones in exchange for our American sack lunches. Now they welcomed us back cheerfully, although a group of New Zealand DVs had landed here too, also marooned by the weather, and with our arrival the little kitchen hut was jammed with twenty people. On the blue flowered oilcloth on the long table was a last tray of big square scones. They looked as if they were made of chocolate. They weren't. They had been in the stove a long time. They were made of iron.

The wind rattled in the stovepipe. The Vandals revealed intimate details of their lives in response to our prying questions.

"It's a nice spot to call home. The buildings are made of polyurethane foam sandwich. The walls are four inches thick. In New Zealand one of these buildings would be a stand-alone outside freezer. When the field parties come here they get the unheated buildings; they're supposed to be tough.

"We have solar panels. We get forty watts. The only drain is our fire alarm system and the radio. We have lights, but we never need them."

Outside was a little trailer with which the Vandals fetched ice from the lake to melt for water. They did not bathe often. Forty-five minutes of work with a pick and shovel on the lake was good for a week's supply of water. On the side of the wagon were the inscriptions "Lucy's Liquor Waggon" and "Vanda or Breasts," with the last word crossed out and replaced by "Bust." At one end of the building, in an alcove, was a fuel drum with a funnel in it for a urinal. Far out among the windblown stones of the surrounding hills was a three-sided shack partially sheltering another drum with a toilet seat on top. It had no door. Beyond it the storm surged at the peaks. Wind whistled around the hut. Again foresight failed me. I looked at the little hut and was glad I would never have to use something that uncomfortable. Everyone was supposed to be tough—except DVs.

In the kitchen building on the table was a big plaid Scotch tape can with a sign on the side reporting the results of the Onyx River Flow Sweepstakes for several years. The Vandals were still collecting bets and guesses for this year, but the sign gave some idea of when the river might turn liquid: "1969: December 30, 2100. 1970: December 5, 1530. 1978: December 30, 0600. 1979: December 5, 1530." In the summer of 1977–78 the Onyx River never flowed at all.

Don Elston sat back in a chair at the table and talked about his project. It was a joint United States–New Zealand effort to chart the geological structure and history of the Dry Valleys. The drill penetrated the permafrost to a depth of about two hundred feet and drew out cores of rock one and three-quarters inches in diameter made of stone or of gravel cemented together by the ice.

"We've done eight so far," Elston said. "We're going to do four more. We're using the subsurface information to piece the geology together and to tie the surface to the subsurface. We want to work out the events of the late Pleistocene, trying to get a handle on that part of the elephant."

Near the door was a bookshelf full of paperbacks. Among them were *Modern Welding*, *The Ashley Book of Knots*, two copies of Peter Scott's *The Eye of the Wind*, *Walden*, and a book called *Snowbound Six*, by Richard Martin Stern. *Snowbound Six* was a dramatic adventure story. It was about a group of people trapped by bad weather and cold in the wilderness of New Mexico, U.S.A.

(5)

The afternoon wore on. Ellen, surrounded by attentive pilots and
crew members, conducted interviews about flying in Antarctica.
Malcolm talked serious science with Don Elston. I walked down
to the lake, drawn by a fascination for the blue ice that, in light
of subsequent events, might have been considered morbid. I
walked out on it. It was surprisingly slippery in the cold wind. It
was shot through with cracks and with tiny columns of bubbles
frozen in place.

Nothing about these antarctic lakes was familiar. None had
outlets; in the brief period in which water became liquid here
they collected salts out of the little tributaries and the ground-
water. The layers of water in the lakes grew saltier with depth,
which meant that although deeper layers were warmer, they were
also heavier, so they stayed down and did not mingle. This concentrated the heat as well as the dissolved minerals: the bottom of
this ice-covered lake had been measured at over 70°F. Not far from
here by helicopter was another body of water, a shallow pond
that was so salty that when the bitter winter clamped down on
Antarctica and froze the heart out of even the stone, the water
remained liquid, reflecting the blaze of the aurora and the arch of
stars, a strange living pool in the hard land.

"I don't know, Larry," Rich Littke, our pilot, said to the pilot
of the New Zealand DVs as they both looked up at a gleam of
sunshine on the mountainside. "This might be it."

Hi ho helo! Everyone bundled back in the machine and went
galloping away again. Up the side of the Wright Valley it dashed,
across an array of rocks arranged by the flexing of frost into mounds
that were so symmetrical they looked like prehistoric barrows,
tomb upon tomb up the hill. We dared the teeth of the Asgard
Range, and nothing gnashed. It was no longer snowing; out the
windows the blacks and browns of distant hillsides resolved themselves into forests of pine, or sagebrush meadows, or little pockets

of cottonwood trees, made into familiar living things by nostalgic eyes and then turned back into rock by the knowledge of reality: the view was utterly unsoftened by life.

Over the ridge, the helicopter rushed down the slopes of a glacier called Matterhorn, flying low across the crevasses like a skier. It passed the tongues of glaciers lapping down the bare slopes: Suess Glacier, Canada Glacier, Commonwealth Glacier. It shot over Elston's camp, the tiny yellow tents staked out on an immensity of gravel. Each tent was eight by eight feet, slept four, and partied more. "We've set places for fifteen people in one of those tents," Elston said, "and sat and told stories half the night." The helicopter stopped and refueled out of twenty-five-thousand-gallon rubber bladder tanks that had been hauled by tractor train from McMurdo to this desolate spit of windblown rock called Marble Point.

The helicopter stopped so Elston could introduce these curious journalists briefly to a group of emperor penguins on the ice near the slowly advancing open water. The penguins waddled flatter-ingly in our direction, as if overjoyed to make the acquaintance of other warm-blooded beings. But when we dashed off in another direction to pursue a rumor of whales at the ice edge, we dis-covered that the penguins weren't interested in people after all: they wanted to meet the helicopter. They wanted to bob and genuflect and get down on their bellies in front of the great red bird-god with the wailing voice of thunder.

Malcolm, Ellen, Bob, and I had nodded to the icons of Ant-arctica. Penguins, weather, seals, glaciers, cold. The day's tour was over. "Coming light, sir. Easy up, sir." The helicopter left the groveling birds without a gesture of hope or salvation, inscrutable to the end, and flew away toward the distant black hump of Observation Hill and MacTown. The bad weather was behind. The clouds that had seemed so dangerous lay back against the mountains in innocent folds of white.

It was late at night. We walked up into town from the helicopter, wide awake and laughing. The night's single dazzling star laid golden spring sunlight on the black rock, on sides of buildings, on the power poles and wires, on the Royal Society cathedral. Sleep seemed a waste of time. We had Antarctica. We had each other. At a party the night before, a solid, unemotional carpenter had been talking about why he came. "It's not the place," he said, "it's the people. I tell you, it's the people." Overwhelmed by the power of the land, we gave in to the power of affection. Like a squad under fire, tossed among glaciers, blown around by the wind, blasted by the light, dismissed by penguins, we had become close. In the late, bright night, Malcolm, Ellen, and I went over to the mess hall, ate hot dogs and chili among the empty tables, talked about love and marriage and war and the majesty of Antarctica, and felt young and riding the crest of life.

Friendships made in Antarctica were doomed to change. Without that mighty third party they could never be the same, and no human being lived for long on the ice. People made lifetime friends here, but had to remake them when they got home. We sat talking as if the light of Antarctica had driven through us and laid open each other's most precious hopes, but in just a matter of a few dozen hours the others would be gone north back to the world of real war and marriage and love and darkness, already forgetting the majesty, and I would be bereft of their company, left on the ice alone.

But not yet, not yet. We were still on the manifest for the Pole.

Chapter Eleven

This Awful Place

(1)

I staggered coming up out of the tunnel into the light. It was less than twenty-four hours after the Dry Valleys, but Antarctica had changed again. We were at the Pole.

Equilibrium was gone. Something odd was happening to my breath. It collected in my face. Though I could see it, every crystal, there was not enough substance there for my lungs. I gulped at it. *Mawsoni*. Crabeater. I'd lost my way on the ice. In all the blue-and-white world there was no water sky. A hand touched my arm. Whose was it? My white wool mask was like blinders. I could not see for the cloud I made and the sun in it. A woman's voice: "You okay?" Yes, yes.

"A white desolation and solitude," Richard Byrd said of this place. He flew over the South Pole in 1929, and when he came back that's what he said to Paul Siple, the Boy Scout. In January 1956 a Marine Corps pilot flew across the Pole as an advance scout for United States Task Force 43, which was planning to build a base there. The marine dropped smoke flares, a balloon full of ink, and cutout cardboard models of penguins into the white desolation. He circled. They had disappeared. It was the snow, he thought. Up in this stunning cold the snow must be powder. He could imagine the aircraft sweeping closer and closer to this deceiving brilliant surface, touching down with exquisite gentleness, and being enveloped in frozen fluff. A large white flower would bloom on the high plateau and would slowly drift away, and the pilot's soul would join those of Titus Oates, Edgar Evans, Henry Bowers, Edward Wilson, and Robert F. Scott, enshrined in legend and eternal cold.

The marine pilot returned to the fledgling U.S. base on McMurdo Sound carrying the bad news. For a short time it added to the fears that some raised against the occupation of the Pole: It was very cold; people could not live there. The sun would set in March and rise in September; people could not remain sane there. And now the surface was untrustworthy; people could not land there.

Soft snow and strange sunshine. The sun sets once, rises once. It goes down slowly into a sea of snow, sidling around the horizon and taking the late red sky of west to all points of the compass, every one of which is north. It leaves twilight hanging in the sky for a month and a half. It rises fierce, flinging arms of light around the cold world. "It rolled, heaved and surged like a distant forest fire or like a restless, flaming tidal wave. . . . And we saw strange flashes of light," Paul Siple wrote of the five days before sunrise. The sun sets once, and the temperature goes to a hundred below, but the snow is hard as iron. When the planes touched down there was no catastrophic cloud. Men walked unimpeded on the hard surface, pounded on stakes to get them to stick, made foundations for buildings so big you could get lost in them, took possession of a place that seemed solid as land. They laughed at the rumors. The men were sane; they kept warm.

But the snow moved. It gathered. It felt hard and reliable; it was hard and shifty. Everything the planes brought and everything built was slowly consumed, grain by windblown grain.

The South Pole was a dream, a nightmare. "The Pole . . . Great God! this is an awful place and terrible enough. . . ." Scott cried out to his diary while he was camped at the Pole in defeat, words to be read only months after his death. Scott walked up the Beardmore Glacier, pulling a sledge. He walked back down the Beardmore Glacier, pulling a sledge that bore the tent that would be his tomb and the pages of the diary that would sweep away his foolishness with glory. The Pole was a nightmare, a dream. Comfortable, confident, our group of journalists had flown south in an LC-130. The Beardmore was a staircase no longer, just a checkpoint passing under the wing.

"What else do you have up here as a landmark?"

"The Prudential Rock."

The pilot was quizzing the copilot.

"How much fuel at Pole?"

"They got a 10K bladder that's full and a 24K one pretty near full."

"How much time do you have to report?"

"You have thirty minutes to get hold of them. After an hour you're said to be overdue."

The Transantarctic Range approached and passed under the plane. Glaciers poured down between mountains like water over a five-hundred-mile-long dam of loose rocks. The plane crossed the range at an angle. The glaciers looked smooth, seamed with lines of stress and blue icefalls, pouring water stilled and softened by a time exposure of centuries. The range rolled away close to the course, like a freight train on another track slowly drawing away to a siding a thousand miles away on the Weddell Sea. Behind it the surface was flat and high. The ice was dammed, and behind the range it grew and grew and grew, expanding under our gaze until the mountains were gone and from twenty-four thousand feet the horizon in all directions was an unbroken curve of snow. It was six, eight, nine, eleven thousand feet deep, two miles of snow packed to ice, the storehouse of the world's fresh water; the cap of reflection that tossed the sun's light back in its face, fed winter winds across the globe, and sent its creeping fingers of cold into the depths of all the world's seas; the face of the earth that shone.

Get out of the plane. Walk slowly. Put on your fur-backed bear-

paw mittens. Put on your balaclava mask. Pull up your hood. In
your enthusiasm do not walk into the propellers. Your enthusiasm
may be hypoxia, the drunkenness of too little air. You may be sick
with joy. Walk slowly. The air is very thin. Amundsen-Scott South
Pole Station is at 9,300 feet above sea level. It has an effective
altitude of 10,600. Walk slowly. Do not run up the stairs. Do not
run. "You will have strange feelings here. You may have a headache, nausea, shortness of breath. Anything beyond that, see me."
Dr. Michael Beller, station physician. All arrivals are the same:
The doors open, the warmth of the cabin makes a fog at the
doors. You feel the sting of the cold. You stagger out with your
survival bag. You are high, you are heavy. Your space suit is un-
gainly; your arms stick out from your sides. You look around.
Flags; a tiny barber pole with a silver ball on it in the middle of
the flags. A huge silver dome; steam rising from vents. A ramp of
snow down into a big square door in the dome. A sign above the
door: United States Welcomes You to the South Pole.

(2)

"It was 47 degrees below zero Fahrenheit when you landed. It was
minus 67 when the first flight came in this year. The highest
temperature ever recorded at the South Pole was minus 7.5 degrees.
The lowest was minus 117." The standard briefing was given in
the South Pole library. Shell within shell, the people at the South
Pole lived warm. The dome was shelter. It was calm in there, but
the frost remained. You could drive a front-end loader through the
door, and people did. The cold came in, too, stronger than a
D-9 Cat. The light within was dim, shaded from the glare by the
overhead expanse of aluminum. This metal sky colored day and
night inside; within the dome the light was a cool metallic blue,
like twilight on a quicksilver sea. The lights of the interior buildings shone warmly out onto the snow floor. The air looked as if
it should taste like water stored in a can.

The sun came harshly into the dome through a cluster of openings at the peak. A shaft of light blazed in at a shallow angle at this time of the spring, and moved slowly around the huge room, making a spot of light on the upper reaches of the dome. The light swung like a planet around the central fire. At the edges of the holes in the roof was a growth of bright white rime ice, as if the light drove in so hard it scraped on the metal. Through the dazzling holes could be seen, if the angle was right, the American flag that flew at the dome's peak. From the twilight inside the dome the flag looked bleached; all those stalwart colors blown pale and inconsequential by the raging antarctic light.

Long orange buildings were stacked up like cargo containers on the snow, one and two stories high. Their precious cargo was warmth. Their doors were like air locks. The warmth was like oxygen. Without it we would all soon die. We would go spinning away into the whiteness, pale and stiff in our red jackets.

Within the containers were people. The population of the South Pole today was sixty-nine souls, including the visitors: Malcolm, Bob, Ellen, Guy Guthridge, and me. Outside the containers was the food—boxes of frozen beans and frozen bread; cans of frozen sauerkraut. It was dinnertime in the mess hall: Chinese chicken and egg rolls. The cooks were the antarctic C.I.A. contacts—they were graduates of the Culinary Institute of America. After the bland Navy food at McMurdo, the South Pole cuisine was magnificent.

There were stairs outside the buildings. Up the stairs, down the stairs. Our footsteps rang, bunny boots on metal. Through the fuel arch, where great black bladders lay on the snow like huge hot-water bottles, blanketed with insulation. Dick Cameron was here too, bearded and happy. We followed Guy Guthridge around. We never took off our coats; we sweated in the warm rooms, grew chilly in the dome. The grand accumulation of South Pole science piled up against us, drifts of golden leaves. We were like children, stuffing pockets that were too small: Give us time to understand. There is no time. Listen, take notes. You reach the South Pole once in your life.

Elmer Robinson, University of Washington, studied the way the ice surface reacted with trace gases in the atmosphere: "Like most antarctic research I'm familiar with, an investigator begins looking at some general aspects of the field, then finds there is little known at all about conditions in Antarctica." The public address system interrupted: "Mike Beller, please call oo6. Mike Beller, please call oo6."

Eric Siefka, communications chief, was twenty-two. He had been coming here since he was nineteen. He would winter here next year. "We do most of the flight following for the continent," he said. "We talk to helicopters around McMurdo." A large wooden mallet hung above an array of radios, labeled Acme Noise Suppressor. Siefka: "We talk to everybody. We're going to have a sign made: Antarctica Control."

Gary Foltz, U.S. Geological Survey, monitored seismographs. "This machine can pick up earthquakes from all over the world. We also pick up a tractor in the dome, or a Herc arriving."

Malcolm: "Can you detect an underground nuclear explosion?"

Foltz: "Yes."

"What do you do?"

"Just pick it and send it to Colorado."

Foltz was solid and unemotional. This year would be his second winter. The first time he spent a year here he and a colleague, figuring their display of modest humming machines bored Distinguished Visitors, made up a control panel with flashing lights and switches that said things like Engage Satellite. The panel was still there. It had no real function at all.

The South Pole was stairs and shortness of breath; glimpses outside of the dazzling permanent day; glimpses inside of the work that progressed here, day to day.

F. Tom Berkey, of Utah State University, looked up into the cusp of the ionosphere, where the earth's magnetic fields, curving to the Pole, made a window in which he could stare into the eye of the solar wind. Ensign Frank Migaiolo, with the National Oceanic and Atmospheric Administration, tested this remote air for any trace of changes in the quality of air on the globe. Migaiolo, also the fire officer of the South Pole Station, watched for the most frightening enemy of explorers of the cold land.

Francis Navarro, a Spaniard and a graduate student from the University of California at Los Angeles, listened to the reverberations of the earth's mantle in response to earthquakes on the surface. When we came to see him he stood in a cluttered room with a globe in one hand and a spool of solder in the other, demonstrating the creation of twenty-seven-day tides in rock and ice and deep, hot liquid: "For our studies we need an earthquake of more than 7.9 on the Richter scale." Navarro would spend the winter. He had recently started a beard. He was waiting for the beard to grow thick. He was waiting, with equal certainty, for the crash of devastation and tragedy that must happen somewhere on the globe, waiting to catch the echoes but not the tears.

The public address system interrupted again: "XD 03 has departed McMurdo Station. Estimated arrival, 10:55 local. Zero mail, zero pax." It was the second half of the double shuttle, coming to take us away. There was a saying in MacTown: "Never wait for the second shuttle." It might not come. But this one would not fail.

Malcolm had carried his Christmas cards in his survival bag; he took them to the post office. The postmaster was Mike Beller, the doctor. Doctors in the Antarctic had to find something else to do or go crazy bored. Beller had a box of cachets, verification of our presence here. We sat at a table in the library, putting "South Pole" all over postcards.

And then nothing was left on the schedule. In the library were shelf after shelf of books, and a television set hooked to a video cassette recorder. Some of the residents were watching a movie. Slowly our eyes were drawn to the screen, to the little blue window on our distant world. The movie was *The Godfather, Part II.* Malcolm, Bob, and Ellen slid into chairs. On the little screen a man was shot in the forehead. He died. On the screen another man got into a car. Poison took effect. He went into convulsions. His heel kicked out the window of the car. He died. Someone was shouting. Someone was screaming, crying. Someone was being buried.

Whose dream was this? Not mine. I dreamed about Antarctica. I left the library. I walked alone through the cold air of the dome. I put on my bearpaw mittens, my balaclava mask, my hood. My eyes flinched from the brightness of the big door. I walked out into the sunshine. It was so strong I felt washed by it, cleansed by the solar wind. Looking in the direction of the sun I could see a very faint glitter in the air. Fine ice crystals, light as molecules, drifted down from the clear sky. The glitter fell all around, almost invisible, dusting the surface of the immense whiteness with a dew of light.

(3)

The barber pole with the mirrored globe that represented the South Pole was surrounded by the sixteen flags of the Antarctic Treaty nations—the original twelve plus four new members. Near it was the stand of arrows, common to all antarctic stations, that bore signs pointing in assorted directions, each sign to the home of someone who had been here. Memphis, London, Lisbon, Los Angeles, Miami, Tehachapi, Billings, Eugene. The flags were official. The arrows represented longing. Here home mattered more than country. The taller of two stands was topped with a wooden fish and pointed to Salmon, Idaho.

This was not the real South Pole. Where was it? In the neighborhood of the barber pole was a one-acre grove of bamboo stakes. Within these transplanted tropical woods was hidden the South Pole, the real pole, the true axle of the earth. I wandered around. I found it. The real Pole was modest. It turned out to be a little imitation of the big barber pole stuck into the snow. It reached my waist. On top of it was a small knob. That was it, the heart of the whirl.

The real Pole was not celebrated with international flags. Next to it on a bamboo stake flew a single drab, dark blue flag bearing the insignia of the U.S. Geological Survey: crossed hammer and pick.

I stood out on the hard snow, looking around. My head hurt, softly, dully. My eyes ached. I wrote notes on my notebook. The pen froze and faded away. I got out a pencil and wrote with it clamped in my mitten. In the distance was the faint mutter of generators. A plume of steam rose from the vents and drew together in a long, low cloud that drifted—north. The paper of the notebook crackled as I turned a page. It was brittle. It tore; it broke. Nearby noises seemed very loud, loud as all others were distant. The flapping of the USGS flag. The sound of the paper. The scratch of the pencil. The harsh sound of breathing, like the puffing of a lung made of tin cans and parchment.

The South Pole was advancing across the ice. Its position from year to year was marked by metal posts. Each stood about ten meters in front of the previous one and was labeled with copper: "Jan 1, 1983." "Jan 1, 1982. Set by T. Henderson, K. Covert. USGS." The posts cast long shadows in the low sunlight, the golden morning sun of spring. The earth's core remained in one place. The ice moved, thirty feet a year. Nine thousand vertical feet of ice, a thousand miles wide, moving ten meters a year, moving toward South America, moving toward the distant sea, cold, hard and alive.

As I stood at the Pole, it seemed that someone was walking in the distance. The single figure was alone. It strode across the ice three hundred yards away. It did not pause or wave, although I was the only other figure on the white expanse. It appeared to be coming out of the featureless distance and walking with simple resolve back into the featureless distance. It was up-light, a silhouette made thin by the glare of the sun. It was Shackleton, finally making the last ninety-seven miles to the south. It was Amundsen, looking for the glow of light on the snow. It was Scott, free of the sledge at last. It was Titus Oates. "I am just going outside. I may be some time." I will be forever. I will walk through the meaningless years in the light of the Pole and cast a long shadow.

The figure was a South Pole scientist. He passed, following a distant line of flags, and went into an outlying building where machines monitored the cleanliness of the air. I knew where he had been, and perhaps that is why the silhouette had made no sign to me. He had been down an illicit hole.

The place he had come from was called Old Pole. It was the labyrinth of structures that Paul Siple and his men had built and lived in during the winter of 1957 and others had occupied until 1974. Old Pole was now a hatch over a well in the snow fifty feet deep. Old Pole was finished. Old Pole was drawing away from the Pole itself with the ice, being inexorably removed from its setting of glory.

Old Pole was out of bounds. It was invisible from the surface, buried and nearly crushed. It was buckling and collapsing under the smothering of that snow that had seemed so solid a foundation. At another base that was dying under the snow, people had reported rivets popping out of bent steel like bullets, firing down the frosty halls. Shot by the wall, crushed by the ice: somebody could be killed. You are a USARP; you are forbidden to go down Old Pole. Do not go down Old Pole. Do not go.

(4)

You were not permitted to go down Old Pole. But people went down anyway. The life everyone led in Antarctica was so strange that even the most recent past was legendary. People went down through the hatch to glean valuable hardware from the debris, or to bring up food that had been frozen there since 1974; but mainly they climbed down the blue ice tunnel to wander through the cold hallways of the ghost town that was the first city at the bottom of the world; to be a part of Antarctica's history.

An arrangement was made. In the interests of history I was escorted to Old Pole. It was possible that someone wanted me to expose government waste; Old Pole was littered with thousands of dollars of equipment that might have been salvaged. But I was already bewitched by the continent, too enthralled to worry about money. Antarctica was hope and hardship and beauty; it was worth the price. So in the collapsing clutter of Old Pole there was nothing more important than the glimpse of lives that had once also been captured by this terrible, enchanting landscape.

There were four of us. We had bunny boots and wool masks and coats and double layers of underwear and headlamps lit by batteries warmed by our bodies. We carried hissing gasoline lamps that steamed and cast a cloudy light. The faces of the other three were hidden by the masks, where the frost grew at their mouths like stone crystals. They were, for the sake of protecting the guilty, Robert F. and Ernest and Roald, and I was Titus. We were ghosts, floating among the ruins.

We moved rapidly through the buried halls. We walked so fast it seemed we were pursued. We were. We were chased by the cold. We moved urgently, like criminals. The cold was the officer of the law.

It was sixty below zero. When Paul Siple arrived at the South Pole he dug a hole to measure the temperature within the ice. That would be roughly the annual mean temperature at the Pole. He dug for four days and excavated a pit eighteen feet deep. The thermometer registered sixty-two below zero. Now that had become the temperature in his old home, where he and seventeen other men had spent the first winter, 1957. It was winter there forever, down the blue walls of the hole by ladder and rope to the snow-dusted plywood at the bottom and the shadowed memories of ghost towns and ice.

"The roof had sagged under the crushing weight of ice," Richard Byrd wrote of January 1934, when he returned to Little America on the Ross Ice Shelf, which had been abandoned for four years. "Several of the main beams had cracked. They lay splintered across the top bunks. A film of ice lay over the walls, and from the ceiling hung thick clusters of ice crystals, which were brighter than jewels when the light caught them." In Byrd's old station the telephone rang when cranked, and the lights glowed faintly, and there was a frozen piece of roast beef with a fork stuck in it resting on a table. Men left in haste and the things that seemed part of life stood and cooled. In Old Pole the plywood floors were strewn with T-bone steaks, white beans, and a fine gravel of frozen broken eggs. The place was strewn with artifacts of the twentieth century:

Bean with bacon soup. Plastic bags of hot dogs. A sign on a door: "Check electrolyte level at least once/week." A room entirely lined with copper mesh. An exercise bicycle. "All aboard!" shouted Roald. "Hell with that," said Ernest. "Look at this fan," said Robert F. "Is that ancient or what?"

A table was strewn with playing cards. "Operation Deep Freeze," it said on the back of each card. "Task Force 43." There was a Christmas card: "Love, Mother and Dad." In his old camp Byrd noticed an accordion, boxing gloves, and a phonograph that played "The Bells of St. Mary's." In Old Pole the debris was the same. We rushed from room to room. The cold pressed closer behind.

Walls of white leaned in upon us. Leaves of frost grew from the walls. We brushed against them and flakes glittered in the lamp, falling in the fog we made with our breath. Wires hung across us, brushed against us like webs, glistening with frost. Doors had the names of offices painted on them. We walked on tilted wooden catwalks. We hastened, hastened, the cold marching at our heels. The steel arches were crumpled like tinfoil under the weight of the snow. Ice crystals grew on the roof and formed on the electrical wiring. Ice crystals grew in blooms. The headlamp caught a little fake garden behind a picket fence, a garden made of plastic flowers. Next to it was someone's vegetable garden, growing big green plastic peppers. Everywhere were photographs of women. Most wore nothing in the cold. Their skin colors tended to blues; their smiles were antique.

A bowl of cereal stood on a table in the galley, flakes in a puddle of ice. The town was a labyrinth; here and there, rarely, a shaft reached up to the outside world, and a little spot of blue light filtered through the snow. Floors humped up into the rooms. Ceilings were crooked, bending to meet the floor. How deep would this little city go before it was crushed to a flat layer of wood and meat and photographs of women, a smudge of the twentieth century moving slowly north toward South America? Some of the support beams were split, showing fresh jagged wood. Wires festooned the place, caught us around the throat, brushed against our heads and dropped ice down our necks. Robert F., Ernest, Roald, and I rushed in the white halls. I tripped on steaks and frozen instruction manuals. The library was almost empty. There was one remaining rack of Ellery Queen. Roald followed the shelves around, speculating about what literature the departing Americans thought important: "The religious stuff is still all here." Ernest was the boss; he swept up a handful of hard candies, two cans of Pream, and a box of beef jerky. "What a score!" he said. The words were muffled in his mask.

My head hurt. I got out of breath easily. A thermometer reading down to 30 was just a little glob of red nestled in its bulb. It was here to record warmth, to record the pressure of that life that had gone. We moved in a fog of our own making; the lanterns smoked and steamed and our breath made huge clouds. The headlamps cut through it in beams. Everywhere small electric motors were stored in closets, waiting to whir. Stuff was scattered right and left. Someone had ransacked it, but there was a sense of wild abandonment, as if suddenly it was too much—the dark, the loneliness, the weight, the slide of the brute ice—they all threw up their hands and chucked the books and the meat out in the halls and fled, mouths open to the killer wind, out into the snow to run north in all directions and disappear.

There was a smell down here, a bad smell, like something rotting, but without ferment. It was a hard flaking away of odor. It was the smell of dried fear and frozen excrement. At one place where steaks were splayed out of a box, someone long ago crapped a hard mound.

In the bar a can of Piels Real Draft Premium Beer had exploded and made a permanent head of frozen foam on the side of the can. It looked like insulating foam but smelled of beer. My feet were starting to get cold; I must keep moving, pacing around. Keep moving, keep moving. The flexible cable from my headlamp to the batteries at my chest was hard as copper from cold. It whacked me in the nose. It knocked frost from the mask onto my cheeks behind the stiff wool. Frost grew all over my face. My eyelashes tried to freeze together. I took my hands out of the big mittens to take a photograph and they got covered with frost too. Surely the wood was splitting around us and the steel buckled just from the cold.

In some of the rooms there was snow on the floor. In some places it was as fine as talcum powder, in some places it was like beach sand—but everywhere it was dry, dry as dust. Then we opened a door into a room where the ceiling had broken and there it was: snow cascading down and forming a little glacier, dense and deadly. It filled the room. It was as if I had opened a door on a live malevolence, the awful thing hidden behind all these doors decorated with humorous remarks and naked women: the antarctic nightmare. Scott had stood here and felt it pressing down on the arch of his courage, distorting it, crippling it, breaking it in: this terrible place.

A chill that was not just the raw cold ran through me. There was no mercy in this moving ice. I looked at the ice-filled room. I could not pull away. I saw an ending:

The snow is pressure. The nightmare grows. Roald and Ernest

and Robert F. are ghosts. I am Titus Oates, inside Old Pole. I may be some time. I am running through snow. The snow is light as powder, deep as the sea; I sink. At the bottom of this sea will be white living trilobites, huge, armored seals. I am running, running, running through these halls, accompanied by cardboard penguins and balloons full of ink, and I open the last door at the end and call out to see it there—the bland, hard face of death.

No, it cannot be. Roald! Ernest! Does it look this way? Did it come upon you this way? They are gone. They were never here at all. I have been stumbling in the wind. I open door after door and there it is: cold, white, implacable, heaping down from above. The shaft up has clamped shut. The ceiling has fallen in. I have waited too long. Old Pole is going down in the sea of ice.

The hissing dies. The lanterns go out. The headlamp goes dim. The batteries at my heart go quiet. Still I open doors to stare at rooms filled with snow. The structure cracks as the ice moves. Rivets fire down the halls, ping and whine. I am flowing toward South America. I have time now, time to get there. I find matches and cook steaks over heaps of smoldering instruction books, filling the air with the smell of meat and killing gas. Byrd sat in his hut alone at Advance Base on the great Barrier in 1934, breathing carbon monoxide from his stove; they came and found him in August when he was almost dead. No one will find me. I am a thousand feet down. The ice creaks in its journey. I can hear the groan of the earth below. I slice green peppers. I sit on the bar and eat the steak and gnaw on the frozen beer, and it gets completely dark, until at last my eyes, wide open, see dimly by the soft, deep, permanent blue.

(5)

The man I called Ernest came to get me. My feet were cold. We climbed back up out of Old Pole and hoisted a big hunk of copper—some kind of valve—out with us. On the way back to the dome our Spryte broke down, but Ernest opened it up, played with the engine, and got it going again. Inside the dome the light was metal blue, and the lights of the little buildings were warm. Outside, snow drifted gently against the walls.

Chapter Twelve

On the Radio

(1)

I love you. Take the money out of savings. I love you. Pay the doctor first. I miss you. I love you. Please disregard the letter.

Every day the messages went out from McMurdo, from the little hut up the hill from town, the ham shack. By Marsgram or by ham patch the connections were made, day after day; always a man to a woman, or a woman to a man, making the fundamental link across the miles. Navy personnel, civilians hired by the National Science Foundation's contractor, helicopter mechanics, the men and women building the new power plant, truck drivers, scientists—all called home. My arm will be all right. Call Ma. Can't wait for February. Can't wait for October. I love you. Wait for me, honeybuns. Please send me some letters.

"ABQ, ICE. How are you doing, Frank?" Radioman First Class Craig Reynolds sat at the radio, leaning into the mike. Across the world, on the frequency of 13975.5 kilohertz, from the state of Vermont, U.S.A., where it was winter, came a reply:

"Just fine, just fine. Still got my coat on, just got home."

The room was small, with a linoleum floor inlaid with the inscription "1982," and stained plywood walls that bore a map of the world and a green, green poster of New Zealand's South Island. On one side was a bank of radios like the instrument console of an aircraft. From it Reynolds played the frequencies and drew from them the voices of home: VKT in California, LVP in Maryland, ABQ in Vermont. They were all amateurs, like Reynolds, who was doing this on his time off. When the connections were made the operators at the other end either sat back to receive the teletype of the Marsgrams or made collect calls to numbers Reynolds gave them. If the number was answered, someone in McMurdo got on the phone, was connected to the ham shack, and talked to home.

It was a cumbersome arrangement; a globe balanced on a half duplex wire.

"How are you? *Over.*"

Reynolds flipped a switch. Frank in Vermont—ABQ—flipped a switch.

"Fine, *over.*"

Frank flipped the switch back. Reynolds flipped the switch back. The voices from the phone and from the radio went on. They had been warned that this was public air on which they spoke, but the spark they made on this rare contact was bright and intimate. The two men were like producers in a studio, sitting stoically behind the scenes, selecting images from the monitors, while the story of love and longing surged around them.

I sat and listened. I had come to interview Reynolds, but I had a hidden agenda. I wanted to talk to my wife. In this cold, bright, exciting world the strongest emotion was affection for others of our kind. Bonds were made quickly here—a warmth toward one another extended to ward off the enveloping cold—but they were seldom expressed. The movie of Ernest Shackleton's expedition had shown the men hugging their dogs, and everyone understood the need. There was nothing else to hug. When Joe the Drug Dog was brought to MacTown to do some of his disagreeable research, he romped around town like a big puppy and everyone with a clear conscience loved him, but because of the sensitive nature of his job no one was allowed to lay a finger of friendship on that big pattable head. It made everyone moody. "To be able to expend emotion down here is extremely valuable," said Jeanne Williams, who was here for her second winter, with her husband. So people called home.

The sense of adventure carries you about two weeks, a Navy psychologist had said. I'd been around McMurdo longer than that. Now, with my colleagues of the press gone, I was assailed with thoughts of my family. I could make only a small public gesture over the radio, and it was certain that someone among the helo crews and pilots was even now sitting at his personal short-wave listening in with delight, but suddenly it seemed to be something I could not do without.

I was last in line for the ham patch. Only one of the Marsgrams on the wall was not between man and woman. It was a telegram that came in to McMurdo in response to a Marsgram out. The McMurdo resident had sent a query to the head coach of the professional football team he favored. The team had been losing. The original Marsgram was not there, but from the response it must have read something like WHAT THE HELL? The answer was personal and apologetic:

HARD TO PIN OUR PROBLEM TO ANY ONE AREA. WE HAVE LOST FIVE BALL GAMES BY SEVEN POINTS OR LESS. IF WE COULD HAVE WON ONE OR TWO OF THOSE NOBODY WOULD BE SAYING, "WHAT'S WRONG?" WE STILL HAVE A CHANCE, AND NOBODY AROUND HERE IS QUITTING.

It was signed by the coach. You may be an important man in the city, with secretaries for your phones and fifteen sportswriters clamoring at your door, but when you get a telegram from the Antarctic, you answer it yourself.

In the ham shack a rattling noise like the sound of a helo grew on the air.

"SWP, ICE," said Reynolds. "Looks like we got the wood-pecker again." The sound whacked into the room, destroying communication. It was as if a phantom helicopter crossed the ionosphere in another dimension, borne on billows of radio waves, chopping them into turbulence with its blades. "We think it's some kind of radar," Reynolds said. "But we don't really know what it is." The noise slowly subsided.

"SWP, ICE. Let's try again."

It was my time. SWP dialed my number at home. I waited, unreasonably tense. Ham patches were known to yield unusual results. Once, during the first winter at the South Pole, the U.S. contact got the number wrong but the man who answered it accepted the charges anyway. He may not have been entirely awake; where he was it was 1:30 in the morning.

"Hello!" said the man at the South Pole, whose name was Willi. "May I speak to my wife?"

"Huh? Who?"

"To my wife!"

The two men managing the conversation with their switches must have been drawn into the drama in spite of their detachment.

"Who is this calling?" said the voice in the States.

"This is Willi calling from the South Pole."

Sure. At 1:30 in the morning. Slam!

In the McMurdo ham shack I waited. I was sure my number had been dialed correctly. In a moment now I would break the long silence.

Then:

"ICE, SWP. Line's busy."

(2)

"Mushrooms! I said *mushrooms!*" The voice on the radio was urgent. It was Monday morning on Mac Sideband.

Life on the ice was attached to the radio as if to an iron lung. Cut the ties and it would cease. Every morning at about eight, Shaunessy Everett, who worked in the Chalet for Antarctic Services, walked over to the Navy's headquarters building, past the two big anchors that leaned together at the door, and went upstairs past the weather office to the room down a hall. It was the little room that housed the radio transceivers collectively known as Mac Sideband. Orange lacy curtains shaded the room from the constant sun. On shelves were stacked rolls of military type 1, class 2, grade B, three-copy canary teletype paper.

On the morning of the mushrooms two conversations were going: one between McMurdo and Christchurch about the purchase of a 300-baud computer modem, the other between Everett and the science crews who were living in tents and the insulated canvas huts known as Jamesways all over western Antarctica. Communications were good but not perfect. One of the crews, two women camped out to do geological mapping at a desolate place called Helms Bluff, had been ordering up items for the next regular helicopter supply drop, and the urgent mushroom message was in answer to Everett's question "Did you really say you wanted four cans of hot mustard?"

Coms were not profound. They were calls into the wilderness: Are you there? Are you alive? What do you need? Like a hen counting her scattered brood, Everett called the science groups one by one and got her food orders, her announcements of camp moves, her logistical requests, her reassurance. For that hour and a half each morning Mac Sideband became the round table where the scientists gathered to get their shields repaired and their bravery replenished by contact with the vast enterprise that sustained them.

"Hi, there, Shaun, we're all fine here. How are you?" It was Don Elston, who had been with us on the helo, calling in from a different gravel-field camp in the Dry Valleys, friendly as ever. His crew had drilled two more holes and their crates were getting full of cores.

"I'm doing real well, Don," Everett said. "Hugh and Gary got back into town last night. They don't like the bunkroom but they'll get over it. I have no new traffic for you."

The next call was from the Roaring Valley, a name that can only refer to wind on a continent that is otherwise silent. There a group called Sierra 075, from Northern Illinois University in DeKalb, was studying ancient bits of the earth's crust embedded in younger rocks. Patterns of rocks and fossils studied in recent years—including a fossil marsupial, found in 1982—strongly supported the idea that Antarctica was once the central mass of a continent scientists have called Gondwanaland, which since broke up into Africa, South America, Australia, India, and other fragments. At least one person who subscribed to this theory posted a sign at the South Pole that bore the slogan Reunite Gondwanaland! but Sierra 075 wasn't being political. Some of the rocks it studied resembled those found in Australia, so the goal was a deeper understanding of how the continents were linked and parted.

"Sierra One Seven Three, Sierra One Seven Three, this is Mac Sideband, how copy, *over*."

"Sideband, Sierra One Seven Three."

After the faint scratchings of teams calling from the nearby Dry Valleys, the voice of Robert Bindschadler of the National Aeronautics and Space Administration—one of a group studying the great white sliding skin of the elephant seven hundred miles to the southwest—nearly blew Everett's ears off.

"I don't believe it," she said aside, but it was easy to imagine a reason. There were no mountains around Bindschadler to break up the transmission: he was genuinely on the ice. He was camped near an area called the Siple Coast, which, with a thousand miles of ice plateau on one side and the Ross Ice Shelf (about the size of France) on the other, looked about as coastal as a North Dakota winter prairie. His group was among four studying what had become one of Antarctica's glamour issues, the west antarctic ice sheet.

It was good to hear his voice. Bindschadler had been marooned in MacTown with Jay Zwally (who had speculated about the numbers of Kiwis in the truck and the brine channels in the big ice cube) and several others while trying to get to a place called the Crary Ice Rise, on the Ross Ice Shelf, just off the Siple Coast. There were six of them; I had talked to them one night before one of my own journeys, and when I returned several days later I found them still waiting for weather to improve so they could be flown to their new base. They had picked up a slogan in the interim: Free the Crary Ice Rise Six.

They weren't exactly radicals, but what they were studying had the potential to reshape the world. If the ice sheet were suddenly removed, much of what it covered would be below sea level, so the sheet in effect was resting on the sea floor. This was thought to make it less stable than the larger east antarctic ice sheet, whose foundation was higher. Geological history indicated that the western ice had fluctuated widely; if it were to fluctuate soon by sliding off into the sea, it was so enormous that worldwide sea levels could rise twenty feet, forcing much of civilization to flee for higher ground. In our conversations in the lounge of the California Hotel, Bindschadler and his group had insisted that this was not a Big Splash problem; even the most dramatic scenarios called for Act I to run at least two centuries, but since the ice sheet's fate might be linked to very small temperature changes caused by the carbon dioxide greenhouse effect, and since many other global effects attended even a few inches' change in sea level, the west antarctic ice sheet had become, relatively speaking, hot news.

The Crary Ice Rise was near one of several streams of ice that flowed through the sheet a bit like rivers, a bit like ocean currents, and a bit, one scientist said, like gravy on mashed potatoes. Each was thirty to fifty kilometers wide and moved up to one thousand meters a year—fast, for ice. Ice streams were the drains for the ice sheet, so they were the key to whether the whole thing was pouring away.

The work consisted of planting flagged bamboo stakes in perfect circles on the ice streams to measure the stresses going on in the ice by how the circles bent. The human stresses were not insignificant: ice streams almost by definition were sown like minefields with crevasses that could eat you alive.

None of the scientists at work on this question had ventured a resounding prediction on the ice sheet's future. "It's a very real possibility that it might collapse," Jay Zwally had said. "But we don't even know what it's doing right now." Another scientist, Sion Shabtaie, of the Geophysical and Polar Research Center of the University of Wisconsin, worked on a study that indicated the sheet might not be doomed after all. "We concluded not that the sheet was disintegrating, but that it was growing," he said. He grinned. "We are reevaluating our thinking."

Bindschadler had nothing new to report to Everett. The ice sheet wasn't going to cut loose today, anyway. He did, however, have a rather forlorn request, considering the coincidental history of flight delays he had already encountered. The work was finished there and he wanted a Hercules to come and move him to the next site. He signed off while I wondered what time it was out there; since the sun rolled around the sky at about the same height day and night and the only formal occasion of the field day was the contact with McMurdo, it was the practice of at least one project leader to ask his team what time they liked to get up in the morning and then decide which time zone applied based on that preference. If they liked to sleep in, well, hell, then Everett's 8:00 A.M. would be a lazy noon at the ice rise and they'd work until midnight.

The proximity and meaninglessness of the time zones here had many effects and applications. In 1957 Catholic meat-eaters at the South Pole figured they could avoid Fridays altogether by walking around the world at the appropriate time of week and crossing the international dateline before dinner.

On the wall of Mac Sideband was a plastic-covered board. On it were written in grease pencil the numbers and locations of the scientists in the field. The sheet represented a remarkable scattering. Everett was in Camelot and her knights were in London, at Hadrian's Wall, in Rome, in the Alps, somewhere outside of Algiers, or on the southwest coast of Norway—each with a long wire running from lance tip to tree, solar panels propped up on the horse, trying to get through to home.

On the board was Sierra 099—Don Elston, at the lower Taylor Valley. Bindschadler was there: Sierra 173, at Siple Coast. Fifty-six Alpha was at Cirque 6 in the Dry Valleys. That was one of two teams led by George Denton, a legendary figure in antarctic research, who had a glacier named after him in the Dry Valleys and who worked so hard, it was said, that he was the only man on the ice who wore out two pairs of bunny boots in a single season. Denton was still alive, of course, because of Twitty Conway's prescience. Denton, too, was involved in glacial research, and his teams were gathering the evidence to refine a three-dimensional computer model of the greatest extent of the ice during the peak of the last ice age.

Sierra 172 was at Reedy Glacier in the Harold Byrd Mountains, way up near the southeastern tip of the Ross Ice Shelf, looking at sediments in rock blown clear of snow and ice by the katabatic winds that roared down from the high plateau. Sierra 041 was out in the opposite direction, at another curious Dry Valleys lake, called Lake Joyce, where the interaction of trace metals, chemicals, and nutrients could be studied in a closed system where things like sewage and smog still had no effect. Sierra 164, Ian Whillans' group, was out at Upstream C, another flow on the Siple Coast, planting stakes and looking out for crevasses. Sierra 063 was a thousand miles away, at the Thiel Mountains, conducting a joint project with the British to learn more about the way the two main pieces of the continent, East and West Antarctica, had moved and joined in the long span of geologic time. Sierra 150C and 151 were sharing a camp at Upstream B, on the edge of another of the Siple Coast ice streams, S-150C drilling an ice core and S-151 working as part of the overall study of the west antarctic ice sheet. Sierra 081B, directed by another indefatigable antarctic hand, Phil Kyle of the New Mexico Institute of Mining and Technology, was perched on the rim of the summit of Mt. Erebus, gazing down into the fuming crater.

Other members of Phil Kyle's group were scattered on volcanic rocks at the far reaches of helo travel. Dave Johnson and Bill McIntosh, who worked with Wes LeMasurier on the *Polar Sea,* were out working for Kyle with another student, Ingrid Klich, near Minna Bluff. There if they didn't get to the rocks the rocks came to them.

"You'd climb up a cliff to get samples," Johnson said later. "Rocks would come sailing off the tops of the cliffs. You'd hear a low humming noise. You knew it was a rock, so you'd duck, and then the rock would come over like a flying lawnmower blade, end over end, and would explode down below.

"One time we were collecting in a little valley. We sat down for a while, then put the crampons on and climbed up this ice face. We came down, skirted across the ice, and just as we got to the side, a huge boulder came off and exploded right where we had been sitting. It was not more than ten minutes since we had been there: 'Ingrid, did you see *that*? It was right where my bun marks are.'

"It was geology in action. It was dangerous, but that's part of the business. We did get some good samples, and that was the thing."

On the radio Everett ran down the list, sometimes talking through a relay named Barbara at the South Pole, eight hundred miles away. And one by one the teams checked in. It was a routine day. Bindschadler wanted to move, or at least be an alternate mission to be pulled out if someone else's weather went sour; Elston had to come to town for a DV tour; a photo flight had to be coordinated for the scientists studying the flow of the ice sheet; and Sierra 164, Ian Whillans' group, had a list of seventy-three food items that it wanted sent up on the next flight. The only typical thing Everett had missed was the wake-up song she usually got from the two-woman crew at Helms Bluff. Christmas was approaching; the day before they had greeted her with "*Oh, little town of McMurdo, how dingy, dark are thee.*"

Everett described the occasion with delight to her boss, who was standing at the radio today. He was a tall, solemn representative of the National Science Foundation. Perhaps irritated at the increasing chorus of female voices that were enlightening the southern air, he grumbled bureaucratically. "Not very professional," he said. "*Not* very professional."

"Aw," Everett said, defending her troops. "It cheers them up in the morning."

(3)

The Doggo was shouting into the telephone. Everyone could hear him outside the padded booth. He was talking to the vet in Christchurch. Scott Base's fifteen sled dogs were his responsibility. He was agitated.

The postmaster leaned over the counter to talk to an American who had walked from McMurdo to mail some letters with Kiwi stamps.

"Dog got in a fight," he said sadly. "He's got a lump on his old man."

The postmaster at Scott Base was a kind man. He had a gently sorrowful face that held no pain, as if he merely took others' burdens on the shoulders of his own equanimity. He looked like the kindly workman at a fictional hard-knocks boarding school, the one who would let the boys in when they missed curfew. And he had one particular power that made him forever endearing: he held the keys to home. At Scott Base, two miles by dirt road over the hill from McMurdo, there was a telephone to the world.

This was no technological marvel. The United States could have had a radiotelephone link to the phone lines in New Zealand too if it chose. But there were those in the hierarchy of the system who believed, based on a long history of dealing with the emotions of isolation, that too much contact with the family was bad. Once I saw Dick Cameron at Scott Base and said casually, "That telephone is the best thing on the ice."

Cameron came as close as he could to a scowl.

"No it isn't," he said. "It could be the worst thing. When you're away a lot of problems are taken care of without you having to deal with them. When you are in touch you get involved in those problems and they distract you from your work, but there's nothing you can do about them anyway." Cameron was not immune to using the facilities when available—he had once talked from Antarctica via ham patch to his wife, who was in Germany—he just thought it best to have little access to the sounds that fed the loneliness.

So at McMurdo all you could do was get on the ham patch with the leering hordes listening in and speak in generalities to a voice that sounded more like a duck than your loved one. At Scott Base, for less than twenty dollars, you could get in the little padded telephone box and talk on a private line. And today I was scheduled to get in there right after the Doggo was done.

On the walls of the post office were posted New Zealand stamps and newspaper clippings, both reminders of the outside world pressing around Antarctica with its claims of ownership and rule. Stamps were a way of asserting jurisdiction, and one of the clips was a report on a United Nations debate on the Antarctic Treaty, in which the honorable representative of Malaysia had called it "restrictive and exclusive." On the wall the world busied itself with Antarctica: New Zealand claimed; Malaysia complained; Japan explored the continental shelf with an oil company research vessel; and a combined British and American expedition set off for the continent's highest peak, the Vinson Massif.

In the post office a young woman named Bronwen—who looked so gentle that I could hardly believe she was the same person who had gone charging up an ice cliff on a rope a few days before during a survival school I attended—hand-canceled the stamps. *Thump, thump, thump, thump.* The Doggo's voice, calmer now, came faintly through the door. On the wall was a poster: Fire . . . Is the Great Antarctic Monster.

Outside the window, in a gently falling snow, Scott Base's fifteen huskies, legacy of the old days, kept for sentiment as much as use, yowled, paced, or slept at the ends of their tethers beside the edge of the sea ice. Just off the beach, pressure ridges rose in frozen combers; the sea ice, blown by a wind far offshore, buckled as it moved past Pram Point. Lieutenant Doug Hocking, the U.S. Navy's chaplainesque public affairs officer, was already planning a surfing expedition.

The leaders of the Kiwis was Norman Hardie, a small, gently humorous man who was so wiry that he looked wizened. He had been in wind and sun most of his life. New Zealand explorers think of Antarctica and the Himalayas in the same context, and Hardie was a climber of almost legendary achievement: eight Himalayan expeditions including the first ascent of Kachenjunga. Here, he was a magistrate and a coroner—another formal little arrangement designed to make New Zealand's claim to this wedge of Antarctica clear, although, in a typically cheerful disregard of all those claims, New Zealand willingly coexisted with the United States's city on the ice right in the middle of the Kiwi sector. It was possible that the balance of payments was favorably affected by the money the Yankees spent on wool shirts, calendars, and stamps at Scott Base.

Earlier, on the press tour, Hardie had shown us through the station, which was entirely linked by enclosed corridors that worked outward from the original building, which was built at the same time Old Pole was put up, during the International Geophysical Year, 1957–58, when the modern exploration of Antarctica began. That room, now used for a temporary sleeping quarters, was filled with signs: Welcome to the Ross Island Hilton; Phone Bookings Accepted; Showers by Request; Room Service, Phone 57. The little room was going to be removed from the station and flown home to Christchurch, where it would become part of a museum. On a wall was another sign: Closed for Eternity—Ed Hillary.

Hardie had shut big doors carefully behind us as we walked down the hall. "Air doors?" someone had asked. "Fire doors," Hardie said. "We have to be fussy with the fire doors."

Finally the postmaster nodded kindly in my direction. I stepped into the booth. There was a sudden muffled silence as I closed the door. Then the phone rang. I picked it up and there, from ten thousand miles away, was my father on the line.

He was nearly seventy-five. We had been distant when I was younger, he and I, because he had spent much of my childhood traveling in his work. He had crisscrossed the world while my mother and I stayed at home. He had seen India and Africa and Scandinavia and South America. When we were together more, while I was a teenager, we had been antagonists as often as friends. Now he was retired and traveled little, and we had developed an affection that I valued more than I had ever expected.

I had nothing special to tell him except to ask him to give a message to my wife, who was not at home. So I looked out the little window at the ice and told him what I saw of this strange place. I tried to say something about the snow falling, the grainy shape of the base of Black Island where it emerged from the lowering storm, the waves of ice piling up against the shore, the spires of ice the waves lifted that were blue in the shadows as if glowing with the sea's own incandescent cold. As I told my father about the weather of Antarctica today, it seemed that without an actual intention I was trying to tell him that I knew what took him away from us then and that I understood it, and to tell him that I was out there now, seeing the far reaches of the world as he once was, and to give him some of that old sense of being a part of the distance that he must miss.

When I hung up I knew that Dick Cameron was right: it was hard to make the contact and then so quickly give it up.

(4)

"I was trying a month and a half before I got through to my girl-friend," Craig Reynolds said, as the ham operator in Florida tried my number one last time. It had been busy twice. "Phone was always busy or she wasn't home or something. I must have put through a hundred and fifty calls."

This was very encouraging. I uttered sympathies, but my sincerity was limited by my narrow focus on present needs. Forcing someone to hang up the phone from ten thousand miles away by ESP is difficult.

There was a long pause. He was dialing again. In the ham shack it was quiet. There was a distant thump of helo blades and a distant rattle of the woodpecker on the air. Then the voice came back.

"We have a connection. Go ahead."

So, at last, we threw our voices out into space, with all our love and a few watts, skipping our longing to be together across the light. There were others talking in the background, on other frequencies, and across the world we human beings spread our net of affection for one another, trying to hold that warmth in, to give us time to turn this newfound ability to link one to another no matter where he or she calls home into something more substantial than just waves, something strong enough to bind us against the woodpecker, against the accumulating weapons of the mighty but lesser force of hate.

"Debbie! Debbie, how are you? *Over.*"

"Mike! You sound very strange."

I love you. I miss you. I hope you will get the letter.

Chapter Thirteen

The Big Game

(1)

A pilot was eating bite-size Shredded Wheat from a cereal box in the van that ran back and forth from MacTown to Willie Field. He offered one to a loadmaster who was sitting next to him.

"Sorry," said the loadmaster. "I'm trying to quit." Silence came down on the shuttle again.

It was Thanksgiving morning. Maybe that's why we all seemed sad. The wind blew. It crackled in the little red and green flags along the road. It was far warmer here than at the South Pole, but today even this mild cold seemed too bitter to live in. High of 15°F; wind gusts to twenty-five. Nobody seemed to feel much like talking. Thanksgiving was the last big celebration on the ice until the Christmas season came, bringing its load of loneliness; last night, Rob Robbins said, it was "shit and giggles all over town."

From Willie Field—the permanent airport out on the McMurdo ice shelf, five miles from town—McMurdo was a black smudge on the distant hills. The airport was a small city, by itself one of the larger villages on the continent, with maintenance men and aircraft mechanics and cooks making a population of about a hundred. After several years in the same location it was sinking into the ice and advancing toward the edge of the seasonal sea; a crew was busy moving the whole town back up the ice conveyor to what was now called Willie Three—the third since Richard T. Williams and his D-8 went through the sea ice in 1956. Like the South Pole, Williams was still in the same place in his tractor somewhere on the bottom; like the South Pole marker and the ice, Willie Field moved.

The McMurdo complex, which included Willie Field, was so much a town that it had community events. Or perhaps the events were part of its desperate effort to seem to be a town. For Thanksgiving there was going to be a parade, followed by a football game. I had come for the game. It was the annual Penguin Bowl between the Navy and the civilians, who were called the USARPs.

I was early. People were putting finishing touches on tractors that would become floats. I walked aimlessly in the white snow streets of Willie Field, and then it happened.

The wind had become calmer. I was less cold. The parka hood curtailed vision. I walked down a small slope. Suddenly there was a loud crackling sound. I looked around. Nothing was moving. The crackling sound was right here. I looked up.

It was a curious sight. A power pole was crashing down on me with absolutely no provocation. I was offended. It looked like a huge club with arms. It was a great writhing, jerking thing, with strands of unraveling wire, flailing at the air. The lash of God had found me at last.

I scrambled to get away. The pole fell at me. The living wires came down across my path.

It was as if a rogue wind had whipped across the ice, without disturbing even the snow, to break the pole right off and fling it at me. For a moment the air above seemed full of jerking black whips. Scrambling backward on the snow in my bunny boots, I briefly contemplated what would happen if the wires came loose and started to flail across the space in which I was, loosing all that tension in a sudden attempt to wrap me in buzzing light.

Then I had escaped it. The wires did not part. They hit the ground in front of me, jerked and writhed, and were still. The pole had broken off about two feet up from the base and the wires' tension had yanked it out onto the snow. It left a stump of huge golden splinters.

I looked around, perhaps a bit wildly. The problem was easy to spot. A forklift carrying a metal bin labeled For Water Melt Only held high in its arms like a butler bringing tea had walked right into the wires at a corner behind me and yanked the thing over.

People were running. I seemed to be a spectator at a curious play. They were running very slowly on the snow. Everything was strange: clear, calm, silent. The people running seemed to make no sound. I was transfixed. I had felt a breath colder than any antarctic wind; I was coming back slowly into the embrace of life.

Out of a building almost buried in snow emerged a beautiful woman wearing fatigues and a green parka: blond hair, thin gold earrings, a face like a Gypsy. A wind-weathered, lovely warm face. She ran at the wire. I yelled, "Don't touch it!" She leaped the wire. It was me she had come to touch. She put her hand on my arm and looked at my face.

The strangeness ended. She asked if I was okay. I was fine. The forklift driver stood beside his big yellow machine, and someone cursed him. The curses went on and on. The driver was a civilian. Officers in uniform approached with walkie-talkies. They spoke solemnly to distant places. There was a siren, but it was only the airfield crash truck warming up for the parade. The beautiful woman in fatigues said simply, "It's over." It was. She drifted away, as much the gift of God as the strike of the hot wire, draining away the fear with her flattering concern. I wandered from the scene. No injuries, no inquest. In a few minutes the big game between the civilian USARPs and the Navy would begin.

Soon the site was deserted, except for the pole on the ground and the forklift, and the poor driver, who still stood ten yards from his disaster, staring. He was a civilian, but he stood at attention, thinking, Court-martial, court-martial, firing squad. He had a fresh face and a little mustache, and his cheeks blazed with the cold.

I wouldn't have felt nearly so sorry for him if I'd been dead. I was lucky; a fine, embarrassing end this would have made. In Antarctica there were more noble ways to die. Falling down a crevasse, crashing on a remote glacier, or slowly freezing in a distant tent were honorable ways of making a departure. But I could not expect to have had even a fish hut named after me if I'd been bludgeoned to death by a power pole.

(2)

The Navy team warmed up doing formation shoulder rolls in the snow. The USARPs gathered in a loose knot at their end of the field around a couple of bottles of Jack Daniel's. The Navy men all wore fatigue pants and white waffle-weave long-john tops. The USARPs wore their baggy black comedy-team trousers and a loose collection of plaid wool shirts and sweaters. They staggered around stretching halfheartedly, and occasionally stopped to look at the Navy men, who were now doing precision jumping jacks, with apparent awe. On the shoreward side of the field the green ranks of the Navy fans looked smug, while up and down the assembly of red-jacketed civilians on the opposite sideline ran mutters of concern.

On the Navy sideline Captain Brian Shoemaker stood foursquare in the snow, looking cheerful and confident as always.

"They don't play full contact football elsewhere in the Navy," he said. In Antarctica the Navy boys were tough.

Shoemaker was a small, slender man with large eyes. He carried himself like a soldier, and he had run in the Marine Corps Marathon, but he had a big grin. He also had a twist of white canvas in his pocket. This was the skin of a snow snake. The snake had been killed by a truck on the way to the McMurdo dump, and already the station biologists were determining its taxonomy. If you believed this he was prepared to tell you about the nurses at Marble Point, where the Navy, which never built anything until it had put a hospital there first, maintained a facility with one doctor and eighteen nurses. Since there was nothing else there, the nurses were wonderfully lonely.

One year Shoemaker and several pilots convinced a new helo pilot of the existence of the yearning nurses, then tantalized him by sending him off on flights to everywhere except Marble Point. When they finally granted him a mission, the pilot landed eagerly at the point and emerged from the helo bearing gifts of nylons, perfume, and candy he had brought from the Ship's Store. But at Marble Point there was only a tiny fuel hut and a group of fuel bladders that stood alone on bleak, windblown black rock. When he got back to McMurdo his colleagues greeted him with a sign that read, "Welcome Home to the Lothario of Antarctica."

Some people on the ice called Shoemaker the Shoe. A lot of people called him Sir. One or two even called him "that cocky little bastard." He was sure of himself, at least. And he seemed sure of his men. He stood on the sidelines awaiting the massacre.

The Navy men finished their warm-ups and came cheering out of a huddle. The USARPs straggled into position. Referees made gestures. The USARPs were in trouble right from the beginning. They had to kick off. Navy received, ran it back in a cloud of snow, and began what was expected to be the first of a series of drives at will through the demoralized civilians with two runs and a completed pass for a first down.

The referees had to line the ball up with yard markers—flagged bamboo stakes—on the sidelines; chalk lines on the field would not have helped. First down! On the Navy sideline one of the troops holding the down markers cheered and waved his pole. It had begun.

But then something unexpected happened. The Navy juggernaut was stopped. Fourth down; no gain. The USARPs took over. It was first down going the other way. The men in the funny black pants weren't looking drunk and foolish anymore. They were tackling hard and moving quickly; they were slapping hands and grinning.

The demolition was not going to be so easy. The USARPs' casual ragged look had been the game's first fake. The civilians were as prepared as the Navy. They were tough, too.

It had been this way for twenty-five years, to the eternal irritation of both commanders and scientists on the ice. The alliance between the armed forces and the civilians in the U.S. program was like that between rough wool and skin—necessary, but not always comfortable. Marble Point was an example, in Shoemaker's mind. Its reach of bleak gravel was bereft of nurses, but it was the best place for a permanent hard-surfaced runway. Why keep hitching Willie Field up the ice every few years when you could build your house and your runways on rock? It would be expensive. It might force cutbacks in the science. But it made everything more permanent. And besides, the Russians had all those bases. . . .

And this cut deeper into the differences in perspective. Down there, hidden at the heart of all the U.S. activity on the continent, was the shifting, ghostly idea of presence.

Presence was what the Navy team had asserted with its crisp shoulder rolls and jumping jacks. Presence was the sign on the door of the tunnel into the dome at the South Pole, where the United States made a point of claiming no land and recognizing no claims, yet announced to all, "United States Welcomes You. . . ." Presence was Kiwi Ross Dependency postage stamps and the appointment of Norman Hardie as coroner. Presence was U.S. C-130s and camouflaged C-141 air force transports landing on what Kiwis thought of as New Zealand's ice. Byrd dropped more than one U.S. flag out of his airplanes. There were flags and tins bearing claims statements on behalf of various countries in unlikely places all over Antarctica. In 1938, Nazi Germany, wishing to establish presence in Antarctica, sent flying boats to the ice to drop swastika flags tied to javelins every fifty miles across the continent. One report of this effort claimed that the pilots, confronted each flight with the massive rise of the ice plateau and a fuselage weighed down with five hundred pounds of javelins, carried the symbols just out of sight of their support ship, then dumped the whole load. So, buried in the ice somewhere in the area claimed by Norway, small pockets of very intense Nazi presence work their way over the years slowly toward the sea.

In the exhortation supporting the U.S. antarctic program, signed by the U.S. president, the notion of presence was invoked before any mention of science: the program, the memorandum announced, would maintain "an active and influential presence in Antarctica. . . ." The Soviet Union, which recognized no claims, had established bases in the logistically horrible but otherwise quite logical pattern—in terms of presence—of one in almost everyone else's claim. Feeling responsible to follow the president's directive, the Shoe found the Russian action frustrating. As a military man he thought in terms of competition. To him there was a base gap in Antarctica.

"In 1961 the Russians had two stations," he said one morning a few days before the big game. "Now they have seven. We started with six and this year we're going to be down to three." (Tucker Scully, director of the State Department's Office of Oceans and Polar Affairs, argued that the U.S. presence was better served by its capacity to fly LC-130s to any point in the continent to establish temporary bases than by making permanent camps. "You don't have three guys holed up there all winter with an American flag under their armpit, but I think that's as good a presence.")

"Do you think we should build new bases?" I had asked Shoemaker.

"We should go back to some of the places where we've been."

But on Thanksgiving afternoon the Shoe wasn't thinking about aggressive Russians, just those damn USARPs. The first half ended with a stalemate. The Navy sidelines were shocked; the civilian sidelines were startled and happy. The game's public address announcer, who commented vigorously but vaguely on the game from inside a historic old aircraft control tower that was so warm and crowded that its windows were utterly fogged, announced that all the USARP vehicles were illegally parked and the penalty for a parking ticket was death, urged that participants keep their ticket stubs (the game was, of course, free) for the drawing for a free tour of Antarctica, and thanked the sponsorship of a firm called Weddell Furriers. During halftime the seven-member Bunny Boot Marching Band, led by a drum major who marked time with a pool cue, offered renditions of "Anchors Aweigh" and the Marine Hymn. Science was then served by a Navy man who, researching the effects of cold upon human pigmentation, ran stark naked from one end of the field to another, starting off pink and ending up blue.

The Navy came booming out of its halftime shelter, a hut called Storm Dome, wrested the ball from the USARPs early in the second half, and, taking advantage of an impromptu glissade by a defender, completed an eighty-yard pass play for the game's first score. Red-jacketed fans could be heard offering the USARP coach another bottle of Jack Daniel's. The cheering of the Navy side, led by the sailor carrying the down marker, was only slightly dampened when the team failed to run the ball over for the conversion, leaving the score 6–0. Now, surely, the rout would begin.

But the civilians held on. The field became soft and treacherous. Snow flew. Bodies fell and slid. Boots churned for footing. The third quarter ebbed away, and the lead remained precarious. The redcoats on the sidelines began chanting, *"Use-arps! Use-arps! Use-arps!"* And suddenly the funny black pants were driving grid east, pushing the Navy presence back into its own territory.

(3)

The Shoe's main antagonist on the ice was Edward P. Todd, although antagonism is too strong a word. The two men drove hard in slightly different directions. Todd was the director of the National Science Foundation's Division of Polar Programs. When he was in McMurdo he was a DV as well as an executive; he was there to gaze through the vast thick lenses of his glasses at everything that was going on and pronounce it good or otherwise. He was a big, wry, friendly man, with a sense of humor that was sometimes heavy but always dry. His jesting was camouflaged by those deep lenses, which made his gentle eyes look enormous and severe. When I first met him in Washington I thanked him for the invitation to visit Antarctica and he stared at me and said, "You probably do not deserve it." I had smiled uncertainly, humbly agreed, and got out of there fast. I only found out when I met him in McMurdo three months later that he had been joking. Todd kept granola bars in the many pockets of his parka and offered them to others at any excuse.

Todd was the man of science. His allegiance was to the pursuit of knowledge. Presence was an unfortunate necessity, an excuse to spend money on the vital work of getting to know a continent. In the years since the IGY his point of view had been in the ascendancy in the Antarctic. There had been one surge of armed force: In 1946 the United States assaulted the continent with four thousand troops in Operation Highjump, what one author called "D day in Antarctica." But the treaty, which came into force in 1961, had demilitarized the continent and made science king, so Todd was actually Shoemaker's boss.

This line of authority was tense and not always clear; as had been true since the IGY, when Byrd was in charge of the U.S. program but Admiral George Dufek, technically his subordinate, took command on the ice, small resentments flowed. Todd at least had some sympathy for the Shoe.

"This command is at the bottom of the list of commands that get you somewhere in the Navy," he had said one morning as he walked out of the mess hall. "So a young officer who has worked his way up to captain is assigned this command, which is a disappointment, and comes down here only to find out that he's not really in charge."

For several years the National Science Foundation and the U.S. Department of Defense had been renegotiating the terms of the memorandum of understanding that described their cooperation in Antarctica. Both sides fought for a larger role, the Navy to take over some of the construction and maintenance jobs that had been done by the civilian contractor, and the Division of Polar Programs to expand civilian duties. Behind the apparent self-interest were different notions of Antarctica's future: Todd saw it as growing in importance as a laboratory and monitoring station for the rest of the world; Shoemaker saw it as a potential arena of dispute as the world reached down to the freezer for resources.

Out on the field of snow, neither side gave much away. But the USARPs drove steadily grid east, in spite of determined efforts by the frustrated Navy down-marker bearer to stretch the first down rope. Led by a twenty-three-year-old construction worker from New Jersey named Chris Keri, who had learned to throw gentle passes to receivers whose feet moved fast but whose progress was agonizingly slow, the USARPs drove sixty yards to score. Keri, whose beard was full of frost, ran the ball across for the extra point.

On the somber Navy sidelines the Shoe was as cheerful as always. He talked about beating the Kiwis in a cricket match played with a tennis ball, and of the first antarctic marathon, scheduled for later in the year. On the field the Navy took to the air, but it was too late. In the end the USARP team intercepted a desperation Navy pass and put the game on ice.

The civilians got the Penguin Bowl trophy, a towering structure donated by a California trophy-store owner who must have put on all the extras in the shop, including five brass football players, one angel, and one half-naked man with a wreath, all stacked on three tiers of bowls, columns, and arches. Keri, the day's hero, said modest quarterbackish things like "The line did a great job." Everyone packed up and went back to the Hill for a magnificent navy Thanksgiving dinner. No one was sad. The civilians were in charge for today, but it had been very, very close.

Only one person remained at Willie Field. Leaving in a truck, I glanced over at the scene of the morning's falling antarctic tree. There was the forklift. And there was the forklift operator, standing at attention on the snow. Someone must have told him to remain with his wreck and then gone off to watch the game. He stood there contrite and cold, his lesson learned. The one thing that this delicately balanced system could not tolerate was error. Yet error had occurred.

Chapter Fourteen

Blue Ice

(1)

As if to give homage to the hazard it was to undertake, Hercules No. XD 05 took off from the ice runway, turned grid east, and crossed the ruins of a Lockheed Super Constellation. Good omen. I had said my prayers and made my amends because it seemed the reasonable thing to do. We were going to the blue ice near the Allan Hills to drag the skis on an untrodden surface and see if we could land.

Out the porthole the old Constellation lay half drifted in, with its triple tail section missing one fin and its wings invisible in the snow. In 1970 it made a whiteout landing after five approaches and slid off the runway. The ice broke it to pieces. Sixty-eight passengers and twelve crew were aboard. All survived.

Everyone survived the last trip to the Allan Hills, too. Three days ago Brian Rich took a Herc up to the Allan Hills and thrashed the skis around on the sastrugi until he got an unsafe light on the nose ski. The ice was so rough the copilot had a hard time reading the airspeed. Shortly after that, Rich got an unsafe light on the main skis. He decided it was time to go home. "My main thought was if I had set the nose ski down, the nose ski would have joined us in the cockpit." Now he was going out there to try again. "The plywood must get through." Last night I had the big eye, lying awake, thinking about the flight to Allan Hills.

The plane droned up the Taylor Valley. Thin clouds hung on the ridges, folding down over the edges like the ice. From the flight deck the valley was a long trench, bounded by brown and black layers of stone, digging back into a high whiteness that seemed without definition, like the waking end of a dream. The lines of color in the rock were straight as fences; the white snuffed them out at the valley's end. We flew grid east, climbing: 7,500; 8,500; 10,000. The terrain rose against us. Rivers of ice poured down out of the clouds, and the mountains became ridges struggling above the enveloping mass, then nunataks holding their heads out. Then, just as the ice conquered all, everything vanished. We were over cloud. The plane slid out over whiteness as if over unformed land, waiting for the world to take shape beneath.

In the back of the Herc there was a bundle of equipment for Sierra 058, for whom we were trying to find a landing site. It was a curious stack. In it were a couple of snowmobiles, a big bunch of bamboo stakes, a mound of boxes, some Scott tents, and several Nansen sledges. It seemed odd to find wooden sledges carried so carefully in this howling aluminum chamber: they were a part of antarctic exploration in just this form all the way back to the beginning. They were long, slender constructions of rope and wood that looked like the bare ribs of an aircraft. They looked anachronistic. They were not. They were built that way because Nansen and then Amundsen, who refined them, had the right ideas. They were made of New Zealand red beech, bamboo, and nylon rope. Their runners were coated with a synthetic skid material that wouldn't go splintering off at a hundred below. They weighed about seventy pounds unloaded, and could carry half a ton.

Before its work was done here, VXE-6 would drop nine people, nine snowmobiles, and thirteen Nansen sledges on the ice near the Allan Hills. The team, led by William Cassidy of the University of Pittsburgh, would be out for fifty days. It would cover five hundred miles. On the plains on which it traveled the wind always blew, scouring the snow from the ice and leaving it clean and blue. And out on the blue ice, where the snow never remained, there lay stones. The stones had come from space.

This was the gold of Antarctica. Guy Guthridge: "A scientific bonanza." In 1969 a group of Japanese glaciologists, surveying across the ice, picked up some rocks, looked at them carefully, and discovered they were meteorites. Altogether they found nine. Only four had been found in all previous antarctic exploration. Nine in a year! The rush was on. Now in a good year Cassidy's team would find over a thousand specimens, the fragments of fifty to two hundred actual falls. So since 1969 one-half to one-third of all meteorites available for study in the world had been harvested from the blue ice fields of Antarctica.

"It's a big Easter egg hunt for grown-ups," John Schutt had said. "They're just lying on the surface. I've found two or three hundred of them, and I still don't tire of it." Schutt was the team's mountaineer. He was small and lean, with ragged hair and a cheerful smile that revealed a chipped front tooth. The tooth and something wiry about him made him seem worn but tireless, like a man who walked steadily uphill on a field of loose rock. He had been working for the meteorite team for four years.

Each specimen he and the eight other team members found would be picked up with forceps and put into a dust-free sterile bag. That bag would be sealed and put in another bag. The whole thing would be kept frozen all the way from the Allan Hills to the Johnson Space Center in Houston, where it would get the same kind of care and scrutiny given to rocks from the moon.

Most of the meteorites, of course, had come from farther away than that. Among the specimens the team had found was a rock that seemed to have come from Mars. Possibly whacked off the surface of its home planet by the impact of another meteor, it had somehow found its way to the sky above Antarctica, and had been drawn to Earth. This rock, whose origin was interpreted from its composition, furnished a useful anecdote for speakers who wished to promote the value of antarctic research. In the anecdote Congress, moved by its inscrutable wisdom, demanded a program to retrieve a seventeen-pound sample from the surface of the Earth's red neighbor. A committee of senators took testimony from the National Aeronautics and Space Administration: "Mr. Chairman, it will cost thirty billion dollars." It took testimony from the Pentagon: "Mr. Chairman, it will cost fifty billion dollars." Whereupon a little man in a white smock with a lapel pin that read "NSF" came in carrying a sack. "Ah, Mr. Chairman . . ."

John Schutt was in the aircraft now, sitting up front with the pilots and Cassidy, plugged into the headphones, watching out the windows as, slowly, the low clouds over the plateau faded away and the plane came out across the sunlit blue.

(2)

We had left our Earth. We had slipped into a crevasse in time and had fallen out. We had escaped the shadow of mortality. We sailed free. I kneeled at a porthole with my nose to the Plexiglas like a child. We were borne grid east on a sea of light.

The surface below us was brighter than the sky. It ranged out to infinity, shining, to a horizon that curved softly in a haze of brightness. The surface was infinitely varied. Right below a field of sastrugi reached out across it like a fan of riffles blown up on water. Farther out, a formation of vast crevasses, all bridged and half-hidden by snow, ran straight and parallel toward grid north like drifted-in highways in the world we had left. They were so straight they must have been engineered, drawn across the face of this foreign empire by men whose blood ran cold and fluid with glyco-peptides. But the broad paths to nowhere were abandoned, the engineers gone.

Everywhere were the fields of blue. They emerged from the white of the snow in gentle swirls of a square mile or two and in vast landscapes of blue that reached out to the world's edge to make a union with the sky. The blue was pale; fair. It was neither luminous nor translucent. It was the color of a windy sea and calm milk, equally mixed. It was the color of a cold eye. It was the color of morning on a planet whose sun burned no red. It was a blue of heartlessness and a blue of pity. Up-sun it turned to the silver blue of steel; down-sun it became light blue as a blanket, but cool as a shadow in snow.

So we flew between sky and sky, the snow on the blue like cirrus clouds beneath us, sun shining from the ice above. The meteorites gathered here, it was thought by some, because the moving ice pushed upward on a swell of the distant hills, the wind blew it away by molecules each year, and the rocks embedded over the miles and the centuries were left on the surface. But there seemed to be a more fanciful explanation. As we crossed this new world, where the boundaries of light were so mingled, it seemed that the blue ice was a window, into which the meteorites, like birds deluded by reflection and hope, flew to die.

(3)

On the horizon a line of low clouds lay dark against the white, looking like coast. As we turned, the shadow of the aircraft appeared and disappeared from view out my porthole; since our turns were subtle and hard to judge in this directionless land, the shadow took on a purpose of its own, and it seemed that we were accompanied by a ghost.

PILOT: What did you call that real hard snow? Stirge or something?

SCIENTIST: Firn. F-i-r-n.

NAVIGATOR: Real close to stirge.

Our shadow grew. The plane was descending. "Not any lower than five hundred," Rich said to the copilot. Out the window the relief of the snow increased and the huge roads of the snow-bridged crevasses swept past, wide as interstates. "We used thin aluminum tubes, six feet long, to probe the layers of snow and ice," wrote Vivian Fuchs about his journey among crevasses on the plateau, "and we assumed the area safe if resistance was still encountered at the full depth of the thrust. . . . A hole would be cut in [each ice] bridge until it was possible to thrust one's head far enough in to see the width and direction of the crevasse. Hanging down over a bottomless pit, with sloping blue-white sides disappearing into the depths, gave the impression of gazing into deep water. . . . We . . . were bringing the vehicles forward . . . when we were surrounded by a rumbling noise like underground thunder: at the same time there was a shuddering and gentle collapse of the whole snow surface. Suddenly two enormous holes, 30 to 40 feet long and 12 feet wide, appeared on either side of the track just ahead." The LC-130 would test the surface with its skis while all on board hoped that this strange shifting landscape would not engulf it.

"In a ski drag you're just dragging a physical presence across the ground," Rich said once. "You're looking for anything." Crevasses, snow humps, invisible pinnacles. "You cross at about five hundred feet. You put it up-sun, put the sun over it, put it down-sun, put it across-sun. I've spent a lot of time looking at crevasses this year. You see if you can get an angle where you can see them. Sometimes you make three, four, five passes before you see the crevasses. When you make the drag you're still flying. You're at 105 knots, plus or minus. Anytime you want to you can still go flying." Rich smiled. "Even the drag doesn't guarantee you there isn't a crevasse there. It doesn't sanitize the spot. You don't know anything until you actually come in and set the aircraft down and it disappears."

The crew began a landing checklist. The loadmaster back in the cabin buckled himself in tight and grabbed the nylon webbing of his chair. The plane swept low, and through a nearby porthole I could see the sastrugi grow. It looked as if the snow were strewn with long lean boulders just beneath its skin. I held on.

The history of flight in the Antarctic was burdened with disappearances. In 1929 Larry Gould's Fokker monoplane vanished, but not in landing. It had been flown 135 miles from Little America to a camp near the Rockefeller Mountains. There was no blue ice there at first, but it came. The three men in Gould's party camped by the plane and a wind blew up, slowly scouring the snow away from their campsite until the tent and plane stood at the edge of a growing pool of blue. This was not a breeze. The three men sat in the plane to use its radio, and the airspeed indicator registered ninety miles an hour. The engine's oil was thick as crude with the cold, but the wind spun the propeller. Once Gould, grasping a rope with which he tried to hold the plane down, was blown horizontal like a doll on a string. The men crawled into the tent and spent the night in a din of flapping canvas, and while they were asleep the plane flew itself away.

The wind was a powerful but poor pilot; the plane made it half a mile and crashed. When the team found it the next day the three propeller blades were curled forward, aluminum petals wilting in the cold. No wonder it met grief. The wind had flown it backward.

The sastrugi raced past. I thought of the helicopter crewman: "Easy down, sir. Six inches to your toes. Easy down." In my bunny boots my toes tried to grip the floor.

COPILOT: 110, down 2.

NAVIGATOR: 25 feet.

COPILOT: 105, down 1.

"It's hard to believe we do the things we do with the airplanes," Brian Rich had said one day at a party given by NSF for the press. "But a Herc's built like a tank."

COPILOT: 100, down 1.

Bang!

The skis hit with a whack. They hit again. Then the whole plane began to rattle. The humps of sastrugi, dazzling in the view from the dim interior, raced by, shapes on a platform passed by the downwind express. We hit them as we passed. The load of sleds bucked in its straps. We bounced around in our seats like potatoes in red burlap. We crashed along, but the hardness we slammed against had a fraction of give, a core of softness. We touched the snow, and the snow gave.

Through the tiny glimpse of window I could see the long horizon. For all its roaring thunder the plane was very small. On the expanse of the continental plateau it was just a little bright nib, drawing a plume and a shadow on a thousand miles of snow.

Then, without a sensation of pulling away, the plane took to the air. Softness prevailed. The sun rose again on the wall. We turned to come back to the mark we had made.

In just the time it took to make the turn the mark had vanished. Fog slipped across the white-and-blue landscape. The scratch in the snow, the line drawn with the silver tip of the pen of antarctic science, scratched with the sharp fingernail of the men of the Navy, disappeared. But we could not loiter for the wind to blow the fog away. XD 05 had to go back for fuel.

For me, the trip to the Allan Hills was over. I would disembark, because I had other places to go. Much later Brian Rich would tell me about the return later in the day, when he landed on the ice and let Cassidy and his team get their first breath of the wind in which they would travel for almost two months. "They were so excited, it was great. It meant that they didn't have to go in with helos and traverse sixty miles. It was a real up experience."

"This is like nothin' in the world," J. J. Miller said once. "If I never do another whiteout landing that would be fine. But this— flying around on skis and stuff, nobody gets to do that. Ski take- offs, ski landings, rocket-assisted takeoffs—it's a hell of a lot of fun. In terms of a pilot's airplane, with landings and takeoffs and chal- lenges and making the plane do what you need it to do, nothin' comes close to this."

"As a professional military man," wrote Captain Marion E. Morris, who once flew in the Antarctic, "I was involved for all too short a while in an endeavor of peace; an endeavor which taxed my ability as strenuously as any of the times of combat. . . ."

The Hercules returned to McMurdo and landed. On the planed- snow runway it was like gliding onto butter. The engines reversed. A cloud of snow rose over the plane. The roar that had supported us ran down through an octave of harmony and diminished. The scientists got out; the Navy men got out. They conferred together about the route back. Among the warriors and the men of knowl- edge there was no discord on the ice.

Chapter Fifteen

Survival

(1)

Just like government work. I spent two days and a night wet and cold learning how to survive in the snow, then at last they sent me out to the field—to the driest place in the world. Now, newly competent and confident at falling down snow hills and building igloos, I was strapped into a helo, all crumpled up like an accident victim into a very small space among Scott tents and food boxes, with one foot going to sleep somewhere under the seat and the other propped up over there like a stranger in a white helmet on top of a bag full of mail for Vanda Station, heading for Victoria Valley and a hillside of rocks and wind.

Snowcraft Survival School was designed to teach you how to keep Antarctica at bay. It had begun in the second floor of the Berg Field Center one evening with basic instruction in climbing a rope on prusik slings and fitting crampons to boots. There were fifteen of us, including several Kiwis, who were clad in yellow. No racial distinction here, just parka colors. By the end of the evening we were all hunching ourselves up and down ropes hung from the rafters like a crew of semicoordinated monkeys.

On a wall in the Berg Field Center was a huge photograph of a leopard seal loitering around a tiny ice floe on which a penguin stood. The penguin had made a small mistake. It was isolated on the floe. Now it would die. Antarctica had no mercy. Find a crevasse unexpectedly, you die. Lose your way on the ice, you die. Neglect your cooling body, you die. Step in the wrong place, you

184

die. On December 14, 1912, Belgrave Ninnis of the British Royal Fusiliers, who was called Cherub, stepped off his dog sledge in the land his team leader, Douglas Mawson, called the Kingdom of Blizzards. He stepped off and the surface opened in a puff of light snow, and he disappeared. He was never seen again.

We practiced falling. We fell again and again, diving down a hillside scarred by others. The hill was very steep. The instruction was simple. Dive down it until the snow flies. Yahoo! Death looms. Dig in ice ax as brake. Stop. Life saved again.

We fell in twos on a steeper pitch, roped together, while one partner broke the tumble with the rope wrapped around his ax and boot. Many lives were saved. The sun shone, the air was still. We were around the corner of Ross Island's long promontory, near the bay called Windless Bight. There was no wind. In the still air we shouted and cheered.

We may have been overheard. Somewhere out here was an array of microphones installed by Sierra 108, directed by Charles R. Wilson of the University of Alaska. In a hut on the other side of the hill Wilson's technicians listened to infrasonic waves—extremely low vibration sounds; the deepest songs in the world. Some of the vibrations had a period of a minute between the peak of each oscillation. This was not the sound of drums or cannon; it was the slow throb of the earth itself. Kay Driscoll, the winter-over technician for Wilson's project, had told the press group, "We get mountain association waves, when the jet stream interacts with the ranges. We see low-pressure systems going up and down. We get the shock wave induced into the atmosphere as the aurora goes into its breakup phase and goes into its descent."

"Could you hear a nuclear explosion?" Malcolm asked.

Driscoll: "Yes."

Malcolm: "Might be a good verification technique."

Driscoll (reluctantly): "Yes."

We flung ourselves off the mountain. The mountain hummed. We tumbled and slid in the snow, headfirst, sideways, backward;

snow down the neck. An earthquake in New Zealand murmured. We offered ourselves as hostages for the training of our companions. Without fail, our companions held the rope. A newborn Herbie throbbed in the far distance. Antarctica was cheers and singing in the cold.

The shock waves of bodies in training colliding with snow fled in the dry air. We adjourned to a little A-frame hut in which teacups hung from the ceiling, to discuss shelter. Instructors went through the options. You could dig a trench in the hard snow, and put little sleeping platforms off it and cover it with blocks. Quick, easy, warm. Or you could build an igloo.

"But remember, you have to sleep in it tonight whether you've finished it or not."

You could make a pile of gear—sleeping bags, packs, anything big—pile snow high on top of it, pack it down, then tunnel in and remove the gear, leaving a cavity that could be hollowed out. Simple, adequate, warm. Or you could build an igloo.

"An igloo is a little tricky to build. The tendency is to go around and around and then you wind up with a cylinder that goes up and up. And remember, you have to sleep in it."

"Who wants to build an igloo with me?" Gregg Stanton, the intrepid diver. Silence. "I've always wanted to build an igloo," he said. "Anybody want to work on it?" Silence. What was this? Stanton was from Florida. To acclimate for diving in Antarctica he had gone diving in Florida's cold springs. The water had been seventy degrees. He was prepared. Sure. He knew about igloos.

At last I could see there was no option. Everyone else here was practical. They were planning trenches. But someone must build an igloo. So I joined him. I, too, was prepared. I had lived in California, where people think about igloos every day.

Stanton was serene. I worried. He was the engineer and construction crew. I worked in the mines, sawing blocks out of the snow. It was firn: f-i-r-n. It was hard and light. If you dug a snow cave in firn you could seal in the door and breathe through several feet of it. It could be cut into blocks with a saw. A piece two feet square, ten inches thick was easy to carry, and easy to lift into place on the wall.

Stanton measured and ruminated and fitted blocks into walls. I quarried and brought him blocks. The survival school crews built their homes next to the area lived in by last week's school. Their trenches and mounds were already drifted over. Their little village looked like a ruin, already tumbling before the inexorable antarctic wind. All our brave little shelters were doomed.

Other teams were belowground before we had our walls up to the second row of blocks. Then both my fretting and Stanton's serenity became more pronounced. Trench builders started dropping by, making cheerful observations about the comfort they were soon to experience below the surface. Stanton smiled. I kept sawing. The others went smugly back to their trenches.

At least we were learning fast. We learned first that to prevent an igloo from becoming a cylinder you have to lean the blocks inward, and leaning blocks tended to fall off the wall. Firn was a marvelous building material, but dropped from any elevation it became powder.

The blocks, initially crude cubes, grew more sophisticated. In the cutting they had to be beveled on all sides to tilt and gather toward the middle. We built little towers out of ruined blocks to hold the first blocks of each row up, but found that as soon as three or four blocks were in place, they leaned against each other at angles and held each other up, like drunks on a street corner. We boiled snow over a gasoline stove and made tea. We drank some and used the rest to glue the blocks together. It make them look as if they had been anointed by a dog, but it worked.

The sun rolled around the big blue sky. A gentle plume rose from Mt. Erebus and blew nowhere. Antarctica was benign today. It was tolerant of our endeavor. When Larry Gould and his colleagues tried to cut snow blocks out of firn near the Rockefeller Mountains to build a wall around their restless airplane, the wind took the blocks and flung them at the builders' heads. Our igloo was whimsical; put a little sting in the air and we'd be right down there in the pits, grubbing out a trench with the rest of them.

But in the clean and pleasant sunshine we raised our dome. Ever anxious, I became an expert with the saw; the blocks were marvels of precision, eyeballed to fit. Stanton grew insouciant with his competence; he popped the blocks up on the wall at remarkable angles and they stuck. Now, by God, using tea was cheating.

Observers became respectful. One even posed for a photograph beside our house. I had to kneel to cut out each block; my knees became raw and proud. At last, to finish, we completed an arch across the top and filled it in with firm firn wedges.

Inside, the light was cut into blue squares, like luminous blue tile. We could sit up in there and stay dry. Ask them in the trenches about that. Down in those close quarters they looked up from prone and got snow in the face. I suffered a small setback in the process of making the igloo comfortable when the pressure stove caught fire and threatened to explode until we dumped snow on it, but the brief conflagration just sealed the walls. Next door, where David White, Stanton's field leader, was building one of those domes made of snow piled on equipment, the residents found themselves jammed in a space just big enough for two rolled-up sleeping bags and a shovel; but we could stretch, breathe, and converse.

Late in the evening White, a small, wonderfully good-humored man, came over from his snow heap for a visit. He was thoroughly damp from the excavation he'd been doing, and was not so charmed by the conditions in what we could refer to, with disdain, as his hovel. During our conversation a brief, plaintive observation escaped him.

"Do you ever wonder," he said, "just *why* you're here?"

This was a question others shared. "Sometimes," a woman at the Biolab said once, "I get to wondering why the hell I'm here. Then I think, Where else would I rather be?"

That was not White's meaning. He was delighted to be on the continent. But he could think of a number of places he would rather be right now without leaving Antarctica. His room at the California Hotel, for instance. He didn't object to being in Antarctica; he just didn't see much need to learn how to live on the ice. It was an understandable sentiment: the farthest he would get in his work from the safety of McMurdo was a diving hut about three hundred yards out on the sea ice along the Willie Field road.

I should have shared his good-natured frustration; my skills in cutting blocks of firn would come in mighty handy out in the dust of the Dry Valleys, where I was scheduled to go. But I didn't. I was drier than he was, first of all. We all knew, too, that the survival school simply made us more competent in the cold. And tonight Stanton and I had achieved a simple thing, and we felt a simple pleasure. We had made our shelter; it was sound, comfortable, and bright; and it was the best house in town. It was eight feet in diameter. It was five feet high. It felt like a cathedral.

Outside, the world became utterly quiet as the students went to bed, so the occasional sound of footsteps was loud and the eventual absence of them was an enormous soothing peace. My anxiety disappeared, and Stanton was proud. We felt so damn resourceful that we brought the stove back inside, opened a can of freeze-dried pork with a crampon point, and feasted on hash and chops for dinner. We could handle this place, Antarctica. The sun shone upon us, our igloo glowed a gentle blue, the wind did not blow, and Antarctica smiled.

(2)

What continuity was there in this life? There I was, at the South Pole one day, watching football the next, building igloos the next —and then jammed in a U.S. helo called by the radio code words Gentle Eighteen, wrapped around equipment that was bound for a joint New Zealand–Japanese project, myself going to a strange and obscure place in the Victoria Valley to visit some strange but not-so-obscure people. The only continuity was the unending drama, and the drama was not in us, but in the place we so briefly inhabited; the continuity was the continent. Gentle 18 flew out across Warren Zapol's fish hut, across roads heading to nowhere marked with the long shadows of flagged stakes, across the long straight track of Lyle McGinnis's seismic research journey across the sea ice, where he shot ten-pound charges of dynamite at intervals and listened to the layers of sediment on the sea floor whisper back their echoes of depth and history. The track and the little regular blooms left by the shots in the ice looked like the course of a one-armed cross-country skier three hundred feet tall. The helo crossed a cluster of huts at a place called Butter Point, where the Kiwis were assembling a camp for an offshore geological drilling operation the next year. It crossed a single yellow tent pegged among stones near the foot of the Meserve Glacier. The mark of the human species was odd and scattered, and sometimes its purposes seemed obscure, but Antarctica was a single presence, serene and magnificent; and cold.

"Easy down, sir. One foot. Six inches to your toes. Easy down, sir." There was a flurry of action, people, work, noise. The helo blew dust. Four of us were running back and forth, loading boxes, unloading boxes. Introductions were made in this rushed meeting. Hello. Mike Malin, hello. Dean Eppler, hello. Talked to you the other day. Going to spend a few days. Here's my gear. Let's put those boxes over here. . . . Helo blades thundered overhead, blowing dust. *Whack-whack-whack-whack.* Sunlight flickered under the blades. Here was a curious plywood box labeled Din Din. Here was a cardboard box labeled Used Food. *Whack-whack-whack-whack.* Sweat grew like frost in the small of the back. "You know," Eppler said, "when you've been snowed out four days, when that red bird comes in it's really very nice." *Whack-whack-whack-whack.* "*Roger,*" Malin said to the pilot. "See you in three days."

Silence.

Cold.

I was out on the ground. Suddenly the helicopter was gone. It was like being tossed through a time machine, tumbled end over end in a tumult of noise and voices, and then hitting the ground in an alien world.

The air was thin and cold. The land was entirely without sign of life. We were out on a rocky hillside. The rocks were rounded brown granite boulders. Between the boulders were small drifts of pale brown sand and of snow. The snow was thin and scabrous, gritty with the sand that had blown on it since it fell, and rotted by the dry wind. The surfaces of the boulders were roughly polished. Except where flakes of surface had recently broken off to show a pale, coarse interior, the rocks had a patina to them, the color and feel of wood stair rails in an old fish cannery; it was as if people with callused hands had been rubbing them for centuries.

The helicopter's sound vanished into an enormous empty space, so clear it might not even have contained air. The slope dropped away from where we stood at 2,450 feet above sea level toward the pale blue ice of Lake Vida, then rose again miles off in a long smooth rise seamed with parallel stripes of dolerite. It rose to gentle distant benches—stones, stones, stones, sweeping fields of stones rising again to distant high valleys: McKelvey, Bantham, Barwick. And above the valleys were the tiered mountains of the Olympus Range, grid northeast; the St. Johns Range, grid southeast; and in the far east the Apocalypse Peaks.

Up among the peaks and ridges, two thousand, three thousand feet above us, twenty miles away, a layer of fog rode high, half concealed behind the stone, showing only glimpses of a long whiteness behind the mountains. It looked like the poised breaking of a wave, coming across the dike.

But it was not fog. It was the rim of the eastern plateau. It was ice.

The helicopter banked away behind a jagged ridge of dolerite, and it left a huge silence, deep as the whole valley, wide as the continent. In all this valley today there were three people: Mike Malin, Dean Eppler, and me.

Malin was waving around a hand-held transmitter. He saw me looking around in awe. He grinned like a conspirator. He said:

"This is about as close as I can get to Mars."

(3)

The next thing he said was:

"Where's your chair?"

Mike Malin knew how to live in the field. He did not believe in the pursuit of hardship. When the people at Berg Field Center had asked him what to send out with me he had said one cot, one folding metal chair, one tent. The people at Berg Field Center had said to themselves, "Mike Malin already has two chairs. He has plenty of tents." They sent a sleeping bag and a foam pad.

Malin was annoyed. It was, however, a cheerful exasperation. He had an underlying appreciation for the Berg Field Center. Mike Malin was thirty-three. He was utterly confident. He wore an aggressive black beard, and his cockiness would have seemed arrogance if it were not so wrapped in enthusiasm. As a teenager he had, mostly by luck, flown in weightlessness missions with Apollo astronauts; it seemed he had never been aware of the full burden of life again.

Malin earned his bachelor's degree in physics at the University of California at Berkeley and his doctorate at Cal Tech, and had worked at the famous Jet Propulsion Laboratory in Pasadena for four years, where he worked on planetary probe missions. "It was a political training ground rather than a scientifically rewarding adventure." Now he was an associate professor at the Arizona State University, specializing in volcanism and planetary and polar geomorphology. "One of the reasons I study volcanoes, floods, wind, and things is that in a human lifetime you can see something happen. Mount Saint Helens has changed a lot in a few years." He never hesitated to talk about the things he had done, but he had fun talking about them, which made the difference.

We had a small discussion about where to put the tents, one Scott tent and one small backpacking tent, since all ground sloped toward the distant lake. We moved all the wooden boxes of food and equipment to a little dish of sand. More sweat. Then Eppler started to put it up. He was Malin's graduate student assistant. He was large and moved slowly, but only in comparison to Malin, who was mercurial. His beard was enormous and fair and gray around the edges.

Eppler was the eternal grad student assistant. Because of the nature of the work, which I was soon to discover to my pain, he wore thin gloves with the fingertips cut out of them. They made him look destitute, and the white in his beard made him seem both aged and ageless. Here he was, still in the field in his eighties, poor but marvelously robust, pink-cheeked and youthful, a scientific tramp for whom nothing mattered but to learn, moving with his slow grace from barrel to barrel of knowledge, gleaning what understanding he could find.

There was another way to consider his look of age—that it was premature. Dean Eppler was thirty-one, two years younger than Malin. But he had been out in the field for two weeks, and he had been cold. As I learned that first day, even eight hours when you're cold can be eternity.

The sweat of effort cooled. We sat down to go to work. This was not heavy duty. The temperature was about 15°F. The wind blew gently. The cold came over me slowly, but without mercy.

Mike Malin was studying wind erosion. Among other things, he was trying to learn how long it took rocks to erode in precise amounts, so the erosion itself could be used as a measure of time. The work was like almost all science: painstaking and tedious. It involved bolting precisely weighed and measured rock samples— which had been glued to bolts—onto aluminum racks. The racks were aligned to the cardinal directions and left to the wind. The project would take forty years: three seasons to plan and install, and the rest to come back at intervals and remove selected samples from the racks to see how much damage the wind, the snow, and the sand had wrought.

There were 140 rock samples on each rack. Each sample had to receive a bolt, be mounted on the aluminum, receive a lock washer and another bolt, and be bolted tight. This could not be done in the big bearpaw mittens, which were as voluminous, comfortable, and maneuverable as quilts. It was done in thin gloves.

We sat with our backs to the wind on a stone shaped like a Weddell seal. We put frames together. We took nuts out of plastic bags and put them on bolts. We attached the bolts to the frames. The wind blew gently, inexorably. The cold came softly, like a memory, like a disappointment, like a pang, like a profound and lasting regret.

There was no frostbite. There seemed to be no danger. The nip of the cold on fingers did not seem to be the source of the trouble. My face was chilled, but not uncomfortable. The air was not bitter. The cold that was so strong came from the core, as if it grew in the heart and was pumped out in the coursing of the blood, bringing slowness and hurt to all the regions of the body. My spine, where the sweat had been, was a rod of cold steel. My legs were gelid. I congealed. Malin and Eppler laughed and bolted, bolted and laughed, bolted and told stories about astronauts and flying, and I slowly drifted out of the conversation, neurons becoming lazy with stoking the furnace, limiting their dwindling attention to the complexity of putting a nut on the end of a small black bolt.

This was turning into a difficult task. Which way does the nut turn? That way. No, I guess not. This way. Of course, Oh, here's another one. Let's see.

I was disappointed. Was I truly just a DV, to be coddled and watched over and shown carefully to his warm room at night? And yet within that disappointment at my fragile strength lurked a willingness to assert those rights. Call the helo! Find an excuse!

How important is it really to spend three whole long frigid days with these people, attaching bolts? Let's get on with other things. I just remembered something I must do. An interview with the weathermen, in their big warm room. Very important! An interview with those poor, unfortunate Navy cooks, slaving away over their hot stoves. Vital! Not a moment to lose. An interview with the sauna in the California Hotel. An experiment with sleep.

Sleep! I would become an expert on sleep. I would become a specialist in sleep. It was late November. I would be able to sleep until Christmas, if I could just get warm.

Chapter Sixteen

Easy Up, Sir

(1)

"No matter how cold you are," Mike Malin said, "you do acclimate to it." We were all in the Scott tent. On the floor a small one-burner pressure stove roared, heating water. I sat on a chair very close to it, trying to go up in flames.

"If you were out here for five or eight days or something," Malin continued sincerely, "you would find it doesn't bother you as much." He glanced at Eppler. "Maybe you don't acclimate," he said, "but your brain becomes desensitized to it."

They had quit relatively early. They had noticed my discomfort. I was showing familiar symptoms. Malin had seen Eppler do the same thing early in their fieldwork.

"I can tell when he's gone farther than I can push him," Malin had said. "He gets moribund. Sullen. Doesn't say anything." My sentiments exactly. So we had burrowed through the tube door of the Scott tent and found within a golden light and what seemed to be about a cubic foot of warmth around the stove, and the two men tried to reassure me that things would get better. They were like a team of paramedics working knowledgeably over my prostrate hope. A little heart massage, a drip of IV.

"It becomes routine," Eppler said, "because it's something you deal with and you don't think about it too much anymore." Like Malin, he paused to assess his observation. They were, after all, scientists. The determination to utter truth guarded their thoughts. He continued, "Except every once in a while you do, in fact, get pretty chilly."

We laughed. Laughing helped.

"I like fieldwork," Eppler said, "but this isn't necessarily what I enjoy doing in terms of the climate. Mount Lassen, in California, where I did the work for my dissertation, is more my style. It would get down to forty-five at night, so it was brisk and refreshing, and it would be up to eighty in the day, so you didn't have to freeze your kazoo off."

"Oh, it's all relative!" Malin retorted. "Sure. Before he was here he was complaining about all those days he got rained out in California. Rain!" With great pleasure, we laughed about rain. It was unlikely that the Victoria Valley had seen rain for a thousand years.

Soon after he arrived in Antarctica, Eppler had written a letter to a woman back home. In it he said approximately this:

"This place is sometimes very much like beating your head against the wall. When it's really cold, you really don't like it. Particularly if you have to be outside working. Then when the sun comes out and the wind stops, you forget all that, because you're just agog at what you're seeing. It's so beautiful. There's something about it that's so exotic that you forget how unpleasant you can feel while you're here and just sit there in awe. I'm glad I did this."

There was a hierarchy on this team. The two men were friends, but you knew who was the grad student, who was the Principal Investigator. Malin got the Scott tent, in which four could sleep, for his own. Eppler slept in the little backpacking tent. He also did the cooking and the cleanup. I found out my place soon enough. I roomed with Eppler.

Malin was so ebullient about what he was doing that his assertion of these little privileges of rank, which not all took here on the ice, earned no rancor. Malin was a rare phenomenon: a cheerful and indefatigable man. Being around him was like keeping company with an endless, multicolored phosphorous sparkler.

"I find lots of things interesting," he said. "I like to work on them."

Among the things he was working on were cameras for photographing the surface of planets and of Halley's comet and computer models for reconstructing the geological contours of land from the evidence gathered by geologists in the field. The data would be put in the machine, and the machine would draw a picture of the earth on its screen and run the earth backward in time. This work in computer graphics had led him into movie graphics, and that led him off in many other directions.

Now, in the tent, while Eppler was outside cooking frozen chicken from the Din Din box over a balky two-burner gasoline stove in the −15° evening, Malin mused about what creates the perception of reality in a photograph. If you could identify the characteristics of a photograph by number, you could create something that looked like a photograph with a computer program, and make frames of a movie that would look like life, digital images of reality. "I'll have a palette of numbers; a palette of textures." You could have a palette of skin tones and one of expression; you could capture a famous face—even a face long dead.

"It would be fun," Malin said, "to make a sequel to *Gone with the Wind* with Clark Gable and Vivien Leigh."

There were no limits in Antarctica. You could look out the door of the tent at a palette of all the grandeur in the world. In this brightness the stars were invisible but close. One of the experiments Malin was doing here as what he called a "bootleg project" was to see how metal eroded in the windblown sand, because he could apply that information to photographs of the sand-pitted legs and bodies of U.S. lander probes resting on Mars and learn about Martian wind.

"The earth and the other planets are all so closely linked in my mind," he said. "I can't separate my work from one to the other. They're all part of the same family. They're siblings. You can learn a lot about someone by studying his brothers and sisters."

There was a noise from Eppler outside, muffled by the double walls of the tent. It sounded like a grunt.

"What?" Malin called.

"Nothing," Eppler shouted back. "Just yelling at the chicken."

(2)

It was morning. Mike Malin was emerging from his tent. I could
hear him from my nest in the sleeping bag. He was thrashing in the
canvas. That tunnel door was always trouble. You had to crawl out
like a dog, or like a spaceman in an airlock. Malin's voice went
ringing across the dry landscape.

"Hatch coming open, Houston."

It was eight, just before Shaunessy Everett's radio roundup.
Eppler was out of the tent and pumping up the stove. Malin was
up and out and singing. No wonder; music was just as familiar to
him as the red plains of Mars. As a teenager he had been a talented
musician on the trombone, and had turned down a scholarship to
Juilliard to attend Berkeley. "He's done more shit in his life than
the law allows." Eppler. The song this morning was from *Fiddler
on the Roof*, adapted to Antarctica: "*Sunrise, sunrise; sunrise,
sunrise.*"

Go away, sunrise, this sleeping bag is warm.

The cold of yesterday had been reinforced by Malin's dark
observations about the likely inadequacy of my sleeping bag. He
had been wrong. The nylon-lined bag had been bitter to slide into,
but in ten minutes I had at last been warm. And now, alas, morning
had come so swiftly, and, alack, my snow-damp trousers, which I
had laid beside the bag for the night, were quite capable of standing on their own.

"Mac Sideband, Mac Sideband, do you read?" Out by the Scott
tent Malin was checking in. There was Shaunessy Everett's voice,
crackling out kindly from her little warm room at MacTown.
Malin, as usual, had a telegram for her to send, about a camera
project back home. No place on earth was out of touch: Malin
sometimes got a twenty-four-hour turnaround on his telegrams,
from send-off to response. Then he gave the Victoria Valley
weather report for the pilots: "Ceiling five thousand broken, wind
zero two zero at eight, gusting to fifteen, temperature twelve, visibility seventy-five miles." When he signed off I could hear Everett

calling 099, two valleys away. "Good morning, Don, how are you today?"

Warmth feeds courage, So eventually I propped the pants up against the wall of the tent and emerged from the cocoon into the chill of day.

And something had changed. The cold was no longer oppressive. It was just another factor to be met in paying attention to this remarkable place. It had, as predicted, become routine. Bolting up the racks became a normal task, attended with laughter and curses but without lethargy. We told stories and laughed. I told Eppler about flying down a canyon east of the Teton Range in a snowstorm; he told me about making a tough approach with the wings loaded with ice; Malin described a ride in a supersonic air force jet. We had a long conversation about systems used for human waste elimination in spacecraft, which led to a philosophical discussion of whether or not an antarctic explorer, faced with the necessity to arise and go forth for relief in the middle of the night, should instead make use of his bunny boot.

This reminded Malin to take a break from work to show me how to use the portable toilet and its plastic bags, because in the Dry Valleys nothing decayed, so all solid waste was carried out. That was what the Used Food box was for.

That little blue-green toilet seat looked cold as the proverb. I vowed to avoid its use. But I was to be here for three days. This would take considerable resolve.

We returned to bolting. The wind lifted the wind sock and let it fall. "It stands straight out at thirteen knots," Malin said. Today it seldom stood straight out.

One row of bolted stones was completed and Malin and Eppler attached it to the rack, lifting it carefully into position.

"Easy up, sir," Malin said at one end of the rack.

"Easy left, sir," said Eppler, at the other.

Malin sang: *"Oh, what a beautiful morning. Oh, what a beautiful day. I've got a beautiful feeling, a helicopter's coming my way."*

Eppler and Malin speculated about what would have happened if Malin had gone to Juilliard after all. Twists of fate. Malin had become a famous jazz musician. The Johnny Carson show: "Johnny's guest host tonight is Mike Malin. Mike's guest tonight is Carl Sagan. 'You know, Carl, I've always been real interested in space exploration.' "

In this good-humored hum, I fell into Eppler's system for keeping his fingers warm enough to work: we bolted for about ten minutes at a time, while the fingers slowly became less and less comfortable, then when we agreed it was too painful to continue, it was off with the light gloves, stick them in the shirt so they wouldn't get stiff, plunge the hands into the big bearpaw mittens, and pray for circulation. Whacking and rubbing the hands together, I could feel the warm blood coming back, trading places with the cold, corpuscle by corpuscle, capillary by capillary, until the precise moment when the whole hand was ready to be called back to duty.

The day before, we had hiked to a dolerite ridge and peered down over it at clouds moving up from the Wilson Piedmont. In Alaska people were fond of saying they walked where no one had been, which was never accurate; that state had been trod yard by yard. Here that conceit was more likely to be true. Few or none could have been here before us. Typically, Malin had shown more energy than Eppler and I, and had reached the ridge first.

That night Eppler had said, "One of the interesting things about being here, particularly in the Dry Valleys, is the idea that very few people have been here. That probably is the first time somebody has climbed up that peak and looked over the side. There's something that I really find appealing. It is a very odd feeling. When we were following Mike up I saw a footprint and I thought, That's got to be Mike's footprint because there's nobody else's footprint that could be out here."

Yet even here the precious untrodden slipped away. We had taken the ridge for ours. Most others had already been conquered.

There were footprints everywhere. Even this continent was nearly all mapped. The geographical unknown was about used up on this earth. "We have looked over the horizons," an Old Antarctic Explorer wrote recently in sadness. "Now we're looking under rocks."

It was a lament for the lost days of walking first on the face of a new planet. But all that was lost was the nineteenth-century glamour of heroic exploration, which had its last glory in Antarctica. The great mystery of the earth remained just as lightly scratched as was the ice plateau by the skis of the LC-130. When Imre Friedman's team of biologists from Florida State University, Sierra 015, looked under the rocks in the Dry Valleys, which appeared barren as the moon, they found a marvelous thing: life. The wind and the bitter dryness drove life into the stone itself, but there, in the microscopic cracks and pores of the crystal, it thrived. Mystery was unconquered. To Malin and Eppler, walking to the ridge where no one had been was tourism; discovering how the earth had been shaped by frost and wind was adventure. They bolted the tiny samples to the racks, taking again and again that infinitesimal, infinite step into the eternal unknown.

Considering this, they ruminated on the future of this place; even out here, where there were no movies, the heat of the rest of the world still shimmered on the horizon, distorting the view. Off in the *fata morgana* of civilization, representatives of the treaty nations met to try to make rules for mining Antarctica that would not infringe on their ambiguous agreement to ignore one another's claims; nations that were not part of the treaty argued that they should have a piece of the pie. Even if the west antarctic ice sheet wasn't getting warmer, Antarctica was heating up.

"My own personal view is that this place should be kept as an international hands-off zone," Malin said. "As a clean lab if you will. It's one of the few places you can go and monitor what's going into the atmosphere. Let's check what we're doing to our earth."

Suddenly a helicopter galloped into our lives. It roared up from behind a hill as if it had been in ambush. Baroom! *Thwop-thwop-thwop-thwop*. Dust, wind, whirl. The time machine, the steed of the knights of science, was out on the open range. It came thundering into our camp in a halo of heat. It was a DV tour. With a sudden flurry it populated the solitary camp with a crowd.

The Distinguished Visitor was Edwin Salpeter, an astrophysicist, one of the developers of quantum theory and a member of the National Academy of Sciences. Salpeter, in his red USARP-issue parka, with his hair swept back from his forehead as if by wind, was wild and happy and alive with energy: he was like everyone else here. He and Malin instantly plunged into conversation so urgent it seemed as if the whole future depended on what they had to say. Eppler conversed with a young woman who was part of the group with equal sincerity. It turned out later that he was suggesting that she trade places with me.

Malin and Salpeter paced back and forth across the crazy landscape, surrounded by stones that had been carved into the images of trolls, monoliths, slugs, monkeys, shark fins, piles of corpses, whales, cattle, Volkswagens, little Buddhas. Malin told him, with all his enthusiasm, about wind erosion, moving sand dunes, and Mars analogues. Then the helicopter whisked the DVs away. Much later Salpeter would describe with similar intensity what enthralled him about Antarctica:

Elsewhere people had developed theories about the earth based on data they already had, he said. In a sense they cheated, making the theory fit the data. In some disciplines you could run an experiment in which the theory (gunpowder explodes) was used to predict the outcome (boom!) and thus you tested it. You could not, however, run similar tests of some of the most far-reaching ideas, like the theory of plate tectonics. But here now was Antarctica, fresh, new, unknown. Bring your old ideas here and apply them to the rigors of this new evidence, and they would come out true or new. This was the experiment, the grandest in the world.

(3)

And now there came a time of decision.

It was midnight and still in the Victoria Valley. I stood a long time outside the tent, looking at the incredible view. The wind sock we had erected for the helo pilots—an elegant gesture, typical of Malin—hung empty on its bamboo stake. Far away, a rim of icefalls at the edge of the Clare Range caught a stray bit of sunshine that poked through the general clouds, and the whole force of the plateau seemed to lie behind it. What kept the ice from these empty basins? And what little push, what little change of heat or cold, could alter the balance and begin the slow filling process again? I stood in the cold, looking right and left, right and left again, trying to absorb it all for a permanent memory, because I knew that was all I would have; the memory could never be replenished. Right to left I looked, a repeating scan, from the hanging ice to the layered palisades of Circe and Dido and Boreas and Aeolus in the Olympus Range, to the huge pale slab of ancient rock just across the valley from our camp, seamed with one gray and two black intrusions crossing it like a track, which pointed to the black peak above that must be part of the same newer stone. I looked back and forth, watching the clouds thin and rise in the hardening cold of the evening—at the great black-and-white valley, all that open rock flecked with sandy snow, the patterned shapes that Eppler and I, bolting away, had pretended were trees (a jagged black outcrop), a road (an intruding volcanic sill), and a hillside covered with mountain mahogany (boulders). Now that the wind had gone the silence was complete; the only noise in this whole valley, the only vibration in the whole basin of cold air, was the breath and heartbeat of the three men on the hillside. It was utterly still, and I walked and stopped, and stood still, and listened past the rush of my own life to nothing at all. Life was very small here, but the rock and its presence was very large. I stood, looking, part of the immensity, feeling neither awed nor dwarfed nor powerful in it, just part of it for too short a time.

Tomorrow the helo would come again, curling up out of the valley below us with a little tremble of air that abruptly became a storm, and would land close to the tent, blowing everything that was loose, including the Used Food box, tumbling grid southeast. The nearby silence shattered, we would fling everything into the helo, tear down the wind sock, and vault the big valley to Malin's next campsite on the opposite slope, where we would unload while the restless machine flapped around our ears; and suddenly I would be sitting strapped in by the open door while the crewman leaned out to begin his litany, and all that remained of these remarkable few days, that were not too long after all, not too long at all, was good-bye. "Easy up, sir. Easy up. Coming light, sir." And far ahead, in the next season, Mike Malin would return to his sites and find evidence that the antarctic winter had assaulted his little racks with winds of up to two hundred miles per hour.

But that was to come. Tonight the valley stretched out in its embrace of quiet and its infinite shades of cool color. And slowly I realized I had a decision to make. I stood outside the tent. The bag would be warm; I had no fear now of the first slime of nylon cold, which my own heat would dissipate. But I stood outside, and the wind remained calm. More clouds cleared away from the distant hills, further revealing the edge of the poised ice. The air was very cold. But I was making up my mind. The sun sent glimmers through the buttermilk sky. Mike was waiting for me to go to bed so he could have his last moment of daily contemplation in this magnificent land. And so, finally, I reached the decision:

I was going to have to use the damn crapper.

Chapter Seventeen

Complete Immersion

(1)

"Easy up, sir." It was morning. We were off. Farewell!

At last: I was going to be warm.

The helo soared up across the stones of Bull Pass, crossing little lakes. Their disks of solid ice looked like blue coins lying loose in the sand. I would miss the remoteness, the peace, the friendship of the Victoria Valley, but now I was going home to the two-minute hot shower and the all-night radiator in the California Hotel.

And then we stopped at Vanda Station, and genuine rotten misfortune overtook me at last.

It started as a misunderstanding. We landed at Vanda to pick up a passenger, and one of the Kiwi Vandals, whose name was Malcolm MacFarland, met the helo. The pilot shut it down and everyone clambered out, and I overheard the end of a brief conversation between the pilot and Malcolm.

"We got it ready today," Malcolm said.

"Got a towel for me?" the pilot said.

"Sure."

I was all cold sweat and shivers from helping Malin and Eppler move boxes. I had an idea what the pilot and the Vandal were talking about, and I exulted. I knew what was going on: they had built a sauna. That must be it. No wonder everyone we encountered down at the little enclave of outdoor freezers looked so pleased.

That was not it. My analysis was faulty. They were not pleased because they were going to share their comfort. They were happy because they were going to see us suffer. Summer was bringing its whiff of warmth to Lake Vanda, and the ice near the shore had grown thin—it was now only about a foot between the surface and the water. That morning the Vandals had gone out about twenty yards from shore and hacked a hole through it. They put up a sign and opened the most exclusive bathing organization in the world, the Royal Vanda Swim Club.

Like lemmings, like condemned men drawn by compulsion to examine the pockmarked wall, we wandered slowly down to the stony shore. An inevitability settled over us. I made a fuss with my cameras, as if to tell myself that my business here was photography and notes, not participatory journalism, but I knew. I, too, was going swimming. A young Kiwi visitor had the same reaction. He kept saying, "I'll go after lunch. I'll go when I've got some soup in me." Then when I looked around he had a glazed look in his eyes and he was putting his shirt down on the rocks.

The hole in the ice was seven feet long and three feet wide, about the size of a coffin. Loose ice lay scattered around it where the sadists and masochists of the morning had flung it in their enthusiasm of digging. Perhaps it was just my imagination, but already ice appeared to be forming on the surface of the surly blue-green water in the hole, the only wet part showing of Vanda Lake. That water was not like the salt slurry at the lake's bottom, which was tepid. Up here it was just a fraction above freezing.

There was no chance of reprieve. The helicopter pilot stood next to me, already stripping off his long johns. His name was Randy Rothchild, and he was a steady, methodical person; unemotional, almost sedate. He was red-headed and taciturn. His skin seemed very white.

I pushed back the hood of my parka. The wind nipped at my ears. I took off the parka and put it lovingly down on the rocks of the lakeshore. It had served me well. There was a chance I might live to need it again. I unfastened my belt. We had already been informed of protocol. The only items of clothing the rules allowed were socks. They kept you from sticking to the ice.

"Polar exploration," wrote Roland Huntford in the book *Scott and Amundsen,* "[was] a moral source of suffering." "I wanted to feel my body aching," wrote Wally Herbert, an English explorer, of his sledging in the late fifties, "while my mind ordered, 'This is your heritage.' " It was indeed. "One aspect of the English romantic movement," Huntford wrote, "was to equate suffering with achievement."

Antarctica was rich in one resource: hardship. But in today's era of well-insulated buildings and gourmet mess halls explorers in search of true pain sometimes had to help things along. Even those who had no icy water available managed to make do. Winter residents at the Amundsen-Scott South Pole Station called their organization the Three Hundred Club. The first day of winter in which the thermometer dropped below −100°F, they cranked the sauna up to 200°, got in there and cooked, then dashed outside and ran around the stake that marked the Pole. Almost everyone joined. And although most polar bear clubs in civilized places permitted bathing suits, Antarctica was stark: at the Pole, as at Vanda, the only clothing allowed was footgear.

One day in early 1912, members of Douglas Mawson's expedition to the South Magnetic Pole found to their dismay that a box they thought contained vital stove parts (warmth was a preoccupation then, too) had fallen into seven feet of 30°F seawater. Mawson, who was later described as "tall and powerful, a commanding leader," stripped and plunged, rescuing the box after three dives, thus probably inaugurating the tradition of voluntary nude swimming.

Mawson, who went on to endure much greater suffering, has been immortalized by, among other things, having his name given, suitably, to Art DeVries's antifreeze fish—*Dissostichus mawsoni*. But his plunge also established a standard of futility that Vanda swimmers nobly upheld: When his men opened the precious box that he retrieved they found it didn't have stove parts in it after all. It contained four dozen tins of Australian jam.

When Mawson climbed out of the water he said with a grin, "It was not a bit exhilarating." And another phrase that seemed appropriate as I removed my shirt and put it on top of the parka was written by Robert Falcon Scott when he knew, in his tent, that he was doomed: "We shall die like gentlemen. . . ."

At Vanda the swimming club book contained a whole pageful of rules: (1) No togs allowed; (4) Complete immersion must be achieved; (6) No restriction on photography; (10) A fig leaf may be worn but must be a natural fig leaf, and must be naturally green without artificial aid. But the most important was unwritten. Although women now made up about 10 percent of the personnel at McMurdo, and some had even joined the Royal Vanda Swimming Club, people still lived by male standards. Herbert, the man who hoped for the agony of sledging, titled his 1968 book A World of Men. So the unwritten Vanda rule was simple: A gentleman, presented with the opportunity to swim, swims.

So we did. Rothchild walked calmly to the hole. He carefully adjusted the sign the Vandals had put up—an old swimming-safety poster displaying a buxom beauty and the legend Everybody Needs a Buddy. Like an old proud nude pirate walking off the plank as if it were a curb, he stepped down into the water, the first American to join the club this summer and one of only a hundred or so individuals of all nationalities who would join it all year.

It took but a second. Rothchild submerged—and came up a different man. His entire personality changed. He leaped to the surface of the ice. He shouted. He uttered expletives. He ran to the shore. He flung clothing around, trying to get arms and legs into it all at once. And then it was my turn.

Mawson was said to have begun his plunge "without a word." I was up to that, at least. My jaws were locked. I nodded a brief farewell to the spectators, who seemed unduly amused. I glanced at the small pile of clothing I was leaving. I would return. I walked to the hole. Small pieces of ice floated gently in the water. They were very pale blue. The blue did not, today, look beautiful.

I stepped in and sank. My head had to go under to earn club membership. My feet touched the stones or the ice of the bottom, my poor head felt the world close with a splash above. All around was whiteness and blueness and cold. I was immersed in Antarctica.

And then I, too, underwent a profound psychological and philosophical conversion. I gained insight, understanding, and resolve. As the water closed over my head I knew that all the mistakes I had made in my life led inexorably to this moment, and that at last and forever, whatever other foolishness I should commit in the future would never come close to this.

(2)

A few days later Dean Eppler did the same thing. When he climbed out of the hole and ran to the shore he found that the cold had turned his mind into lemonade-neuron slush.

"As I rocketed out, an endless stream of obscenities escaped from my mouth while the rest of my body went into shock from the intense cold," he wrote later. "I scrambled across the ice toward the pile of clothes, continuing to bellow while the assembled spectators greeted my initiation into the club with raucous laughter and catcalls. Reaching my clothes, I realized that I had no idea what to do next; my cold-numbed brain simply ran out of ideas, and I stood for several seconds trying to figure out what I was supposed to do.

"The familiar sight of my red parka started some wheels turning, so I put it on. It was a start, but socks and a parka are not much help in a twenty-knot wind and fifteen-degree-Fahrenheit temperatures. Particularly when you are wet. Mike [who joined the club more than once and did not repeat the experiment on this occasion] finally took pity on me and yelled, 'Start with your underwear!' "

The human need for ritual reached all the way to Vanda Station.

Like Eppler later, we all trooped up from the beach to the main building, to get inside, to sign the book, to revive on potato soup, scones, and jam. Each swimmer had earned for his trouble a small round jacket patch, and esteem, or at least a reputation of sorts, among his peers.

The helo roared away from Vanda Station and went charging up the Onyx River toward the rise of the Wilson Piedmont and the sea, leaving the land of backward rivers, the land of falling ice, the land of lost seals, the land of fishless lakes that never thawed or never froze: the Dry Valleys.

The pilots were hotdogging it, zinging through the crazy valley right on the deck, like warriors. Yahoo! Tough we are. The helicopter shot over two Kiwi backpackers who were moving up the valley toward Vanda and the big surprise that would welcome them. Someone on the intercom made a sound of machine guns. The backpackers waved cheerfully and were past. The river had not yet thawed. It was still glazed or dry. The helo wove its way along its track a couple of hundred feet up, at a hundred miles an hour, following the glitter and the stones.

The pilots were still thinking about the day's achievement.

"It's amazing," Rothchild observed on the intercom, "how fast you dry off."

They stopped at a New Zealand hut at the inland edge of the Wilson Piedmont, where it lapped up the valley and was called Wright Lower Glacier. The Kiwi hut was a single room standing on rock with the huge curve of the glacier rising behind it. Scale seemed wrong. In a normal world the hut should have been bigger and the glacier smaller. The glacier was a big old snowdrift, and the hut was a matchbox. The glacier was a heap of slag from the frost mines; the helo was a little red toy.

We picked up Kiwis, boxes full of samples, and a container of used food. Gentle 18 was again bulked out. I sat in twisted discomfort with my feet jammed sideways by a yellow duffel bag, my movement constricted by bags of trash collected from Malin's camp and by sample boxes, my arms draped over a long Scott tent folded like an umbrella. The helo lifted off and conquered the glacier, going right up its flanks.

I put my chin on the Scott tent and stared out what I could see of the window, and I wondered, Why am I here? Where would I rather be?

There should have been many choices to make from my store of longing and cold, but there were none. Outside the window a snow slope quilted by frost polygons flashed past, and I knew I would remember this journey all my life, and would find good memories and friendship and recollections of adventure in it as long as I could value anything. You grow older, you sense the light or shadow of the things you do cast ahead of you on the path; I sat there in the uncomfortable clamor of the helo and looked at light that ran far ahead. I was content. This was not a moment of life soon to be gone; it was a place so searing and true that I could always return. The constant pressure of time that drives the present was utterly released, so for ten minutes or more I floated free, like Mike Malin in the jet with the astronauts when he was a kid—floated free without the pull of the future or the drag of the past, hurtling across the ice, happy.

A voice came over the intercom. Pilot or copilot:

"You know," it said, "that soup was just what you needed to warm up your gonies."

Chapter Eighteen

No Forgiveness, No Revenge

(1)

On the bulletin board in the hall outside the mess hall in Mac-Town were signs:

"Chapel of the Snows II presents *Gospel Road*. Featuring Johnny Cash and June Carter Cash."

"Movie Sunday 4 December on O side of mess decks: featuring *Conan the Barbarian.*"

"Attention Non-singers. From Chapel of the Snows II. For Non-singers Christmas Choir. No talent preferred, but not required. If you feel you don't have any talent, but love to sing, then WE WANT YOU!!!!! No auditions."

"Sunday Evening: Dr. Lyle McGinnis will present 'Uplift History of the Transantarctic Mountains.' "

"Dial A Prayer—414"

"Forecast 2 Dec: Max —3 C/+27 F. M —10 C/+14 F. Wind 2kts 10kts gust." A fine summer day.

"HELP—Volunteer Referees needed for Volley Ball and Basketball."

The last sign had been defaced. Beside HELP someone had written, "Let me out of here." In small print elsewhere on the sign were the words "No blood, no foul."

On the big blackboard in the Chalet the flight schedule for incoming C-130s was written every day. Francis Williamson, chief scientist for the Division of Polar Programs, had written in the appropriate places. *"Event:* Aooo. *Aircraft:* XD 13. *Departed:*

Tahiti. *ETA*: MCM, 1900. *Cargo*: o. PAX: 100 16-yr.-old cheer-leaders. *Mail*: 16,000 lbs. USARP."

Lieutenant Hocking was organizing a golfing outing in which the players would hit orange balls from flag to flag down the Willie Field road. I was back in civilization. After just those four days, McMurdo seemed a tumult. Certain hopes reawakened. On the flagpole at the California Hotel there flew a red flag. The mail was in. I ran up the stairs. The box was full. I flipped through the stack. Palmisano. Palmisano. Palmisano. Nothing else.

"For many people here, there's a lot of pain associated with not having daily contact with those things that are important to them." I was talking to David Honea and Jeanne Williams, one of the very few married couples in Antarctica. It was dinnertime in the mess. "You can either maintain the immediacy of those memories and needs in your mind," Honea went on, "and suffer the pain of it until you can once again satisfy those needs, or you can put them in a cubbyhole and you don't address that cubbyhole until you can do something about it again. I think that's what happens to your sexual needs. After an initial period of time of preoccupation with it, people go into some stasis period where they may still talk a lot about it but don't get the same rise out of it . . . so to speak."

Taped to the milk machine in the enlisted side of the mess decks was a long piece of paper:

The flow rate (fcm) of chocolate milk is dependent on several factors such as the viscosity (v) of the milk, the height (H) of the milk in the can, and the force (F) exerted by the gravitational field.

i.e. $fcm \sim HF/v$

Now the viscosity of the milk is proportional to the percentage dry matter of the pasture growing in the field, while the height of the milk in the can is proportional to the number of cows milked, which in turn depends on the production of the size of the field (A) and the number of fields (N) under grazing (i.e. $H \sim NA$).

F (of course) $= Mg$

Thus fcm~mg × NA/%DM

This is called the unified field theory, and while reluctant to compare myself with Einstein, I must admit that he was unable to come up with such a solution (neither to the problem nor to chocolate milk).

The mess hall was the core of life at McMurdo. Here science blazed away over the steel trays. Here I had once seen Mike Malin and Bill McIntosh arguing at length about volcanic rock in Iceland and the interpretation of hyaloclastites. Here Salpeter had ruminated about the global experiment of science on the ice, his hair swept back from his animated face like gray fire. Here were the chocolate milk signs. Here, one evening, a half dozen U.S. Army officers wearing parodied dress uniforms waited table on a group of Navy officers, paying a debt incurred by that year's Navy football victory.

"Pure science," Ed Todd had said that night, "was never like this."

We were leaving the mess hall that night in a wind. Todd was nostalgic; it was probably his last journey south. He was retiring; not by nature, more by fate. "It is time," he once said, looking at me through those huge lenses, "to give the pleasure of bureaucratic management to a younger man."

Now he said, giving in to wistfulness at last, "I am always amazed at how much my children eat."

We walked a few paces.

"You mean these people?"

"These kids at the tables," he said. "All these are my children."

The day was so fine that the roads were muddy. We squelched along past the Bean River and the park. In due time Lieutenant Hocking would erect a sign prohibiting the walking of penguins except on a leash.

I asked Todd about the complexity of the U.S. program, with its Coast Guard icebreakers, its Navy pilots flying National Science Foundation planes, its Army and Air Force contingents, its civilian contractors, its endless complications of weather and distance. He glanced at me with that enigmatic look cloaked by the thick glass and offered me a granola bar pulled from the sleeve pocket of his parka.

"Any graduate of a management school would turn green at this operation," he said. "Not with envy but with nausea."

"Yet it works."

I couldn't tell through the prism if his look of amusement was tired or pleased.

"A lot of the younger people," he said, "and some of the older ones as well, really love Antarctica, and want to make it work."

(2)

Antarctica! Now, still dazed by the four days in the field and the Vanda swim, I seemed to watch McMurdo from a place apart. Eight hundred people lived in this city. They all stared out at Antarctica. The scientists in their red coats and their speculative eyes; the civilian employees of the contractor, Antarctic Services— ANS—bouncing around in their strange tracked vehicles or their bulldozers; the Navy men and women in green, griping about the cold and revering the helo pilots. Antarctica! Bleak stones hemmed them in, U.S. safety rules prevented them from exploring the nearby surroundings, and Herbies roared down the alley to drain the warmth from their fingers and scour all color from their faces; but like Shackleton they chose to return to this harsh place again and again.

"You don't see people talking about being here as much as you might think," David Honea said. "In terms of saying, This is really neat." He laughed. "Most of the conversations are probably the exact opposite. But when the experience is over and they talk about it in retrospect, people think, For all the bad things I said about it, it was okay."

Honea chewed on a toothpick.

"A lot of times it's not easy to articulate to yourself what you

have experienced here," Honea said, "much less to somebody else."
We had been talking about the journalism about the Antarctic,
which he thought concentrated too much on bizarre stories about
human behavior, about men who fought with two-by-fours over
women, or loneliness in the long night. He was enormously serious.
He was a big man, with thick black hair and a thick black mustache. He seemed to observe everything he said, to watch the ideas
forming steadily in the air so as to make note to himself that they
were sound. He appeared to be eating the toothpick. Honea was in
Antarctica with his wife, Jeanne, working at the satellite-tracking
station. He was going to spend his third full year in Antarctica. The
place meant more to him than he had yet seen recorded.

"You're always hearing, 'I got so crazy there I barfed down my
shirt,' " he said. "Those things exist. They always get a rise out of
anyone. But I hate to think this is the whole motivation for being
down here. The articles that focus too much on those stories don't
capture the essence of Antarctica."

A sailor came by and handed Honea a list of numbers to take
back to his tracking station. He was not distracted.

"A lot of the impact this place has on people is very sub-
conscious," he said. "It's like— You know, if you could go back in
time to the pioneers who went west, who experienced hardship,
infinitely more so than what it is to spend a winter down here—if
you could ask, 'Why did you do that? What drove you?' those guys
would say, 'I wanted some land,' or 'The Lutherans were persecut-
ing me back in Philadelphia.' That's what they'd *say*."

Honea watched this idea. The toothpick twitched. Yes. It made
sense. He went on.

"Those are the things that are easy to see and talk about. But I
don't think they are the primary motivation. These experiences
communicate to a person on much less than a vocal level. They're
satisfying needs that are pretty deeply buried in human beings."

I went back to the hotel. There, in the sauna, was Lyle Mc-
Ginnis, of Louisiana State University, who had been shooting at

the sediment out on the ice. He was an austere, thoughtful man, who maintained his reserve even sitting naked in steam. I remarked that for all his years of research on the continent he qualified as an Old Antarctic Explorer. There was a long silence. A gaffe. "At least," I said, "you're used to being out in the field."

"Yes," he said. "I find it cool and refreshing."

What the hell. I took the Eppler Memorial Shower. Three and a half minutes of illicit bliss.

The sun moved around the earth; I could not sleep. Restless, late at night, I went down to shoot a few baskets in the empty gym, a battered blue Quonset hut with a battered plywood floor and busted lamps on the walls but with the smell of dust and sweat like any other gym in the world. For a few minutes, taken by the old familiar aroma and the solitary thump of the ball, I went away into memories of other times.

I came out of the gym, and there was the white shining Sound and the Royal Society Range, white on white, gray on white, distance upon distance, all empty. But not quite empty. Somewhere out there were George Denton; Don Elston, with his lined, almost apologetic, friendly face; the four Vanda Vandals, with their magnificent dare to the cold; and Mike Malin and Dean Eppler, surrounded by more emptiness than can be found anywhere else on the planet—all surrounded by rocks blown smooth, tongues of ice lapping down hillsides, and the very beginnings of life fermenting in soft spots in the rock and in the glimmer of warmth under the cobalt blue splintered ice.

This place was not safe. You developed rogue affections. You fell in love with ice and wind. The ice and wind had no feeling in return. Scott was still here. The ice had taken him; no forgiveness, no revenge. Shackleton died in the ship coming back south; Amundsen vanished on a flight into the ice and wind of the north: "Oh, if only you knew how splendid it is up there, that's where I want to die."

Men and women here had affairs of the heart, brief and fleeting.

Was this indulgence, or was it part of the wildness of the place? This was not war; people were not going out from here to die, but that power was in the air: they were confronting the cold of the universe, they were pushing their humanness into places immensely hostile, immensely indifferent to their warmth. One day they were on the Hill, writing letters in the lounge to people who could never understand, or over at the Officers' Club building bridges of affection to people they would never see again, and the next they were scattered out on the Siple Coast, on Ice Stream B or the Crary Ice Rise, living in tents beside a three-unit Jamesway and digging their toilet pit with a gallon of gasoline poured in a hole and burned. The LC-130 flew away and who knew when it would return? It was like war, the craziness and the hardship; it was unlike war: the achievement was not ruined by tragedy.

And through all experience here ran the tick of transience. These things will not happen again.

It was the night of a magnificent day. I had gone through the whirl of the time machine again and was back from the field, from a time that was both very unpleasant and highly enjoyable. Immediately, just as swiftly as that helicopter, Gentle 18, soared up out of the Victoria Valley to replace those four days of silence with the *whop-whop-whop-whop*, the squawking of radio traffic, and the clatter of MacTown, those four days had became mythical, a time of cold black-and-white light and windbrushed rocks and a silence ringed with high ice. I had returned, had found myself eating apple pie, cookies, steak, soup, broccoli in sauce; and the helo pilots had invited me to a toga party in building 202. "Leave your inhibitions behind." I thought this time that I would keep my inhibitions to myself; I had spent enough today. I had gone through enough time zones.

But I was too restless to put the day away. Tired, sleepy, alone again, I walked out of the California Hotel at eleven at night, unable to close my eyes on the light. The town seemed deserted. No one was in the streets. The ground was frozen hard. There was no wind. Some DVs—congressmen and senators—were scheduled to arrive in the night or morning, so the flags were up around the bust of Byrd on the flat place in front of the Chalet. I wandered around, seeing no one. I didn't want to go get hot dogs and chili at the mess hall, because it would remind me of the press group, now so long departed. I didn't want to go to the Officers' Club, because it was one step back from Antarctica. I wanted to breathe this cold air; I wanted to look at the mountains. I wanted to read the words of hope on the bust of Richard Byrd.

The sun shone on the side of his face. He was glorified, a far-seeing, handsome aviator, larger than life. Behind him the Royal Societies rose into a roof of thin white cloud; as always they seemed lighter than rock, a living shape of the continent's dazzling spirit, robed and haloed by the light. On the base that held Byrd's face were inscribed the dates and names of his expeditions. I stood beside the stone and stared out across the ice of the sound, where the long straight roads between the flags led out to Warren Zapol's hut, to the ice runway and Willie Field, to the seal-viewing chamber—the diving bell, that little dry place under the glowing ice. Nothing moved; no trucks, planes, helicopters. The engines of the city were only a faint undercurrent of life, as hard to notice as the sound of my own heart. Back when the press group was here, Karl Kuivinen had described how the ice preserved the years, made note of the passing days of warmth or snowfall. How would it record this perfect day, with the sun on the mountains and every breath of air cold and sweet and pure?

Byrd's words were cut into the stone: "I am hopeful that Antarctica, in its symbolic robe of white will shine forth as a continent of peace as nations working together there in the cause of science set an example of international cooperation."

Fine words. Fine words, in a world in which fine words so often turned to ash, as Malcolm knew better than I. But here . . . This was a place of unusual dimensions: the cold, the dangerous weather, the strangeness, the affection for others that came undemanded, and the hope that not all fine words were empty.

Human beings have hopes for what they can control, and for other things they have awe. In the face of all solemnity, the awe breaks free. Byrd also wrote, describing land he was the first to see, ". . . [A]nd yet one could not exult. Nature had worked on such a large scale and with such infinite power that one could only gape at her handywork with open mouth and say: Holy smoke!"

Over on the other side of town, out by Derelict Junction, which I could see between the buildings, through wires, pipes, and red flags on stakes, there was a stir of movement. Men appeared. They were wearing sheets draped around their shoulders, fastened loosely at their waists, and bunny boots. That was all. Their flesh was very pink. They swaggered up the street, knees and shoulders bare to the cold. They chanted, and the chant drifted over to me distantly. "Heelo! Heelo! Heelo!" they shouted in unison. "Heelo! Heelo! Heelo!" Holy smoke! Arms on each other's shoulders, the half dozen men turned a corner and headed for warmth in the Officers' Club. The silence came down on McMurdo again, and the sun swung endlessly westward, circling this, the top of the world.

THE CAPTAIN
AND THE HERO

Chapter Nineteen

Character

(1)

Bright and alone, the research vessel *Hero* floated on the skin of the night. Snow fell around it and disappeared with a little hiss on the black tension, as if each spark of white were extinguished by the darkness. Snow petrels fluttered around the mast, in and out of the ship's glow like white bats from the ice caves of the south. Lights shone ahead, luminous distant blue-white shapes. They looked like a cluster of homes, seen from the fields, in which children watched television.

From the open door of the pilothouse there flew a single teabag. It too caught the light. It looked like a mouse being forcibly evicted from the bar. It arched far out and hit the water with a little slap. The captain was on the bridge.

Looking down from his familiar perch, Captain Pieter Lenie, skipper of the U.S. research vessel *Hero*, could see a stream of light approaching the ship underwater. It was about thirty yards long and several yards wide. It looked like the flow of an aurora. It was greenish orange. It flowed, it swelled and turned, it rose and fell, the individual creatures in it just barely visible, like the grain in a photograph. It was a column of sleet in the porch light, falling slowly past the ship; it was a magic carpet of life gliding through the sea. It was a cloud of krill, the riches of the south.

Lenie went back into the pilothouse and pushed the intercom button. The familiar dry Dutch accent crackled through the ship. "Wild Bill Hamner," he said, "get up here. Kreel everywhere." William Hamner, Ph.D., of the University of California at

225

Los Angeles, chief scientist at Palmer Station in the Antarctic Peninsula, the National Geographic's expert on krill, came bounding up the stairs on command. He looked over the side and gave a little bark.

"Woof!" he said. Then he giggled.

"Hee, hee, hee," he said. "That's terrific. Let's go diving."

Pieter Lenie: About five feet two inches tall; balding; white beard; Dutch accent. Autocratic, opinionated, sometimes remote. He heaved his teabags into the sea or left them in little drying lumps in odd places; he loved to tell stories about his days working up as a seaman, or of flying, or of the Japanese fighter trainer he owned. Lenie's weapon was a long, cold stare that Britte Kirsch, one of the scientists, called the stinkeye; Bryan Obst, the ornithologist, immortalized the stinkeye in a watercolor sketch that he posted in the Palmer galley. Of course, since Obst did it, the stinkeye looked like a bird, not like the captain.

Skip Owen, the curly-headed Maine Islander who had been on the Hero eleven months, liked to describe Lenie telling one of his sailing stories to a visitor. Halfway through, one of the crew interrupted:

"That's not the way you told it last time."

The captain gave him a long stinkeye.

"It's my story," he said. "I'll tell it the way I want."

Bill Hamner: wiry, stocky, curly hair and beard; a son of a Southern California artist. Hamner had a giggle and a toughness beneath it; he liked to say that in the community in which he grew up, people were only interested in quality of work and a laugh. Stu Willason, all energy and anxiety, newly knighted with his own Ph.D., compared Hamner's work—diving to watch krill out in the open sea—with his own, which involved less dramatic but far more tedious trawling and lab work: "Hamner's the cowboy of science."

The Hero: a ketch-rigged motorsailer: 125 feet of three-and-a-half-inch white-oak planking, sheathed at the bow with three-sixteenths-inch steel; a round bottom, the better for popping up out of the ice when caught in a squeeze; a green hull; red sails to take out some of the roll the round bottom gave it; built in South Bristol, Maine, in 1968 for the National Science Foundation; detested at the beginning, revered at the end. When Pieter Lenie came to the *Hero* on April 7, 1972, the ship had already demoralized five captains, and the last in this unfortunate succession called it "that goddamn green dragon." Lenie took over, made a few changes, and turned the *Hero* into a vessel that resembled himself: small, sometimes cantankerous, but highly capable at what it was asked to do. The *Polar Sea* could marshal 75,000 horsepower when it had to. The *Hero* got by on 760. It roamed the archipelagoes and the fjords of the Peninsula, as familiar with the ice and the rocks and the isolated camps as the whales. But now there was a softening of dry rot in the oak and a gnawing of worry in the heart of the National Science Foundation, and the *Hero*'s remaining days in the Antarctic were almost gone. When the captain took the ship north across the Drake Passage in April, he and the ship would leave the south forever, and an era would come to an end.

Down on the deck the divers struggled into their suits. It took about an hour to get ready to dive. That was all right, because it took about that long to get mentally prepared, too. "The cold screws you up," Hamner had said. "You kind of have to be emotionally ready."

They had dry suits like those used at McMurdo; the water was the same temperature—about one degree below freezing. The dry suits sealed at the neck. "After you've been in one of these suits for four to five hours," Hamner said, "it feels like your neck's been inside a Turkish condom." He gave a wicked smile. He was just warming up. His eyes danced. His wife and colleague, Peggy, as kind and patient as Hamner was volatile, just smiled. Hamner went on: "If you're eating garlic and you're a little flatulent, pop the seal and the suit smells like the inside of a Korean submarine."

Snow fell on the deck and made it slick. Bryan Obst and Jim Stretch were going in with snorkles only, to watch the krill's behavior in the dark.

"When you first get in," Obst explained, "it feels like someone's pushing on your head with a shovel. You get the kind of headache you get when you eat an ice cream cone on a warm day."

"Bryan was trained in advanced sniveling at UCLA," Hamner said.

"I got a B in the course," Bryan said. "I deserved an A. The teacher just didn't like me."

He climbed down the ladder and sat on the edge of a black rubber Zodiac skiff tied to the side of the *Hero*. Beneath the ship the school of krill ebbed and flowed in the ship's lights like seaweed on the current. The water was four hundred meters deep.

"Here I go," said Bryan.

He remained on the edge of the Zodiac.

"Here I go," he said.

No action.

"Here I go."

As if he had been shot, he fell slowly backward into the icy water. He sank, then rose with a blast of water and vapor from his snorkel. His voice was resigned:

"I went."

"When you first get in you have a minute of anguish," Peggy Hamner had said, "in which all you do is pay attention to your headache. But then it goes away." Obst and Stretch lay in the water for a minute, then began to swim.

The night became stranger. The two men slowly circled the ship, black corpses in the water, powered, it seemed, by the steam that emerged from their fluorescent-tipped stacks. The ship was a lighted Christmas tree in the pitch-dark night; once when Obst came up he said it looked like Las Vegas. Below it the cloud of krill billowed around the hull as if it were all that gave the

Hero support. Stretch carried a waterproof camera; when he fired the strobe it outlined his spread-eagled body. He looked like a caricature of a man being hit by lightning.

Out in the distance the faint blue lights of the phantom village glowed and moved and changed their shapes. But the *Hero* had no company; it was off no populated shore. The lights were reflections of bits of brash ice and growlers reflecting the ice light on the mast. And yet among them was life. In the quiet of the evening we could hear breathing. It came at intervals, from all around the ship. It was a deep exhale and a long gasp. There was a rattle in the breath, a little hoarseness. A pair of whales circled, going around and around the ship, feeding on the krill, watching the curious sparkle in the night, breathing the cool air.

Warm on the deck, Bill and Peggy Hamner told tales on themselves. The accepted method of examining the contents of a penguin's stomach, which was necessary to the study of krill and their prey, was not to kill it, but to use an enema bag to fill the bird with salt water (through its mouth), then turn the bird over, shake it, and collect what came out. But buying enema bags through the appropriate channels seemed an impossible challenge to even the noted flexibility of the National Science Foundation bureaucracy, so Peggy went to buy one at a Los Angeles pharmacy.

PEGGY, forthright: Where are your enema bags?

PHARMACIST, softly: Over there, ma'am.

PEGGY, loudly: Is this your largest?

PHARMACIST, sadly: Oh, you poor woman.

(2)

The days were full of life and laughter. Following the abundant krill, the *Hero* glided among the bergs and pinnacles on water smooth and bright as steel. "We're tootling around," said Bill Hamner. Minke whales and humpbacks rose and sounded, penguins porpoised, and leopard seals, crabeater seals, and fur seals lazed around on bergy bits, barely raising their heads to watch the ship pass, their orange feces on the white announcing to the world that they were gorged on krill. Skuas and black-backed gulls swooped around the ship but did not follow, since there were no fishing boats here to encourage the habit, and giant petrels soared past on those long, tapered, prehistoric wings. Clouds of Antarctic fulmars and terns passed, casting flickering shadows, and Cape pigeons flashed their elegant wing patterns at the reflections of themselves in the water. Every few minutes a ragged blue-eyed shag, a bird that looked like a black-and-white cormorant that had gone to a cut-rate taxidermist, came beating up from astern, and with a valiant effort cut across the bow and flew away. It was a compulsion, Obst said: shags had to cross the bow of anything they saw.

Stones rose sheer up out of the water; ice hung on cliffsides in impossibly frozen cascades. We passed close to the shore and the water never shoaled. "We put the bow up against the rocks in the Lemaire Channel," Bruce Carter said. "And we had one hundred meters under the keel." Bruce Carter was thirty-five. He was first mate. He hated to see the *Hero* retired: "They finally get a crew that's happy, works well together, then they shitcan the boat." We passed close under Bruce Island, a rough hump capped with a slab of snow.

"Doesn't that look striking?" Bruce said. "Rugged."

I said: "Weatherbeaten."

Bruce said: "Old."

We crept in close to a busted-up wall of ice that led up into an icefall the captain had named Patty Glacier in green ink on the chart, after his newest granddaughter. (The name would not stick.) Arched caves carved by the sea plunged deep in the ice, the blue growing with depth; Hamner was convinced I could sell an article to an architectural magazine comparing them to the Gothic arch. The captain slipped the *Hero* up to within about sixty feet of the ice, and the huge leaning cliff, all smooth white planes and blue cracks, seemed to lean out over the ship. "The captain," Hamner said, "has been known to come so close to a glacier that ice has fallen on the deck." This time the captain withdrew to a quarter of a mile, then blew the whistle at the hanging ice, hoping to break something loose. Nothing happened. Then as we turned away, the water under one enormous ice cliff was speckled with splashes made by delicate bits of ice falling from the top. That was the only movement in the whole violent mass.

Six of us were in the pilothouse: Hamner; the captain; Steve "Clamfoot" Hall, the Californian Indian; Marko, the cook; Bruce; and me. None said a word. The place was too dramatic. The ship came around a point and slipped into a bay. On the port side black-and-white cliffs rose a stone's throw away; we were in 250 meters of water. Ahead, more ice rose, block upon broken block, up into fog. Looking up, I got vertigo. I could fall backward into the sea. This place, too, was on the chart in green ink: Skip Harbor. Inside were a group of crabeater seals on a chunk of ice, but as we slid in, a pack of killer whales went out. There was a sudden sound of quick breathing and a soft splash of bladed fins, and the wolves slipped away.

Whales and ice and penguins. At the end of a dive for krill a group of gentoo penguins came past the Zodiac and circled the little boat, alternately porpoising and then swimming like ducks, craning their necks to get a look inside the big black thing. Bryan put his mask and snorkel back on and slid into the water. "I've been wanting to get into the water with them for two years," he said later, quietly ebullient. Now they swam around him, popping up red beaks almost the same color as the painted tip of his snorkel, then diving under to race around with that marvelous underwater flying stroke that turned them from the dumpy little people they were on shore into projectiles. As Bryan turned back and forth in the water to watch, the others, sitting in the Zodiac, could hear him laughing through the snorkel.

In another little bay with an icefall at the end we moved at half a knot beside a black cliff. Small cascades of ice trickled into the water. With no apparent movement the icefall made a noise like a muffled gun. "The whole thing's going to go," the captain said. He did not blow the whistle. There was a wall with a huge crack all around behind it, a swamping wall.

We were following whales. At last the whales we had seen earlier—two humpbacks—rose to breathe right against the ice. The captain pushed the throttles forward and turned to follow. Sunlight fell in patches on the ice, picking out wrinkles, cliffs, a distant hill. The whales rose three times in succession, then put up their flukes and sounded. The captain drew back the throttles and the *Hero* glided. The whales were gone. Everyone waited. Clamfoot the Indian was up in the rigging, waiting. A small group of storm petrels worked a patch of krill in the distance, fluttering over the water. The captain was a solemn man, but once a crewman had crept up on him by accident when the *Hero* was following whales. The captain was crooning at them. "Come to Poppa," he said.

The humpbacks came up a hundred yards off the port bow, raising their great knobbled heads with a gasp of breath. It was like seeing royalty. The ship was so still all the cameras could be heard. The huge animals broke the water to breathe three times.

"Flukes coming," Wade Church yelled. Wade Church was thirty-three. Someday, he said, he was going to put an oar over his shoulder and walk inland until someone said, "What's that?" —and there he would settle. He did not say where he would go to see the whales that he loved. Now he stood outside the pilot-house, watching the sea. "Flukes coming!"

The great forks of power rose slowly, dripping. Slowly they swung vertical, showed mottled yellow on their undersides against a wall of distant ice with sun on it, and slid away, the sword Excalibur going home.

It was quiet. Again we waited. A single tern flew over. Slowly the turbulence where the whales had gone faded. A faint cracking sound came from the ice cliff, then a dribble of ice. Far out in the path of sunlight ahead the two whales broke the water, spouted, and breathed, going away, two black bent backs in the brightness. A blue-eyed shag flew across the bow.

"Woof!" said Bill Hamner. "We'll just tootle over to Andvoord Bay."

In Andvoord Bay, Hamner's crew went diving. "We're doing classic ethology," Hamner said, "spending time looking at animals in their natural habitat. It takes a lot of time. You've just got to watch them and keep a record of your observations until you have an idea of what makes them work."

They took still and video cameras with them into the water. Peggy Hamner had a cold and couldn't dive, so I went out to watch with Stretch, Hamner, and Obst in a Zodiac run by Skip Owen. The day was still. Snow fell on gray water. The water was thick with brash ice, which collected in rivers of loose white on the surface.

Out on the water away from the ship the quiet was enormous. The brash ice moved in a faint swell and made a brushing sound. A mile away, cliffs of ice cracked. Once in a while a piece of ice broke off and slid into the water, and a few seconds later we would hear thunder. The cliffs rose into mist and emerged as black shapes high above us.

Stretch and Obst belted on their tanks and their weights and tumbled backward into the sea. Bobbing up again to make contact with the camera, Stretch made an exclamation. "What?" I said. But it was too late. He was already going down.

Skip rowed, standing in the boat. We followed an orange ball to which the divers were attached by rope. Around the ball bubbles rose as fizz.

The cliffs thundered distantly. The *Hero* was two hundred yards off; its engines made a faint puttering in the stillness. Snow fell. Somewhere out in the murk was the brief sound of a wave, and then a whale breathed, then breathed again. It could not be seen; the sound made it seem as if the whole landscape were alive.

A strange noise came to us across the water. It was a deep, warbling call, something like the hoot of an owl but deeper and more resonant, strung together. It must have been the song of a seal. A glacier broke off a chunk and the rumble swept across us and disappeared. Our divers came up, removed the tanks, and lay out in the brash ice with their snorkels, their backs shining black in the surrounding white.

Much later I asked Stretch what he had said just before he went under.

"I just said wow," he said. "It was amazing to get in the water and look up and see those peaks."

Skip took the Zodiac back to the *Hero* and helped the divers up the ladder.

"Beautiful," Hamner said when he got his hood off. His hair was sticking out in all directions. His skin was chafed by the mask. His mind's eye was still full of krill. "You could see a lot of their molting today. They are so amazing. Just one of the phenomena of the world."

The three men peeled off their suits. Their faces were raw. They looked battered by the cold, as if the brash had rolled them, pummeled them, robbed them of their strength. Even Hamner looked utterly weary, beaten.

"Hell of a lot of work doing that," I said.

Hamner said: "Woof."

Stretch said: "But we love it!"

Hamner's eyes came back to life. He grinned a great wicked grin. He said:

"Are we *men?*"

(3)

In the afternoon we moved through soft grease ice, and down in the galley crew members and scientists watched *Fiddler on the Roof*. Jews were kicked. War came. Above, the night brought its cool blue twilight and then its darkness, and the krill came up to the lights again.

I went up at the dim edge of the night with Peggy to take a photo of a school of krill that lay right at the surface. I went up with the camera and a big strobe, although she pointed out that the flash would bounce off the surface and not illuminate the krill. We went up to do it anyway. Snow was falling hard, further complicating matters. I set up the camera, set the flash, and fired.

Several hundred thousand krill leaped from the water as if electrocuted. They jumped in unison. The jump was a hiss and a crackle. They made the sea sparkle as far out as the flash reached. We looked down into the water. The school that had been combed smooth with its common movement was now scattered, with krill staring off in all directions with their little bug eyes, still just beneath the surface. I looked at Peggy. She looked at me. We grinned. She said:

"You're going to have to do that again."

Late at night snow fell, and birds dropped from the sky. They hit the deck and Bryan Obst gathered them in. Most of them were Wilson's storm petrels, the small black birds that flickered low across the waves, showing a spark of white tail feathers, and flew home to the shore at night to nests under rocks to feed their young. The snow fell heavily in large flakes and shone around the ice light, and the birds, attracted and confused by these sparks, flew into the mast and the rigging, and fell, stunned.

Bryan swept them up, put them into his pockets, and took them to the lab. He was working as a diver here for Hamner, but he was studying the energy use of storm petrels for a project of his own. This birdfall was manna to him; he suddenly had a whole group of stomachs to suck out and study. He stood in the ship's lab, sucking stomach contents with a tube and a syringe and blowing them into bottles. He talked to the birds—"I know it's uncomfortable having a tube down your throat, but I'll get it out in a minute"—while Stretch and I and Bruce Carter lined up with handfuls of more birds.

The whole ship crackled with life. Wilson's storm petrels fell to the deck; white snow petrels, less foolhardy, fluttered at the snow in the lights like moths; at the surface of the water, krill fizzed at each shadow that passed; and up on the foredeck a single big south polar skua, which had also met grief in the rigging, paced back and forth as if this whole show of antarctic extravagance were put on at its direction.

Then the snow stopped and the birds stopped falling, the skua departed, and the downpour of krill sank away out of the light, leaving only a few stragglers twitching near the surface. On the surface all was black and white again and the teeming life was invisible, like the hidden roar of blood behind a white, calm face.

(4)

On the video Lee Marvin killed another German. The little low room rang with the sound of machine gun fire and cannons. Young boys fought through desert, dying. Almost everybody who was off duty gathered around the dinner table, watching. The mess was bright and noisy. In the hall between it and the galley was a sign, typed on National Science Foundation stationery, dated December 18, 1968, the start of the first season:

> The rigors of the operating environment, the frequent need to serve as host to foreign visitors, and the necessity to retain a touch of civility in tedious surroundings remote from civilization for extended periods lead to the conclusion that it is in the best interest of the United States Government that alcoholic beverages, in modest quantities, be dispensed on board the Antarctic Research ship *Hero*.

Tonight we had all had our one beer or our single glass of wine. The surroundings were not, however, tedious. Outside, in the twilight, the wind was picking up, driving the sea and the *Hero* before it. Inside, Lee Marvin put the knife to another German just as the war ran out. I slipped away and climbed the stairs to the pilothouse. Bruce was on duty. The little room was dim. The wind blew from astern and showed thirty knots on the gauge.

The sea was dark gray. Sleet swept across the ice light. The ship heaved forward on the following swell. It was very quiet. Bruce pored over the radar screen, which revealed mountains ahead.

"We're going into the Lemaire," he said.

We talked quietly about the *Hero* and his own career. "I'm too old for this shit," he said, but he lighted up a cigarette and grinned. "The *Hero* is not the most comfortable ship I've been on," he said, "but she's got a lot of character."

Down in the mess a 1973 Ford Mustang named Eleanor raced through the streets of Culver City, California. The room was full of the sounds of crashing and tires smearing themselves on pavement. Culver City was all adult bookstores and car washes. The massed police forces of ten Los Angeles County towns pursued the Mustang. Most wound up colliding mysteriously with one another, while the Mustang leaped fuel tankers and got away.

After an hour of this I surfaced, climbing back up the stairs to the pilothouse as if slowly awakening, rising up out of a rage of colors and sound into the darkness.

No one was on the bridge.

The *Hero* moved slowly through the night. The tachometer showed 100 RPM, just a purr. I looked out the windows. Snow or rain blew across the ice light on the mast. First, past it, all I could see were the bits of brash ice illuminated by the light. The ice bobbed out ahead of the ship like blue-white lanterns carried across the night by phantoms. Soon there appeared, to port, a slight glow high in the sky, which seemed to outline a ridge. The glow was moon behind cloud. Along the ridge edge was a paleness in the dark that must have been hanging ice. Then, ahead a quarter of a mile, a great black cliff slowly appeared to my widening eyes, a vertical slab in which dark gray seams of snow ran like a skeleton of the rock. The *Hero* moved steadily toward this wall of stone.

Then, as if possessed of its own instincts in this cold world, the *Hero* turned from the danger, slid around the promontory, and emerged into a widening channel. I climbed the ladder that led up from the pilothouse, and there was Bruce up in the icehouse, with the steering device called the dodger, bringing the *Hero* to its night's sanctuary.

In the morning the wind would be gone and we'd continue on to Faraday Base, the British station out on a group of rocky islands south of Palmer, to pick up two Americans. The *Hero* had dropped them off a week before. That day the Brits had shown us around. Like Scott Base, much of the station was connected by sheltered halls. It had a big recreation room and a magnificent bar. There were pictures of the Queen, of Prince Philip, and of Mariel Hemingway. The Brits were tough; they came to stay. "A lot of these lads have been here for two and a half years," said a man called Mouse, the station leader. One of the lads led us around the little archipelago in a dinghy, past an ancient, graying sign that stood on a pile of rock: British Crown Land. Possession! A skua stood beside the sign, mocking it.

Our guide's name was David Burke. He was from the east coast of Fife. He had been here since December 1981. He was going home in March. He did not look forward to the return. I asked him if he felt acquainted with the outside world anymore. "We get the news," he said, grinning. "But I don't want to hear the news anymore. It's just killin' and wars anyway. When the news comes on I go for a walk."

Now, on the *Hero*, Bruce turned the ship toward a lee coast. He brought the throttle back. The momentum died away. The snow swirled at the light. He climbed down from the icehouse and put the dodger away. He turned on the red light above the chart table and wrote in the log: "2145. All stop. Girard Bay; waiting for daylight to proceed."

Below, in the mess, Eleanor died at last in a car wash. The car thief got away. The movie ended. The screen went blank. Someone went back to the VCR and put in another cassette. Lee Marvin returned to the screen and knifed the German once again.

(5)

The days were full of life and laughter. Only once did I see the sadness of the captain at the approaching end of his antarctic career. I stood in the pilothouse one evening while he recalled his past. He talked about sitting in his father's barbershop in the port city in which he grew up, listening to the stories the seamen brought home, developing his life's resolve. He talked about being torpedoed on a merchant seaman during World War II. He talked about riding out a storm in the confines of Crystal Sound, south of Palmer, when the wind at the nearby Adelaide Station recorded 110 knots on the anemometer and then blew the anemometer away. Slowly the light of the outside went dim, the blue of the passing icebergs grew intense, matching the twilight, and then dimmed too, and he became an insubstantial, ghostly little man, silhouetted in the red light of the chart table. Tell me the history of the *Hero*, I said. He looked at me a long time, no stinkeye.

"The ship was built in 1968," he said, "and was taken out of service in 1984. She worked like hell all the way in between. That's about all."

Chapter Twenty

Sacrifice

(1)

Palmer Station lived by the grace of the glacier. The base was two blue-and-white buildings on a rocky granite point just down the hill from the edge of a tongue of the Marr Ice Piedmont, which lay for miles along the perimeter of Anvers Island. Rocks just behind the station were scored, so the glacier had been where the station was, and would be there again. But for now it was slipping back: there were paint marks from another year on the stone several feet out from today's edge.

The glacier commanded the scene. Out the window of my little room, which was outfitted with Navy bunks that folded up into the wall and came complete with metal batter boards to keep you in when the station rolled, the glacier came down to the water's edge in the bottom of the cup of the bay. There, a quarter of a mile from the station, it always moved, calving every day into the bay. Every few hours the thunder rolled distantly into the station and people near windows looked up to see the last trickle of ice following the new little bergy bit, and to watch the slow roll of the surf wash up on the point. When the fresh ice, full of bubbles of air compressed by the years of fallen snow, landed in the water, some of it broke into pieces and floated away as brash. The sea washed against it, the bubbles were liberated, and the whole bay snapped, crackled, and popped.

Palmer was different. It was warm. Most of the month I worked out of Palmer the temperature ranged from about 28° to 40°F. After

McMurdo it was balmy. On the little islands just offshore, moss grew in deep mounds of green; the station got its water from a pond behind the buildings filled by glacier meltwater that didn't even have a skim of ice. The air had a tangible aroma to it, a richness of life.

Most of this was due to excrement. The surrounding islands teemed. The islands were rocky and covered with penguins. The birds stood among the stones, and looked, from the station, like acres of black-and-white daffodil flags, unblooming. From the depth of the pink nutrient the penguins deposited on their rookeries, the plants should have thrived.

Among the penguins small elephant seals wandered like slugs, leaving behind them a trail of brown slime. The enormous males of the species lay in communal mounds, like piles of legless, living Red Angus cattle. An elephant seal was a vast mound of flesh, humping along the ground in waves of blubber, opening one nostril like a hose, leaking yellow snot. Once while two people from Palmer were walking past a mound of seals, a single Adélie penguin came running out from around the pile toward the people, as if at last it had found something that didn't assault all the senses at once with grossness.

The seals didn't seem to mind. They lay together in wallows, blubber against blubber, burping and farting and groaning in their sleep. Up at the station the sound came faintly on the breeze, and it sounded like a distant group of motorcyclists trying without success to start enormous engines.

Skuas bred in the higher rocks of the islands. They were bad-tempered, fearless birds that dive-bombed invaders even after their chicks were gone. Wherever you walked, a skua was plotting an assault. The bird came sailing in from the blind side with its landing gear down and tried to whack you on the skull with its heels. When I wandered on the islands I learned to hold my notebook above my head, warding off attack with a paper plume.

Once I traveled with Stan Scott on his rounds to collect data on plant growth and weather conditions on the islands. We drove from island to island in a small Zodiac, which gave the blue-eyed shags a lot of trouble, because the little boat went about as fast as they could fly. On our way to Stepping Stone Island, about a mile from Palmer, several shags crossed the bow diagonally, but one poor bird, approaching from directly aft, never made it.

Stepping Stone was covered with rocks and limpet shells. Scott had dug into this curious gravel over a foot and had not come to the end of the shells. They were brought to the island by giant petrels, who ate the limpets and carpeted the island with unfinished limestone. The island also was covered with nests, and within each nest lived a single giant petrel chick. The word *giant* was both the name of the species and the description of the chick. Each fluffy chick was about the size of a small turkey. They could not go anywhere yet; if you came too close to one, the chick would open its enormous beak, screech, and vomit on you. For this trait, giant petrels were nicknamed Stinkers by early sealers.

Stepping Stone was also occupied by about twenty fur seals, once the prey of those same first visitors to the Peninsula. Driven almost to extinction by the nineteenth-century killing, the southern fur seals were making a comeback, and this abundant presence on Stepping Stone was a new advance. The fur seals were as beautiful as the elephant seals were ugly. Their fur was sleek and rich, and they moved with alacrity and suppleness across the rock. This movement allowed them to be aggressive, although they had refined a curious tactic that was easy to translate into human terms. If you approached one it would utter an authoritative bark and might even attempt to chase you away by running at you on its long flippers. If, however, you stood and did not yield, it would usually turn abject, sit back down, raise its nose sadly to the sky, and whimper like a puppy.

We ate sandwiches on Stepping Stone, near some of the ubiquitous plots staked out by Sierra 033—Vera Komarkova, of the University of Colorado, who was studying the plant ecosystems. She marked out her rectangles with welding rods, string, and toothpicks, and hoped that the skuas, seals, penguins, petrels, and people didn't destroy them. While we ate, the surroundings were full of action: fur seals growled and whined, petrel chicks hunched around in their nests and stretched their new wings as if in astonishment at this vast growth on their shoulders; their parents circled and circled the island on their strange, stiff, pre-historic wings; and always, in the distance, the glacier boomed.

Near where we ate was a dead skua, with one wing gone and the other one lying nearby, its skull already almost skeletal, and a metal band around its leg. The band was the work of Sierra 012—David F. Parmelee, of the University of Minnesota, who had banded almost every skua in the Peninsula. This corpse was not unusual. There were bits of dead creatures everywhere on the islands, stuck in the guano goo: half-eaten penguin chicks; dried beaks; single curled-up feet; a ribcage, picked clean; a handful of vertebrae like a necklace dropped from the string; a bit of feathered skin.

It all fit. From where Palmer Station stood at the edge of the grinding ice, the world was a simple place: life, death, and fecal matter.

(2)

Satellites roamed the night sky. Space was busier than Antarctica. Bryan Obst and I sat on a rock on Bonaparte Island, across fifty yards of water from Palmer, waiting for thirteen storm petrels to feed their chicks, watching the bustle in the heavens. We could often see more than one satellite at a time, crossing above us with those cameras and those intelligent songs. The air was so clear there was hardly a twinkle; the sky had depth of field. We could tell that the satellites were closer than the stars.

Bryan Obst, Bill Hamner liked to say, was the only man on earth who could produce a bird from a stone. His business here was to evaluate the energy consumption of the storm petrel, which turned the krill it ate into a high-calorie oil. The storm petrel, as a species, was one of the most numerous birds in the world; knowing how it used energy could also contribute to the understanding of krill.

To tie time and quantity together, Bryan raided chicks. He had found thirteen baby petrels hidden in the rocks of Bonaparte Island, and a couple of times a week he went out to the island at dusk, pulled each chick out of its nest in the rock, put the contents of its stomach in a little jar, put the chick back, waited for the parent to come in from its foraging at sea to feed it. Then, just when the chick was feeling full again, Bryan went around and pumped it out once more. He did the job, just as he had on the *Hero*, by sticking a thin tube down the bird's throat, sucking on the tube with a syringe until it was full of orange oil and bits of half-digested krill, then blowing the contents into the jar.

"Taste good?"

"No. Tastes like bitter soap."

Now, with his first round completed, we sat on the rock waiting, as the adults, full of hope and food, came around and vomited into their chicks' mouths. When they were done, two hours later, we could go around again. Science was not always kind.

Across the tiny strait between us and the station, the lights of Palmer glowed out into the night. Behind them the glacier rose, a cool gray presence in the darkness. Under its broad sweep the lights seemed just a couple of specks, shining down on a little apron of trodden snow.

"Looking at Palmer when I first got here," Bryan said, "I remember thinking, My God, there's just two little shoeboxes sitting there. I couldn't believe it was going to be a whole world."

Small waves washed brash ice against the rocks with a sound like the rush of surf. Off in the distance an elephant seal struggled to start its motor. It did not succeed. Below us the Zodiac that brought us to the island moved back and forth on its rope in the surge, a dim yellow shape. In the dark air around us storm petrels flitted like bats, and once or twice one of them cried up in the stones.

I asked him what single experience here represented Antarctica.

"Last year we went out to collect some birds," he said. "*Collect* is a euphemism for shoot. We were in a Zodiac off the *Hero*. The wind came up, and the birds we wanted to shoot, the snow petrels, which are fantastically beautiful little birds, were all around us, but it was too choppy to shoot. So we went back to the *Hero*. But they had decided to trawl while we were shooting. And they expected us to be gone longer. While the trawl was in the water they really couldn't pick the Zodiac up. So we had to follow them for a while. And the weather started getting reasonably rough: thirty- to thirty-five-mile-an-hour winds. I really had a sense of the Antarctic then. When you're at Palmer, it is so comfortable you're buffered from it. But there in a little rubber boat, in the Southern ocean, with icebergs all around, I got a real sense of being in the Antarctic." He paused. A petrel cried. "Part of it being," he said, "that we couldn't just climb on the *Hero* and go and eat cookies."

A skua stood on the rocks to the westward and uttered a sound halfway between a squawk and a cluck. The elephant seal in the distance now sounded less like a motorcycle and more like a very large, dying leather balloon.

"The thing that's so startling about the animals here," Obst said, "is how tame they are, and how close you can get. My first love is behavior. Just to be able to sit a foot or two from a penguin on a nest and have it going through its absolutely normal behavior —vocalization, the whole bit—is wonderful. Binoculars are re- dundant. Species after species. Only a few don't act that way. The gulls are skittish and the storm petrels are little bastards."

The moon rose over the mountains and cast a long line of light down the glacier. A layer of clouds, more like a snuffing of the sky than something made of vapor, slowly came across the stars, moving south. Soon the pack ice would come up the other way, to cover the sea as completely, thundering before the wind. We talked about the mail, which was supposed to have been brought down by a Chilean Air Force (FACH) flight in February. When the *Hero* met the flight there was only a handful of letters, which meant that somewhere a full sack had not got on the plane.

"That was a morale cruncher," Obst said. "It put a hole in the season." Now he was expecting to see that mail on his way out on the FACH flight in March. "I already know what I'm going to do. I'm going to organize the letters chronologically and read them as they were written." He could see each of those letters, every detail. He rubbed in his good fortune at being able to fly home in three hours across the turbulent Drake Passage, knowing that I was sentenced to the last journey out on the *Hero*.

But over the years there had been many slips between the ice and home. One of the most famous was the story of the boxes full of rocks, collected during an arduous season by a geologist and shipped back in wooden boxes by air. The workmen at a South American airport looked at the boxes, said to themselves, "Those are good boxes, and all they have in them is rocks." They dumped out the rocks and took the boxes home. Some weeks later the anguished message arrived: "Where are the boxes of rocks?"

"Americans are strange people," the workmen said to themselves. So they went out to the edge of the airport, where the runway was built up with local stones. They carefully filled the boxes back up, nailed them shut, and sent them north. Bryan was wrong to speak with such certainty of flying home.

The temperature dropped and a breeze came up. Sitting still, we got very cold, and at last it was time to go pump out the birds.

Bryan worked bare-handed in the breeze. The nests were marked with strips of reflective tape that caught the flashlight beam. "No rattlesnakes here," he said, reaching under a rock and bringing out a bundle of gray feathers. In went the tube, out came dinner. Slowly the last bottles were filled. The clouds had crossed almost the whole sky now, leaving an open wedge to the south, where the moon still lighted the distant mountains.

A good surge was running by the time we slipped back across the strait to the station; I had to step into small surf to pull the Zodiac ashore. But there was Palmer, warm and inviting. We went in to sleep, but I lay awake with the big eye in the little room, while the glacier mumbled and the brash ice crackled like fire. There were days when it seemed to Bryan, he had said, that while he was here life at home moved on. People he would have met, or friendships that would have grown, or women that would have found him pleasant to be with, were lost to this cold southern wind. It was not desperation; it was a quiet wondering: while I am away has the world passed me by?

(3)

On Tim Targett's table a small orange fish slowly died, twisting and opening its mouth and gills wide and curving its body in its desire to appear larger and more ferocious to this implacable predator that marveled at its instincts but would not commute its sentence: to be sacrificed to science, to the study of aging by otoliths. In the biology lab were many tanks of running water and much life, but the word *sacrifice* came frequently into the conversation. It rang strangely, as if it were a rite they went through here, letting blood, bringing about death, to satisfy the god. The word implied more of a respect for life than the word *harvest*, which would be used if any of these creatures were ever killed for commerce. But sometimes sentiment recoiled. When a big octopus caught by the *Hero* went under the knife for its otoliths and then ended up in a magnificent feast prepared by Targett and his colleague Richard Radtke, members of the *Hero* crew came parading into the mess hall carrying protest signs: Give Us Back Our 'Pussy.

There was a different sort of sacrifice at Palmer one afternoon. Four of us sacrificed warmth for beauty; we went snorkeling. The Hamners, who had issued the invitation, watched and instructed while we put on the borrowed dry suits: jam feet into suit; pull calf strap tight to keep air from going to the feet and drowning you, feet up; shove hands through wrist seals; shove head, oof, through neck seal. "I love this," Peggy Hamner said, watching.

We rode a Zodiac to a bay by an island. Jim Stretch had a theory about the immersion headache: splash your face before putting on the mask. I tried it. No headache. Just exquisite facial pain.

But once you were in the water, the pain faded away. We swam among brash ice and bergy bits. The tiny icebergs, which seemed so small from the *Hero*, were enormous. Each bore a dazzling bit of white cake on top, but below it was a deep, looming blue, plunging down into indistinct depths. There were lines of frosted ice and lines of clear ice in these frozen boulders. The clear ice was rippled on the surface, and the ripples shone. In the surge the big hunks of ice rolled back and forth like deep-hulled ships, and large bubbles rose from the depths. Underwater the ice crackled, and sometimes the ancient air that escaped could be seen as a fine haze rising from a berg's side.

Individual krill swam around in the ice. I reached out to touch one with my big lumpy black-gloved hand and the little creature jerked in the water. It was the same escape mechanism we had seen in reaction to the strobe, on the *Hero*. The bergy bits had deep fissures and holes; in one crack a tiny school of about thirty krill rose and fell with the water as the berg rocked. In one piece of ice there was an arch and a column; the column shading from white frosted ice to clear ice, making a small crystal palace—and in the center of it a single krill, transparent and crystalline as its environment, glittered with tiny flickers of red and silver. This was the wealth of the Southern ocean, which Russians and Japanese were already coming to harvest, and which so many others thought would be the next great antarctic resource, as great as the whales of the last century. The belly of this krill was plump and green with diatoms; it repeatedly embraced the water around it with its fishing baskets; it rowed with its paired legs; and it had its castle of ice all to itself.

(4)

Later, Richard Radtke said his face got tired from smiling.

"I'm persistent," he had said earlier. "And some people say 'Hell with you,' and with other people we get it done."

This time we got it done. What Radtke wanted was to go to the glacier. All these weeks he had been sitting there in the lab, studying his collected otoliths, the tiny bones of the fishes' ears, in which rings laid down daily would reveal age. All this time he had been walking those laborious crutched steps to the *Hero* and up to the mess hall, looking up at the blue cliffs and the great white whaleback of the glacier, wondering what it was like up there where these coastal pebbles disappeared and it was truly Antarctica. Now, just a few days before the season's end, he had put the team together to get him there.

Radtke was probably the first handicapped person to work in Antarctica. He had multiple sclerosis. His legs were almost useless. It had taken an enormous amount of that persistence to get down here in the first place; now that he was here he had to get to the glacier.

It was a day of goodwill. Everyone was happy. A couple of the civilian contractor's crew had tied two-by-fours to a chair to make a sedan chair; down at the station they lifted Radtke into the front-end loader, drove him the hundred yards to the end of the road, and set him in the chair. He nearly fell out on his face. This required adjustments to the chair's design. That completed, they tried again. It worked.

The day was cool and gray but almost calm. Radtke rode up the trail carried by four men, his big blue eyes and his pale bearded face alight under a yellow helmet, his long, nearly useless legs flopping around, encumbered by an enormous pair of bunny boots, his good humor unflagging as the men hoisted him around: a talkative, brightly alive man, carrying his disintegrating body with grace.

By the time he reached the edge of the glacier the alleged price for this favor, which had involved a six-pack of beer, now became a case, then four cases.

"No," said one of the bearers. "He's only going to find out the price when he wants to go back down."

At the base of the glacier, where the long white slope rose up to dissolve in the sky, several people wanted me to take a photo for the Division of Polar Programs of Radtke lying behind the snowmobile, so it would look as if they had towed him up the slope on his back. This suggestion was eventually vetoed, and they hoisted him carefully into the back of the machine and set off up the flagged trail to the ridge.

For all Radtke's persistence and loquaciousness and slowness at getting around, which had irritated some at the station when the weather indoors had grown close and on edge, to those who went to the glacier with him there was only one memory of the man that would stick. It was that joyful face, that slender, bearded, radiant face, way up in the world of white light on the glacier, gazing out at Antarctica.

The place where we stopped was the end of the trail, where an emergency airstrip had been laid out on the ice with barrels. From here the glacier was a broad white slope, beyond which we could see the islands around Palmer, mountains standing in a line fifty miles long, and a grand sweep of gray sea. The black-and-white mountains that guarded the Lemaire Channel and rose on the edge of the Graham Coast caught the sun where it came out from under the high flat overcast. Layers of stratus gave the sharp rocks mystery, and light shining on snowfields behind them gave them depth. Far out to sea an ancient berg, tilted and eroded into columns and ramparts of ice, stood out in the sun for a moment and then, as the cloud moved, disappeared in the gray distance, just as if it had slid down the waterfall at the end of the earth.

The near islands, their abundance of wildlife invisible from here, threw up bursts of silent spray, and past them to the north a hint of sunshine lighted the reef where the glacier swung around the bay next to the station and came down to the sea. The glacier showed the blue fangs of an icefall, and the blue cliffs where it calved. Beyond the view of ice the high cloud glowed white and showed dark shadow, a reflection of a distant glacial coastline painted in ice blink and water sky.

We stood around, looking at it all. There were a few flags on bamboo stakes, three-quarters buried in snow; there were a few aviation fuel drums; there was a very large silence. Radtke stood on his shaky legs and beamed. And then, far out in the straits between the distant mountains and Anvers Island, the *Hero* appeared, returning from another krill journey to take Radtke and half the others to the Chilean FACH flight on King George Island, to the FACH flight and home.

The *Hero* was fantastically small. In the human scale we had applied to this view, it should have been six times as big. Among the swells we had thought of as waves it looked like a chip. It was a model; a bit of green balsa wood with two toothpicks in it, kicking up a spark of spray in the enormous gray blue waters between us and the mountains. Up on the ice mountain the seven scientists and construction men looked out at the tiny *Hero* in silence. How small they all were, these scientists, these workers. And how brave to go out in the middle of all this majesty, this overwhelming mystery, to continue the painstaking, tedious, and everlasting task—taking otoliths home in bottles, counting the eggs of krill, measuring the fractures in hyaloclastites—of trying to understand it.

They carried Radtke back down the glacier and took photographs of him in his wheelchair against various symbols of Palmer Station: a fuel tank, a six-foot-high penguin portrait. Inside, Bryan Obst was illustrating the menus for the next day's gala farewell dinner party for the people leaving on the FACH flight, and Peggy was looking up the word *fettuccine* for him in a dictionary. "Did you know," she asked me, "that *fettuccine* has two *c*s?"

"Of course," I said.

She looked at me. "O you purveyor of limited truth."

Rich Radtke was taking off his warm clothing down in his lab, the glow of cold and delight on his face.

"Is that Antarctica?" I asked.

"That is Antarctica."

Chapter Twenty-one

I, Polarman

(1)

Before the *Hero* entered Maxwell Bay, taking the scientists to the Chilean FACH flight, the captain said to Bruce:

"You know, planes are funny things."

Bruce said, "Uh, yes." Now what?

"You know, sometimes they don't fly."

"Yeah," said Bruce. As a philosophical observation it was probably correct.

A silence. Then the captain said:

"Load the laundry room up with Tide."

(2)

Skip Owen ran the Soviet flag up the mast of the *Hero*. In the antarctic breeze the three flags flew bravely together: the United States, the Union of Soviet Socialist Republics, and the Republic of Chile. You never would have known. The *Hero* glided into Maxwell Bay, which was also called Bahia Fildes, where two stations lay side by side: Chile's Teniente Marsh Station, to the west, and the Soviet Union's Bellingshausen Station, across the creek to the east. The captain dropped anchor off a big rock and sent a Zodiac ashore.

Over a century and a half ago a curious meeting had taken place in the waters off Deception Island, not far from here. These islands were as far off the edge of the world as anyone had yet sailed; they were the outer perimeter of knowledge and daring. Stories of the

253

encounter differed, but the more dramatic told of a fog in which a small ship piloted by the U.S. sealer Nathaniel Palmer drifted.

"Palmer, it seems, was on watch himself that night," Ian Cameron wrote in the book *Antarctica: The Last Continent*, "and when he struck one bell he was startled to hear an echo. 'I could not credit my ears,' he wrote later. 'I thought I must be dreaming.' He told himself that the echo must be a trick of the fog; but when an hour later he struck two bells, exactly the same thing happened! Each hour, we are led to believe, when Palmer tolled the bell, there came a ghostlike toll in answer out of the night."

In the morning the fog lifted, and there, in that wilderness of ice, were two other vessels. "Unable to identify their nationality," Cameron wrote, "he hoisted the American flag. And the ships he had shared the night with ran up their colours in reply: about the last flag in the world that Palmer could have expected, the double-headed eagle of Imperial Russia."

The two ships were the *Vostok* and the *Mirnyy*, commanded by the Russian captain Thaddeus von Bellingshausen. The small American vessel was the forty-seven-foot sloop *Hero*. The American was invited aboard the Russian ship, and there he said that he had sailed on over the known edge and seen land.

"Among other things," Palmer remembered years later, "I informed him of our Trip to the South in Latt 68 degrees & the discovery of a Land (never before seen) and it was him that Named it Palmers land."

It was the first sight of the antarctic continent.

But this story, like all those that involved discovery and claim, was wonderfully romantic but was not certifiably true. The records of the *Hero*'s voyage were vague, and neither the fog and bells nor the naming of Palmer Land appeared in Bellingshausen's own record of the event. So the discovery of Antarctica remained, like all the questions of ownership that came later, ambiguous.

The *Hero* dropped anchor off the two bases. The land was ice-free but bleak. It was gray, black, and brown; the hills were dusted with green moss. The *Hero* was here to unload a dozen scientists who were to take the Chilean Air Force (FACH) C-130 back to Punta Arenas and thus home. The ship had also brought a scientist named Connie, who was to have spent the winter in Palmer. Connie was ill. While the first Zodiac was ashore with Wade Church, the second mate, who presumably was discussing the flight schedule, the scientists packed up their belongings and joked about food and families they would see now in a matter of hours.

Then the Zodiac came back. There was news. The captain had been right. Planes are funny things.

Hello, the Chileans had said. Nice to see you. FACH flight? Oh, yes. We have a FACH flight leaving in, let's see, twelve days.

Somewhere, communications and logistics had been scrambled.

While the *Hero* and the disheartened scientists waited at anchor as word of the problem flew from the ship to Palmer, from Palmer to Washington, from Washington to Santiago, and then back, in the form of a decision, a new legend grew among the crew and scientists of the captain's prescience.

When the word came back from Washington they were still trying to figure out what he had meant about the soap.

(3)

In the twilight a keening rose in the wind. It was a long, unbroken, high howl, with all the power of the sky behind it. I was walking the mile back from the hotel with Bruce and Ken Lashbrook, a seaman. In the twilight the wind had gathered strength. Once a Chilean Toyota Land Cruiser passed us, sliding around on the soft mud, and we could see the lights of the *Hero* shining out there by the big rock. It was a little familiar glimmer in the broad darkening of the sky, but it was home no longer. I was to stay here on the dark wet rock of King George Island and wait for the *Hero* to come again.

Then, as we passed the battered blue-and-white buildings of

Bellingshausen, the wind rose, and the wail rose in the air with it, an unearthly moan that brought the wind and the night alive with pain.

"You have to walk back alone in this," said Ken, grinning.

But Bruce was more to the point.

"We have to go out to sea in this," he said.

I said good-bye to them at the little dock, where a high-tide line of brash ice glowed softly with the last light. The Zodiac splashed away in the growing chop, and the *Hero* departed. The scientists had to get home, so that whole boatload, every one of whom had expressed smugness at one time or another to be crossing the Drake by air, was now on the way to that dreaded passage. As we had awaited the decision of the National Science Foundation on that matter—go home or go back to Palmer to wait for the flight—Obst and Stretch had offered to hold a contest for guesses as to what the decision would be. The winner, they said, would get five scopolamine seasickness patches. Second place would get a handful of oyster crackers. Everyone had known what the decision would be. Leave Connie to catch the FACH flight, but take the rest across the Drake.

At my request I disembarked to await the *Hero's* return. My stay in the Antarctic was not finished, and I was afraid that if I crossed the Drake once and found myself a day's flight from home, it would be impossible to come back.

So I walked back up to the hotel alone. The keening was gone. It must have been the array of antennas at Bellingshausen, howling in the wind. Now it was full dark. Shapes of hills against the paler darkness of the night sky were hard to judge for distance in the clear air. One hill I thought was a mound was a mountain three miles away. The mud was soft. Once I thought I had wandered off on the wrong road and was headed for Arctowski, the Polish base fifteen miles on over the mountain. I felt more out in the strangeness than ever. I was now completely cut off from familiar things. I was in Chile and Russia all at once, and above all in Antarctica.

A small cry came from the hills. It was a single voice, expressing loneliness. It was a Wilson's storm petrel up in the stones. It cried again and again, expressing what I felt, and I walked on, feeling for the road, unable to see my feet or the ground in the blackness. This place was utterly unfamiliar to me, unknown.

Unfamiliar, indeed. I followed the glow of lights to the orange-and-cream building the Chileans called the hotel and found, in the lounge, twelve young men sprawled around on the chairs watching James Bond on the video.

(4)

I awoke to the sound of the voices of children. Like the woman's laugh through the wall of the stateroom on the *Polar Sea*, it did not seem real. It was a dream, perhaps about my own two kids, playing in the yard behind the house, throwing sand in the spring, leaves in the fall. But I was awake, and outside the windows the dark bare hills of King George Island, Antarctica, rolled down to the sea, and the sea rolled on to the glaciers on the opposite shore, and I could still hear the children.

But there were no children in Antarctica. Long ago, it seemed, I had been talking to Jeanne Williams at the mess in McMurdo. Late in a previous season, she said, one of the few adventure cruise ships that challenged Antarctica each year had docked at Mc-Murdo for a visit and David and Jeanne had been walking in the streets. They had seen two very strange people come walking up on the mud from the Chalet. They were so strange they might have come from another planet. It would not have seemed odd if their feet had been webbed. These people were dressed like everyone else—in parkas, wool hats, gloves, and boots—but they were very, very short.

Jeanne and David stopped and watched these small people, try-ing to figure out just who and what they were. The little people came rolling happily up the road. And slowly it occurred to Jeanne what they saw: *children.*

So these voices were haunting. But they were not illusion. Out in the hall two little boys ran and shouted, and in the lounge four other kids jumped back and forth over a rope tied between two chairs. There was no cruise ship in town; these children were residents of Antarctica. They were the sons and daughters of six families who had been moved from Chile to King George Island in February to the drumbeat of national acclaim: FAMILIAS COLONIZADORAS DE LA ANTARTIDA PARTEN HOY. They were colonists.

"My children were no more than five years old," German Camacho, the base physician, told me later, explaining why his family was chosen. "My wife was a nurse. We were healthy. I told my wife of the possibility to come here. She said, 'Let's go.' She said I work too much in Santiago. See children one day a week. Here I can see all day. We also think it is important to be one of the first families with children to come here. Maybe that is number one thing we think is important."

He had two sons: German, five, and Francisco, four. By the time he and Ana Maria left, the children would be seven and six, and there might be another in the family. The colonists signed up for two years.

For all the glory, the decision had not been easy. Antarctica was a place of hazard and mystery.

"When we were many miles away, in Santiago, we thought many things were dangerous," Camacho said with a gentle shrug. "But now, living here, it is not dangerous."

The children went to school in the room next to mine in the hotel, which had a blackboard instead of a bed. Their mothers sang to them and wrote on the board. They did not teach the children the whole importance of their presence. It would not fit on the board. The importance lay not in the adventure in which they engaged, but in the bare fact that they were here. The most complex layer of claims on the continent lay over the Peninsula, where three nations said they owned the land: Great Britain, Argentina, and Chile. The Antarctic Treaty's famous Article IV said that nothing a member nation did could enhance its claim, but the treaty did not prohibit actions that might enhance a claim in the absence of the treaty. Without the treaty, decisions on who owned what might rest upon the theory in international law of effective occupation, which could include such diverse precedents as having a police force or supporting guano collectors. So Argentina and Chile, whose maps placed the only color upon the antarctic continent and who believed viscerally in their ownership, had applied laws, mailed letters, maintained aids to navigation, and brought children to live in Antarctica.

As wind and rain lashed at the windows, the children raced in the halls and jumped rope. Their feet were light and quick. Their mothers' voices were soft. It was hot new blood in the cold.

Winter was bearing down on Marsh Base. The wind was constant, sometimes throwing snow hard, like handfuls of sharp sand. In the afternoon the mothers packed their children into a Land Cruiser for the ride down to the six cream-colored, flat-topped houses that sat on a slope and made up their town: Villa Las Estrellas—Village of the Stars. The wind nipped at fingers, noses, and ears. They had been here two months and had twenty-two months to go. Perhaps the pursuit of effective occupation was a cynical use of children—except that it was so good to see them. The families warmed Antarctica.

My second night at Marsh the families and officers piled into the trucks and came back to the hotel for bingo night. They all sat around a horseshoe of tables while the children played around their feet. They called numbers, ate hamburgers, laughed and laughed, and I felt so out of place that I left the hotel and wandered back down the mile of dirt road in the twilight to the room where the enlisted men were eating at a long table. No military weapons were permitted by the treaty, but, like the United States, everyone had their soldiers.

I felt so odd and American, standing at the door while the men ate, that I just hung there, the bits and pieces of Spanish I had all clabbered up inside of me, and finally the chief helo pilot—Chilean or American, they were all the same, brave and happy—shepherded me down to a seat near the table's end. After staring at my plate for a while I loosened up. The bottle of Cervesa Pilsner probably helped. Words began to reappear out of the dust, and the men were all very pleased when I pointed at a dish of butter and asked for the lard. They gave me a couple of hamburgers with good salsa and pickles, and we managed to get our points across, about snow, wind, and *frio*, and especially about the famous *El Hero*—except for one sly-looking individual who, from what I could understand, wished to begin an import business with me with boxes of *chamisas*.

I walked back up the long hill to the hotel in light rain. Wet, the mud had a shine and glitter; it was like walking on a path of starlight. Because of ruts I thought once that I saw two shadows moving beside mine. I almost turned, but the shadows disappeared. There were no cries from the birds in the stones tonight, and there were no howlers in the wires, although the rain was windblown. Nations kissed the ground and brought children, but they hugged the foreigner when he stepped ashore. Who owned this harsh land?

(5)

"Do you smoke?"

"No," I said.

"Ah," said Dr. Oleg Struin, of the Soviet Arctic and Antarctic Institute in Leningrad. "Then you must drink."

"A very small amount."

"A very small amount," he said, "very often."

He whisked a tablecloth out of a closet and laid it on a low table beside a couch in his office. From the same closet he removed four cut-glass wineglasses and a bowl of thick cookies. He started a hot plate under a kettle. On the wall behind him was a line drawing of the face of Lenin. Over the kettle was a portrait of Thaddeus von Bellingshausen. In the window grew a tiny orange tree. He waved to chairs. The two East Germans and I sat down. He poured cognac. We raised the glasses:

"Antarctica!"

I was across the creek at Bellingshausen. A Chilean scientist who described himself as a psychobiologist had taken me to meet the East German biologists, three young men from Berlin who were studying birds. We found two of them: Hans and Martin. They swept me off on a tour of the station with as much enthusiasm as if I had brought beer or *Playboys*, although the walls of some of their rooms were already well papered with pages of the latter.

Bellingshausen was old, spacious, spartan, and clean. On the walls were photographs of spaceships and astronauts. The ceilings were high. American stations had blazing green posters of spring on their walls; the Russians, when they weren't officially celebrating space, had quieter reminders of home. On the walls of the meteorologist's office were a cool painting of a winter scene in sunshine, another line drawing of Lenin, a charcoal of fields, and a simple black-and-white photo of a girl in a very short dress carrying milk cans. The most flamboyant illustration in the whole station was a poster pinned up on the back of a door in one of the rooms of the little hospital: it was a large color photograph of a naked woman's torso, printed over with an eye chart.

In the hospital I left my boots at the door and walked around stark rooms in slippers, with the Germans and the two doctors, who, with twenty-five very healthy men in their care, were enormously bored. They longed to operate on Connie, who needed no operation. They suggested through Martin that perhaps I had a pain on which they could practice their acupuncture. I'm healthy, thanks. Why two doctors? A familiar story surfaced here again: Years ago, they said, a Russian physician at a coastal station on the other side of the continent had to remove his own appendix. Ever since, two doctors.

I conversed haltingly with one of them, Alexander, whom everyone called Sasha. Sasha's room was decorated with a single *Playboy* foldout and black-and-white photos of a girl in grainfields. Sasha was tall and dark, a city boy from Moscow. He was one of the few single men on the base. His eyes were bright, and he often laughed.

There was a balalaika on the bed. Through Martin, I begged for a tune. Sasha sat down on the bed. His smile went away. "He says in Russia a man who plays balalaika must put on special face." The face Sasha put on was sincere, solemn, serious, soulful, lonely. The little tune he played was lonely, too, a delicate refrain that reminded us all of places we had somehow chosen to leave.

He put down the instrument and grinned again. He said something and Martin translated. "I have no family." He said something else and waited for me to get it. "I am free man." He laughed.

Paths between buildings were raised from the mud on wooden slats. A single large dog, whose name was Bourra, wagged and barked at us indecisively as we crossed. Outside were large, weathered, orange tracked vehicles and four-wheel-drive trucks. Everything was familiar, but slightly changed. It reminded me of McMurdo and Scott Base and Palmer, but not quite. This place— from the bulldozers and the trucks to the instruments in the weather office and the photos in the satellite-tracking station to the friendly bearded men—was vaguely familiar. This place was like one of a pair of islands on which the animals had evolved varied ways to fill the same niches of survival. The American bases were the other island. Same needs, same struggles, different choices. We had common ancestors, but we took separate ways. It was like looking into the hard, weathered, grown-up face of the brother you didn't know you had.

Then there we were talking with Oleg Struin, the station leader, a bulky man with a mane of black hair, a small mustache, and a grin of ready delight. Drinking tea, cognac, and, finally Czechoslovakian liqueur, we worked our way through communication. He spoke very little English, and I, straining most of the rest of the day to think like a Chilean, kept trying to talk to him in Spanish, which he spoke not at all. We worked out a slow but reliable system: he said something in Russian, Martin and Hans discussed it in German, and then they relayed it to me in their capable English. I'd answer, and it would make the long circuit back, while both of us tried to shortcut it with gestures and short words. We all drank more cognac.

"I, Polarman," Struin said, bypassing Martin. He was fifty-one. He had spent most of his career either in the Soviet Arctic or in Antarctica. "Four years Vostok. One year Mirnyy. Two years here. Nine years Arctic."

"Your family?"

"Wife comes to Arctic. My wife is Polarwoman. No problem."

He had been in Bellingshausen the year before. He had gone home to Leningrad for six months, then returned.

"No problem for Polarman," he said. We raised our glasses to Polarmen.

"Biggest problem is psychological," Struin said. "Food very good. Clothing very good. Condition very good. Is important work all the time. People no work, rest, only dream. My meteorological, he has no time to think of psychological problems; he work every day."

Hans and Martin looked at each other. They both had families in East Germany. They would be away from home for eighteen months, including the weeks coming and going on the ship. Chile flew mail to Marsh Base on C-130s at least once a month, but Russia and Chile had broken diplomatic relations when Allende was overthrown, so the planes contained no mail for Bellingshausen. The separation was complete. They knew about working to muffle dreams. "We work hard so we do not think of it," one of them said later. Now they agreed that this would be their only trip south.

"Ah," Struin said in English, with a sly, happy grin. "I very often listen to this. 'I only want one year. Enough, enough, enough.' Then I hear at institute. I hear say, 'I like to go again.' "

We three did not yet know about this. This strange desire we had not yet experienced. We knew all about the other kind. But he might be right.

So we raised our little glasses and grinned back at the Polarman. Oleg Struin had an antarctic presence all his own.

(6)

Who owned this land? The United States, for all the flags that Byrd dropped and the cairns Larry Gould left behind, made no claim. The Soviet Union, for all its stations ringing the coast, made no claim. Twelve nations had signed the treaty; seven claimed land, five made no claims and refused to honor those that did. This should have been a problem.

I walked back up to the hotel that night in fog. The walk, with its uncertain footing, took about half an hour. Behind me, the lights of the two stations were swathed in a misty glow. John Heap, head of the Polar Regions Section of the British Foreign and Commonwealth Office and informal dean of the treaty system, said once, with his perennial delight, "The treaty says *this*: Here is an insoluble problem. Let's set it aside."

Just like that: set it aside. Claim or no claim. Suddenly all those overheated issues of sovereignty, boundaries, ideology, possession, and jurisdiction were declared insignificant compared with the goal of keeping peace in Antarctica.

I had been on or around the continent for just two months. But already I was rootless. Home to me now was any shelter. The road home glistened, but dimly. It was hard to find my way. Two or three times I thought I heard the breath of the dog beside me, and once I thought I felt the brush of its nose on my leg, but when I looked around there was nothing. I was alone, deluded by the fur whispering at my ears, the wind nuzzling at my clothing.

I slipped in the mud, but did not stumble, did not fall. The dark was very deep; the sky showed barely a glow. The fur-lined hood closed off all sound but my own breath and movement. I was very loud. At last the lights of the hotel appeared suddenly, close. The hotel was on stilts, and lights behind it glowed through underneath. It seemed to float in the fog.

I went to get some boiled water from the container in the kitchen. The visiting Air Force officers were watching a medical drama in Spanish. Blue gowns, surgical masks, and a vast pump or syringe was stuck in someone's belly. I'm healthy, thanks. One of the officers got up to get some butter. We conversed briefly. I told him I had just come from Bellingshausen.

"Life at that base is very strong," he said in English.

"You mean hard?" I said. *"Difícil?"*

"Sí, sí," he said. "Is not comfortable at that base."

"Big work hours," I said in Spanish.

"Sí, sí. Hard."

But what he said first was also true.

(7)

Carne asada for lunch, Russians for tea. Fire in the eyes, fire in the gut. The British ship *Bransfield* came by in the morning to pick up an airplane ski stored at the Marsh airstrip. Somewhere on board was David Burke, of Fife, going home, going back to the wars and the killin' and the news. He wasn't so far from it as he may have thought. "We used to stop in at the Argentine bases," one of the crew members said. "Now we keep our distance." Some of the Brits played a game of pool in the recreation room, and the Chileans put "Strawberry Fields" on the phonograph. You wouldn't have known they claimed the same land.

After the red ship bound for the Falkland Islands faded out into blowing snow and whitecaps like the slow end to a summer movie, the Uruguayan Air Force major whose idea this was started up his barbecue fire. He had one small problem: the wind was blowing so hard that he couldn't cook outside; so he dragged the pile of coal and trash wood inside a big open-ended storage shed and lit it in there.

We are in Antarctica! We can do anything! We can also get burned to the ground. Coal and wood smoke filled the big room, ash floated down like light snow, and an occasional bit of driftwood exploded, showering sparks into a pile of bags wrapped in plastic. Everyone was so happy and careless that I didn't even bother to read the labels on the sacks; I was sure they were explosives. But the fire that all the safety propaganda of the U.S. and Kiwi operations led me to expect was not to happen here.

Smoke and celebration. Connie came down from her sickroom and stood around with the women, drinking hot red wine and eating barbecued lamb and big yellow potatoes. The women knew the isolation of this world of men; they gathered around and worked to make her happy. The men ate chunks of five or six chops with their fingers. Captain Jorge Dumont, second-in-command of the base, a big, booming joker of a man with a kind, sardonic eye, hugged and carried and jabbered baby talk with Gabriele Miranda, the one-year-old daughter of the chief meteorologist. Dumont's own daughter was born in Chile a month after he arrived in Antarctica. When he first saw her she would be a year old. "I get videos on each *avion*," he said, smiling. "I send, too."

Outside, the wind roared. The *Bransfield*, out in the strait by the same name, encountered winds gusting to seventy-five knots. Snow blew across the black dirt just outside the big open door. The wind rocked one of the two Land Cruisers parked there. The other had no suspension left at all. It would not have rocked until the wind turned it over; riding in it was like being dragged around on a plank.

Late in the afternoon I played table tennis in a room behind the kitchen with a new acquaintance, Alejandro Fernández del Río Sánchez. He was a small, intense young naval engineer who was growing a beard and who gnawed fiercely on the unfamiliar fringe of his mustache while he beat the tar out of me. Alejandro leaned hard into everything he did; when he smashed the Ping-Pong ball he was prone on the table.

Then, trading all this heat and laughter for the cool austerity of
the Russians, Connie and I walked across the creek.

In my mind, made sensitive in recent years to the differences
between my society and that of the Soviet Union by daily reminders from my government, I noticed something. As soon as we
arrived, Struin welcomed us effusively, again produced the tablecloth, and took five glasses from the cabinet. He used his telephone, and almost instantly two others joined us, Sasha the doctor
and another man, introduced as Dimitri. Was there a need, I
wondered, for a Russian not to be seen to be alone with Americans? Even in Antarctica suspicion could not be still.

This time we drank Riga Black Balsam, a liqueur black as coffee.
There was considerable discussion about what it was, and after
consulting a Russian-English dictionary, they announced that it
was made with forty grasses. We chased this fiery substance with
round German Christmas cookies and delicate lemon wafers, then
had to try a mixture of balsam and vodka, chased by peppered
tomato slices. Our communication was more stilted than ever,
because Sasha and Dimitri could drum up two or three words of
English between them and I was still thinking in broken Spanish.

We spoke briefly about the Antarctic Treaty and politics. It was
a subject that made our hosts wary, although Struin laughed about
the inspections that were so dear to the hearts of the Americans.

"We no need inspections," he said, grinning. "Believe. No
problem."

Connie asked cool, succinct questions about women doctors in
the Soviet Union and then we broke away into a discussion over
which was the better city, Moscow or Leningrad. Struin pulled out
photo books of his home, and Dimitri resorted to giving me the
metric heights of buildings in both cities in German. Then we
showed each other pictures of our children, and again Struin
triumphed, emerging from a back room with a two-foot-high bronze
relief silhouette of his younger daughter.

We asked Struin to compare the Arctic and Antarctic.

"Arctic has hunting, fishing," he said. "In Arctic small town, ten, twenty thousand. Here, no more synthetic, very good for us. For me natural is better. Here it is more free."

We raised a toast. Struin grinned. He said:

"Antarctic is Antarctic."

On the road to the hotel in the evening twilight Connie was quiet a long time. After the evening's conversation I found myself talking broken English to her: "Is good time, tonight." She said:

"It's too bad we don't know Russian. It was a chance to meet somewhere that is not Russia and not America. You want to be able to say, All this propaganda!"

We walked a little farther. The wind was behind us, easing us up the hill. She said, "All those people looked familiar."

Where have I seen you before? In my family album or in my dreams? Do those eyes of yours run in my blood? Are you my enemy or my brother? Out in the wind of Antarctica the answer was easy. Between Oleg Struin's office and the beach stood another common artifact, a post bearing arrows pointing home, with the distances in kilometers: Mockba 15,200. You wouldn't have known. Our differences ran shallow in the cold.

(8)

"Many people have great emotion to look again at a family, a home," said German Camacho. "We have a Russian grandfather here. When he saw my children he was kissing them, crying."

The children were like fireflies, each a little Tinkerbell. They were fragile, flitting sparks of energy, dashing around in their bright coats and making everyone think of home. "If you want some color," a sailor once said to a southbound group in Christchurch, "take it with you." The children were live color in the black-and-white landscape of King George Island.

But the black and white raged against the color, and the thought came of the twenty-two months in which that color must thrive and grow and be happy. "I don't like snow," German Camacho said. "I don't like ice. I like to look at Los Andes from below. But here I am on Antarctic land. It is my work and for my family. The cold is our biggest enemy."

The families lived in comfortable three-bedroom homes modeled on houses built in the Canadian Arctic. They had American kitchens, and freezer doors on the outside. The housewives bought food from the storeroom next to the table-tennis room and talked to their families once a week for a half hour by radiotelephone.

"Do you know the word *loneliness?*" I asked Camacho.

"*Solitario?*" he said. "No. No. We do not have that. There are many people living here. They are good friends. We know Polish man and Russian, and many people. Argentinian. They are good people. Many people come here from other places. We can talk, we can eat, we can walk, we can play. We can do many things. We begin a new life, not only for us, for all people who are living here. We have a city, a little city here."

The city's hotel was comfortable but spare: a stem of halls bearing small rooms; communal showers and toilets; a kitchen and lounge. It had been the scene, two years before, of the first international conference held in Antarctica. This had been a meeting between representatives of the treaty nations. The meeting had set up negotiations to develop a system for distributing possible mineral rights to Antarctica without disturbing the fragile balance of ownership and nonownership the treaty now preserved. On the walls of the lounge were plaques from Brazil, China, Italy; Antarctic friends.

In the bathroom were two signs:

The first was in Spanish and English:

"Water is difficult to obtain. Don't misspend it."

The second was in Spanish only.

"*El agua no es potable. No la beba.*"

Don't drink the water.

This was why Alejandro was here. He was studying the bugs in the water system, which were encouraged by the hotel's sewage system, which was too close to the reservoir. I was studying the bugs, too, personally and at length. The ailment that the *Hero* crew called the Chilean grunge had found me here.

Near the bathrooms was the only scientific laboratory at Marsh Base. On one of my frequent journeys in that direction I opened the door to look inside.

A U.S. naval officer once observed condescendingly, "If the Argentines and Chileans have a scientist, they keep him well hidden." Perhaps the scientist was in here.

No. The room was about twelve by twelve. It contained no equipment. It contained no scientist. It was full of bedsprings and mattresses, stacked against the walls. When scientists came to Marsh Base they worked in the field.

The U.S. self-righteousness was not accurate; one scientist and several graduate students were at Marsh while I was there. But this was indeed no Camelot of science. Compared to the vast undertaking of McMurdo, this was more an Omaha of science: mostly, except for the complete lack of weapons, it was an air force base.

Back down the road at the main base, where up to three hundred people lived in the summer, the officers ate in a small room apart from the men. After my visit to the long table I was kindly advised by Jorge Dumont that I must eat with the officers. "You understand, please, Mr. Reagan," he said. My own name being difficult, I was president, by acclamation.

At the table Dumont was joyfully in command. He had a facility of expression. He mimed an eating-lemon face, then the face of a drunkard. He set off sparks with his jokes, and the sparks ran glittering around the table through the young men and shorted out at me, the dumb *periodista*.

Dumont put a record on the phonograph and we ate boiled pork on April 2 to the sound of "We Three Kings" and "Little Drummer Boy." The troops in the next room had finished their meal and were now watching a war movie. In our dining room a charge built up in the stereo system and every few minutes discharged, sending a tremendous crack resounding through the speakers. So we consumed our meal to the sound of machine guns and bombs, Christmas carols, the phonograph exploding, and the joyous laughter of Dumont.

"Life is short, Mr. Reagan!" he said. "You have to laugh! You have to make jokes!"

From the officers' dining room Bellingshausen Base seemed farther than it was. "Chileans and Russians amigos here," Dumont said. "But no politicos. No diplomatic relations." Once a young lieutenant went over to trade blue jeans for Russian hats. It was seen as an expedition, and in its overt purpose it failed. When he returned, all gathered around him. "No exchange," Alejandro explained in English after the discussion. "Much vodka." The lieutenant did not appear distressed.

For me it was no expedition. I just walked across the creek. And for a week and a half that became the pattern of my days. I ate in Chile, played Monroe Doctrine table tennis with Alejandro, then walked across the creek to the Soviet Union.

The *Hero* was on its way back across the Drake when Oleg Struin, by himself, knocking my theory about dangerous Americans in the head, took me over to the Bellingshausen mess hall to watch a movie. The title of the movie was, in French, *Sport, tu es paix*. It was about the 1980 Moscow Olympics.

It was the middle of the afternoon. The building was deserted. In a hall an unfinished game of chess stood on a table: black had the king and one bishop, and white had the king and one pawn. On another table were stacked piles of propaganda pamphlets in English. *The Soviet Navy. The United States: The Prop of Reactionary Regimes.* They seemed silly and inoffensive. I stuffed some in my coat; Struin said nothing.

In the lofty dining room the floor was just dry from mopping, chairs turned over on tables. We righted a couple of chairs and watched *Sport.* The movie was impressive; it was in Russian, it was not a propaganda film, and it had marvelous animation and sequences on each sport and on peripheral activity like coaching and radio broadcasting that carried themselves past any problem of language.

The projector was not impressive. The left side of the picture kept going in and out of focus, and the volume rose and fell until Struin went up into the projection booth and, from the sounds of it, disassembled the entire projector, then put it back together four or five times before the sound was right. "Contact loose," Struin said.

We returned to his office and the little glasses. We toasted *Sport, You Are Peace*; we toasted Leningrad; we toasted his boss. "I like Antarctica," he said. "My boss is fifteen thousand kilometers away." Last, we toasted children.

Leaving, we encountered Sasha and Bourra in a hall. We stood jabbering across the dog in various languages for a while and then Bourra started licking my hand. We laughed.

"Bourra: Russian father," Struin said, "Chilean mother."

We laughed.

Struin said something in Russian to Sasha.

We laughed.

I said, in English:

"Diplomatic relations."

We laughed. We understood one another.

(9)

The road home was familiar: the wind and the cold. It was a little piece of raw Antarctica between oases. I strode along with sleet slashing at my eyes. The road climbed a ridge; when it was light you could get a glimpse of surf to the north. Now in the dark the invisible surf roared. Somewhere out there was the *Hero*. Suddenly, again, I was happy just to be here, to be at ease in this roaring, hard, strange world, sharing, for a short time, this hardship, this toughness, with the men and women who lived on the shore of Fildes Bay. I'm an Antarctican; I can sleep on the ground.

The Land Cruiser with the decent suspension came past and the driver gave me a lift.

"Colder," I said in Spanish.

"*Claro*," he said. "But no snow."

"One day," I said. "In morning. Will look out, see snow everywhere."

"*Claro*."

Winter was coming. The *Hero* was coming. El Presidente was coming. The plane that took Connie back to the world would bring a load of journalists. Two days later another flight would bring General Augusto Pinochet, the president of Chile. All week the men had been painting buildings and putting up warnings. By the night before Connie's flight the whole place was staked out with new Off Limits signs and red chains. The president would come to kiss the babies and possess the ground. The only place that was truly off limits to him was Bellingshausen, but no one put a chain up there.

There were those in the U.S. program who deplored these overtures to ownership, but some other nations only smiled. "We look at the whole thing with rather lofty disdain," one diplomat once told me. "You may think you're solidifying your claim, mate, but it's totally ineffective." The great thing about the central ambiguity of the treaty, he said, was that it let people satisfy their jingoism with possessive statements, then ignored them.

The night before the journalists arrived all the young officers shaved off their new beards. They were going home. And something else happened. As if their return to the world of government and territory kicked off a hormonal change, they stopped making happy jokes and started brooding about communism. Dinner was somber, an occasion for demands of me why Ronald Reagan, whose name I bore, was so weak about the Russians. My own impressions of the U.S. administration being somewhat different, I dodged argument. But my friend Alejandro, aggressive as ever, cornered me in the bathroom of the hotel that night.

"We see the problem," he said, leaning forward over a sink. "We see Russians' power"—he grabbed air with his hand and shook the closed fist—"take other countries. We know the problem. We military men know the problem. We cannot turn to Russia." One hand cut across the palm of the other. "We turn to the United States and—" The hand cut the palm again. "We need *strong* government."

At dinner one of the young men had said something very old and very familiar, almost as familiar as all their faces had become.

"If there is a war I will kill a Communist," he had said, "because I have a wife and son."

(10)

The snow came that night, and in the morning the whole world was white. The white did not stay. The ground thawed it out and the mud emerged again. In the afternoon the first plane arrived, after a work crew had persuaded a single thousand-pound elephant seal to vacate the middle of the runway, where it had established a presence during the night. Connie left, and all the young men left, but that night at dinner Jorge Dumont presided at a tableful of *periodistas* that looked just the same.

It was as if I had gone away for a decade and returned to eat again with the same men. Across from me now was an older Alejandro, less eager, a little tired, all his energy now gone into a sageness, a quiet alertness. His English, always the best of the group, was now excellent, and he translated the witticisms of the group. The visiting priest reminded me of the lieutenant who had gone trading with the Russians. He told a joke, and the one who was Alejandro repeated it.

"Someone in Chile goes to the priest, and asks:

" 'Father, is it a sin to eat meat?' And the priest says:

" 'No, my son. It is a miracle.' "

Laughter.

"You understand," said my translator, "this was in *Communist* Chile."

For dessert we ate fresh pears peeled and sliced in thirds. The journalists, eight hours from Santiago, had no special interest in these delicacies, so I collected three dishes of them and ate them all. It had been two months since I'd eaten anything truly fresh. I discovered something: the pears were fruit from another galaxy that extraterrestrials brought in the night to tempt me. I had fallen. I would search for that flavor the rest of my life.

All the plane's cargo had been precious. Before dinner the dining room had been deserted. I had found Jorge Dumont sitting in his crowded little room. He looked up and grinned.

"You see," he said, "no one is here. They are having their sugar—their letters, their things from home."

Dumont's wife sent him a can of honey and six magnificent large red apples, which he had carefully arranged, one by one, on a shelf above his bed. He would eat them, one every other day perhaps, to make them last. They were the most beautiful, juicy, crisp, sweet apples in the world.

He casually reached up and took one of the apples in his hand.

"Mr. Reagan," he said, "would you like an apple?"

I looked at the apple. I would be back in the world of abundant apples within two weeks. He still had a year. I made him put the apple back on the shelf. But that was not a thing to forget.

(11)

In the morning the Chilean journalists milled around with nothing to do but watch the soldiers painting signs and look across the creek at the Russians. And then, without fanfare, a small green ship materialized in the calm water beside the rock, flying three flags. I raced up to the hotel to get my things, but for the journalists the *Hero* sat out there like a fresh pear in the bleak branches of the south; when a Zodiac came ashore for me the journalists respectfully comandeered it to go out to the *Hero* for interviews.

Awash with journalists and video cameras, the Zodiac arrived at the ship. The captain gave the whole thing the stinkeye, but he couldn't escape. He was their man. They rolled the tape, gathered around him, the Antarctic's famous skipper, and pried from him terse observations on ice and ships and wind. But they wanted more. Here they were, awaiting the visit of their president, who was going to kiss the earth and hug children and assure the nation he was standing on Chilean soil. What could be a better addition to this story but a small concession from a United States representative? Of course, he was only the skipper of a small boat; all the more likely that he would say something tactless and useful.

So one of the reporters asked:

"Captain Lenie, who owns Antarctica?"

The captain gave him a long stare. The reporter did not, of course, recognize what it was. Britte would have known immediately. Finally the captain said:

"I own it. I have to have somewhere to run my ship around. And I've been here longer than anyone." He looked at the camera. "It belongs to me."

(12)

I made my farewells to Dumont, and to Camacho and his family. I took a handful of letters to mail for the East Germans. "Come to Berlin," they said. "Come visit." I extended the same invitation, but they only laughed, kindly. I went last to the chief's office at Bellingshausen, to the high room up the slope from the signs that pointed with longing toward Russia. "Good-bye," I said to Oleg Struin. The Zodiac was returning to get rid of the journalists and to pick me up. I gave him a USARP jacket patch. He gave me USSR Antarctica envelopes. "Antarctic Treaty is good mechanik," he said. "Is friendship." I shook his hand and turned to go.

"Come back and sit," Struin said, "when have time to rest."

He walked me to the door. Small hard bits of snow eddied down in the doorway, emissaries of winter. It was getting colder at Bellingshausen.

"Have a good year," I said.

He grinned. No problem for Polarman.

Chapter Twenty-two

Ice and Fire

(1)

The doctor looked up and saw me taking a photograph of the ruins.

"Yes, yes," he said. "This is very important picture." He had deep bags under his eyes. His hands shook. They were spotted by blisters. Sparks had caught him. His men helped him climb down into the Zodiac. They were very gentle with him. He looked around as if he were being followed. "Very important picture," he said. He slipped on the wet rubber and slid to the floor of the Zodiac. His men helped him gently to a seat.

Behind him the ruins smoldered. It seemed impossible that this had been an intact base twelve hours before. Now it was a black heap of burned timbers and twisted corrugated metal. Little orange flames burned in nothing that looked combustible, as if they consumed the iron itself. The place looked more like a wreck than a fire; something had blasted it, crashed into it, torn it to pieces, and thrown the pieces in a pile.

Only the small orange emergency hut at one end of the base had survived. That and the Argentine flag at the top of the hill were still there, and the signs that read in English and Spanish, Welcome to Almirante Brown Base. You Are in Paradise Harbor, Antarctica.

Almirante Brown Base was gone.

The news reached Palmer at about 12:30 in the afternoon. It

278

came from New Jersey. The message from twenty-five miles away had gone fifteen thousand miles. At 6:00 A.M. that morning, the message said, a fire had started at Almirante Brown, just around the corner of Anvers Island, on the shore of the Danco Coast— four hours sailing time in the *Hero*. The station had burned to the ground. The seven winter residents at the station had survived. Most of their radios had been destroyed, but they had managed to get a message out to Marambio, and that base had passed the message to Washington. Washington called the *Hero*'s operations office in New Jersey. The *Hero* was the last ship of the season. It could save these men from a very bad winter.

The captain had the ship away within an hour. He had been quiet since the ship left King George Island. He had taken the ship out on a short, intense science cruise for Stu Willason's group, and had added to the legends when, after the ship had searched for krill for hours without seeing a thing on the sonar, he had emerged from his cabin as the *Hero* was passing through a line of brash and said, "Fish here. It was like throwing the nets on the other side of the vessel; the trawl net came up bulging."

Now he emerged from his melancholy. He bustled around the bridge. He drove the ship himself. He was almost loquacious.

"Well, well, well," he said. "If it's not one thing it's ten others."

A little later he said, "Almirante Brown was like a home. The same people kept coming back year after year. I wish it had been one of the military bases."

Shortly he said, "I know how it feels to be a survivor."

"The skipper's feeling good," Wade Church said. In a somber way it was true. The *Hero* had just been fading away into history; now the little green ship would go out deserving its name.

It was very late in the season. There was a new chill in the air, something hard and lasting. Bits of brash ice that had floated in loose streams a day or two before now lay frozen together in rafts. Ribbons of forming grease ice made streaks of oily slickness across the water.

"Yeah," Bruce Carter said. "It's time we got out of here. I went out last night and saw that snow blowing horizontal. It's time."

Now it snowed in squalls, with sunlit mountains appearing and disappearing behind the veil. The sunlight was a delicate pale yellow on the ice. As the *Hero* turned past Bruce Island again, it passed close to a huge blue iceberg whose waterline was so eroded the whole berg seemed to float six inches above the sea. In the distance the icefalls around Paradise Harbor, appearing through a gauze of snow, seemed no more substantial than the mist. Far above us, up through towering clouds, a patch of deep blue sky appeared; it seemed so warm and distant it might have been a view of the Northern Hemisphere. On a shoreline was a dark smudge: Almirante Brown.

A blue-eyed shag flew across the bow.

"We've been the last ship in here for twelve years," the captain said. "And now we're the last ship to take the people out."

Above the ruins an icefall blazed in sunshine. The captain picked up the radio microphone. The men on shore still had a short-range portable.

"Brown, *Hero*," he said. "*Buenos tardes.*"

It was April 12. On the season's original schedule, the *Hero* was to have been at Almirante Brown Station on this day for a farewell barbecue.

(2)

The seven men stood on the shore. They wore orange survival suits. The captain went ashore. The men embraced him. They each had one duffel bag. They were all ready. There was no time to linger. The season was advancing. The gentle light of the evening was pretty, but it was not kind. White sheathbills, chickens of the south, migrating north away from the onrush of winter, pecked in the ashes. The doctor said something about the laboratory, smoke, explosion, and waking everyone. He climbed into the Zodiac, slipped, was helped to his seat. As Skip Owen untied the little rubber boat from the dock the Argentine meteorologist, whose name was Miguel Frutos, crossed himself, reached out with his gloved hand, and patted the new snow on the shore.

"Adios," he said quietly. "Otro año, Brown."

The withdrawal was quiet. No hard words were spoken. The men were welcomed without fuss aboard the *Hero*. All but the doctor, who was the chief of the station, gathered in a little knot on the starboard side as the ship turned to go. They took stealthy glances back as the ruins slipped away into the distance. Up the hill from the black pile of rubble, the Argentine flag still flew.

Darkness came swiftly. The captain climbed up to the icehouse above the bridge to guide the ship through the bergs. The doctor found his way to the bridge. For a long time he stood peering into the radar, watching the arm of light turn and turn, then he climbed into the captain's chair, where no one ever sat unless the captain was safely asleep, and sat staring out into the night.

It was a strange night. The blackness came quickly, and a three-quarter moon flashed in and out of the clouds like a searchlight on a mountain. The doctor and I were alone on the bridge. At first I did not want to talk to him about the fire; Wade Church had said earlier, "He seems pretty rattled." When the stars came out briefly, we talked about the Southern Cross and the False Southern Cross, and we stepped out in the wind for a moment to see them both. He had been in Antarctica often, and he talked about the cold and of having to amputate someone's fingers ten years before at the Argentine station Belgrano. He talked about the Rio Plata, where a sailboat awaited his return, and I had a sudden image of that lazy warm river, just breeze enough to fill the sails, and the sun.

But even of this the doctor spoke urgently, as if these things were precious secrets. His voice was high-pitched and hard, like the pluck of a stretching rope.

The wind blew fifteen knots and the *Hero* pitched. In the dark the RPM was down to 240 and the ship made three knots, wary of ice. The doctor sat back down in the captain's chair, folded his hands, and began to doze off. His coat smelled of smoke. In a few minutes he woke with a twitch and coughed.

"Is terrible in the fire," he said. "Smoke."

"Do you think it hurt your lungs?" I asked him.

"A little."

Then some of the story spilled out.

"At the moment I am working in radiology lab," he said. "X ray. X ray. Then one of the . . . Then the film burn. Quickly. Fire, fire, fire, fire."

The ship passed beneath a cloud that was edged in silver by the moon. Below, the off-duty crew and the rest of the Argentines watched *Jeremiah Johnson* on the video: Robert Redford stalking through snowy woods. Outside, snow began to fall heavily, and the huge flakes threw the glare of the ice light back in the face of the bridge. All that could be seen past it was the bloom of the whitecaps. The radar became the only eyes. The captain climbed down the ladder for a minute, saw the doctor sitting in his chair, paused only a half second, then went back up to the icehouse, saying nothing. Over the radio came the voices of the Brits at Faraday Base talking to the *Bransfield*, which was north of the Peninsula. At first the *Bransfield* couldn't raise the Faraday contact, then after a series of calls—"Faraday, *Bransfield*; Faraday, *Bransfield*"—a great booming British voice came shouting in across the miles of desolation.

"It's amazing," the voice said, "how when you pick up the right transmitter people respond to you."

The doctor was asleep. The sound of his snoring mingled with the rumble of the engines, with the rhythm of the sonar as the stylus burned the dampened paper, and with the sound of the fans on the windows up in the icehouse. The snowfall grew heavier; the ship pushed through a torrent of light. Then, while the snow continued, the moon emerged, a cold bright eye searching the sea for life.

In all this strange mingling of brightness and utter dark, the ship stirred five snow petrels up off a distant berg, and the white birds gathered around the light. They fluttered and swooped urgently at the mast, made crazy by the dazzle of the snow.

(3)

"We know now that . . . man is able to winter in even the most desolate corner of the earth and survive," wrote Ian Cameron, "but we can not even today be sure of the cost." Frederick Cook was the man who wrote so eloquently about his year on the *Belgica*; the man who was, his companion Roald Amundsen wrote, "the most popular man of the expedition." Yet later, most historians agree, Frederick Cook made a celebrated liar of himself when he said he was first to the North Pole. "How did the honourable and conscientious doctor of 1898 become the charlatan of 1908?" Cameron asked. Something, Cameron concluded, must have happened to him in Antarctica. "It is . . . possible that the strain, hardship, isolation and lack of sun that winter aboard the *Belgica* had a malign effect upon his personality."

The Argentine doctor wandered around Palmer wearing a big orange float coat that he had taken from the front lobby. He caught me at the top of the stairs. He leaned close. "I have film," he said. "I give you. I want four pictures. I lose everything in fire. I give you film. I need four pictures."

I looked at him. In the ship he had been exhausted. Now, the next day, he did not look any better. But he talked on and on.

"I am chief of station Almirante Brown," he said. "You understand. I have no money. I need four pictures." He leaned at me aggressively. Then he thought about the magazine I was working for, *Smithsonian*, which was based in Washington, D.C. "Ah, I studied in hospital in Alexandria. Washington is most beautiful city in the world." Then his face went hard again.

It was an angular, strong face. But it was as if it had lost something, as if the thread that held it together, a twist of sinew or nerve, had gone slack. He was driving his authority long after it had run out of fuel. He stood on the accelerator, changed gears, and went nowhere. He wore the big rubber float coat, with its black crotch flap dangling down behind, and his survival suit—and it was all too big for him. It hung on his body, all baggy and wrinkled, and made him look shrunken.

"Please, please," he said. "Please give me photograph of my station burned. I am chief—"

I escaped to the mess hall. Phil Colbert, Palmer's station leader, was washing dishes, carefully reusing water. Kelly, the U.S. Navy medic, the only military man here, said, "Now there's a man who knows how to conserve his water."

Phil looked up. He was like everyone else in Antarctica; his life had been unusual even before he got here.

"For the four years I lived in Nepal," he said, "I had to carry all my water three hundred feet up a hill to my house. I learned to be careful with every cup."

Kelly was hanging around to watch the doctor. "If I could just get some Thorazine in him," he said quietly to Phil, "it would unwind him."

The doctor began to unnerve the station. People started missing their toilet articles. More float coats disappeared from the lobby. The doctor was everywhere, down on the *Hero* demanding pressurized oxygen with which to give himself a penicillin mist for his lungs, over at a table with Monte Snyder, who was in charge of the Zodiacs, demanding that Monte draw him schematics on a piece of paper.

He could not stop. He caught Phil, a man of dark, compassionate eyes who was enormously conscientious, while Phil was mopping the stairs. "My men need something to do," the doctor said. "They need some work for these days. For psychological reasons. You understand. I am chief of the base Almirante Brown. They need some work."

The *Hero* was to take the doctor and his men to the Argentine base Jubany on the way to the Drake.

"Let's go on twenty-four-hour emergency and leave tomorrow," one of the crew members said. But that was not to be. "We will leave," the captain said, "promptly at eight A.M. on the morning of the fifteenth of April." That meant *promptly*; the captain had at least once left the chief scientist of a cruise behind on the dock when he was five minutes late. The scientist had to rush out to the departing *Hero* in a Zodiac.

No one would risk being late for this 8:00 A.M. departure, because the alternative was winter. Even the raging Drake held no fear like that. "I'd rather puke my guts out for six days than spend eight months here," said Stu Willason. He had been here all season. He was tired. He was worried, a short-timer in a war zone. Two days left. The house of cards had stood the season, but now the wind rose.

"We've got to get out of here," he said.

"Please, please," the doctor said. "Take photograph of me. Take photograph of my hands." He held them out. The blisters had popped. The burns were bright pink spots. "Take photograph of me here." He went over and stood at the wall at attention beside a coiled fire hose. "Please."

Early in the morning, before light, I went into the bathroom and there was the doctor, washing clothes in the sink. There was a tin of grease or shoe polish on the floor beside him. The washing must have hurt his burns terribly. He had roamed the halls until 2:00 A.M., and now here he was again. He pointed to his eyes. "The cornea," he said. "You understand." I did not. He scrubbed in the sink. "You give me photograph of my base burned, tomorrow, please. I am chief of the base Almirante Brown. I need for information. Please. I pay you."

"No!" I said. "No! I will *give* it to you."

The faint smell of smoke that the Argentines had brought to Palmer on their clothes remained in the air. He turned again to the sink. He washed. A cold wind rubbed against the window.

"Night is bad," the doctor said. "Because *dolor*, you understand."

(4)

In the morning Phil raided the doctor's room. He found a pile of float coats, several bottles of shampoo, shaving kits, and somebody else's foot powder. I worked in the Palmer darkroom and gave the doctor and all his crew photos of the disaster. But the doctor could not let up. Now he wanted more photos, of his hands, of his face. "I pay, I pay." Much later, when all the debris of his flight through our lives had been collected, a box was found, full of toilet articles, with dental floss wrapped around and around it. In the magazine rack of the *Hero* he left an old copy of *Time* magazine, on which he had written messages to someone: *"Dios." "Patria." "Hogar."* God. Country. Home. Inside the back cover were what seemed to be accusations: *"Yo no me rindo. Cap Lenie no me dio mata fuego. Pedi por favor."* I do not surrender. Captain Lenie did not give me fire extinguishers. I asked please.

I do not surrender. When the ship left him at Jubany Station, from which he would be airlifted home, he sat at the long table in that station while his compatriots watched him carefully, and wrote a long letter for the captain to take with him, pausing in his haste only to ask how to spell Monroe Doctrine and Eisenhower.

In the last days of the Palmer season, while the doctor rampaged, the scientists and crew watched movies. Up in the Penguin Bar at Palmer and on board the *Hero* the movie that everyone saw was *One Flew over the Cuckoo's Nest*. Over and over on the little screen Jack Nicholson was lobotomized and killed.

The last night at Palmer, Colbert and the captain talked outside Colbert's office. "I guess he had been going off the deep end for some time," Phil said. "They were talking about relieving him long before the fire."

The captain looked out in the hall, where the doctor was sitting surrounded by several of his men, who had plenty of work to keep them busy, taking care of him.

"It could happen just as easily to me," he said. "Just as easily to you."

Later, the oldest of the Argentines talked quietly to me in the lounge. "Bad for *el doctor*," he said. "We call it *loco antartida*."

Chapter Twenty-three

The Captain and the Hero

(1)

"It was weird comin' in," said Marky, the Hero's oiler. "And it's weird going out."

At 6:30 the morning of the departure the doctor met Bruce in the hallway at Palmer. The doctor gave him a small salute. "I'm ready," he said.

Like high school seniors on the last day of school, suddenly aware that a good part of life was ending, the people of Palmer played out the time. We had a running snowball fight for much of the last two days, and the little village of two buildings, which had been fragmented all year and lately was almost sullen with weariness, became young and one. After the snowfall the sun emerged, and when the work of departure slackened, Clamfoot lay on his back on a plank by the Hero, catching the last warmth of summer, chewing gum and blowing big pink bubbles. Out in the penguin rookery the little black-and-white shoots of life dwindled away as the penguins moved out toward the ice edge, where they would spend the winter; those that were left played at courting and building nests of stones, as if spring had already come.

In the dark of the morning the moon was full. People carried their last belongings to the Hero almost in silence, moving without haste in the cool light. Six men would remain, alone at the station from April 15 until December, passing weather reports, jokes, and chess moves up and down the chain of outposts on the Peninsula. They were ready for the summer tourists to leave. The continent was theirs.

Someone got out the box of cachets so the winter-overs could put "Palmer Station" on their last letters. In the box was a little yellow sheet of folded paper, unsigned. On it was written:

From me to you
Bright lights and promises
In the winter
Water colors

Without commotion, the *Hero* left Palmer Station. The moon cast a lingering silver light on the glacier. Behind it, day showed an arch of pale blue. The crewmen put up the sails. The moon sank and the sunrise turned yellow. The lights of Palmer went behind the rocks of Bonaparte Point and disappeared. Captain Lenie did not look back.

Just before midnight the night before, I had walked out between the two buildings at Palmer. The moon was big and bright. The sky was clear. The stars were dazzling. The glacier shone. The bay was full of brash ice, crackling. The brash ice moved, slipping out to sea. The bay looked like it bore living crystal. The air was sharp and cold. My eyes full of the beauty, I came back in and stuck my head in Phil's office. He was working on his season-end report.

"The moon—" I began.

He grinned. "I know."

"Antarctica— It stuns you."

"That's why I come back."

(2)

Antarctica was always farewells. Everything was too long until suddenly it was infinitely too short. This was the last ending of the season for the U.S. antarctic program, but the start of all these good-byes had been almost exactly two months before at the South Pole. Now, as the sun rose in a clear sky to bring a blush to the hills of ice and a brazen scarlet flame to the sails of the *Hero,* the last day at the Pole seemed to have been yesterday.

It was the morning of February 11. At Palmer the good-byes were informal, but South Pole was the center of the U.S. program, and the closing of the station, the partial abandonment of its nineteen winter residents, was a matter for ceremony. The sun was already low: there were only six weeks more of daylight, then six months of twilight and darkness. The little barber pole with the mirrored globe on top that represented the South Pole cast a long shadow. The snow was faintly golden. Strange thin clouds slipped along just above the horizon, like wolves.

In the mess hall under the huge shining dome of Amundsen-Scott South Pole Station, speeches were made by the visitors, who represented the importance the United States placed in this station built at the apex of all antarctic claims. The nineteen sat in the middle of the room; the people who were going to leave were already withdrawing from them, standing around the edge of the room. The winter-overs sat silently, patiently enduring this last formality, this last toast to their daring, to the tedious, dramatic thing they were beginning with such simplicity.

They had been restless for twenty-four hours. Most of them had been up most of the night, watching *Airplane II* and *Animal House* in the library or drinking in the bar. In the morning one had announced to me abruptly that he was going to quit smoking. "The store won't be open for four or five days, so I won't even be able to buy cigarettes." Another had talked to me about my children and then said, "Maybe it's time I settled down and did that." He thought over what he had said, then added, "Don't mind me, it's just this day." The station leader had talked to me about his departure from the United States months before: "I was thinking, Look, I'm going to be away a year. Don't blow up the world while I'm gone."

Now they were calm. The moment they had been anticipating for weeks had arrived. Soon they would begin the task. There were

a few short speeches, and the plane would leave, drawing a con-
trail arrow north, taking away summer.

In the crowded mess hall Ken Moulton of the National Science
Foundation told them that they were select indeed; they were
among just five hundred people, living and dead, to spend the
winter at the Pole.

"God bless you," Brian Shoemaker said. He wore a pair of
bunny boots that endorsed his nickname: on the toe of one was
written "Bigus" and on the other "Footus." He told the crew he
hoped to drop mail and fresh food to them from an air force jet
at the peak of winter. The airdrop was important, Shoemaker said
later, for the U.S. presence.

The engines of the LC-130 were running. The nineteen stood
together by the barber pole for photographs and popped the cork
off a bottle of champagne. Then they began to drift away, some
back to their science work—monitoring satellite data, reading
particulates in the air, recording particles from the sun, tracking
the echoes of a recent earthquake—others to various vantage points
to watch the plane leave. By the time they were relieved in
November they would know each other by the sound of their
footsteps, by the tick of their minds. "You're an open book by
the end of the year," a previous winter-over station manager had
said. The people here knew that it wasn't the bitter cold or the
long night that would test their courage; it was the thing that was
so hard for us all—just getting along.

The exhaust of a tracked vehicle made a cloud as we walked to
the plane. It was forty-three degrees below zero.

All the days I had spent at the Pole I had been dazzled by the
sunlight and dizzied by the thin air. I was drunk and happy. I
thought odd things. I daydreamed. I thought of experiments and
imagination. Here was the first modern continent, described by
science, settled without nationality, used without waste, governed
without borders. Antarctica was full of squabbles, but they all
stopped at the one point of agreement: the place was too precious

to waste with war. Antarctica allowed us to imagine the world at peace.

We got into the airplane. One of the winter residents came in and counted passengers, cursed us all cheerfully in farewell, then got out and went to stand alone by the aviation fuel pump. The crew chief closed the door. The plane began to get warm. We took off. The enclave below suddenly seemed tiny on the expanse of golden snow. The dome was no larger than the mirrored ball on the barber pole. We made one low pass and then departed straight into the sun, as if planning to take it away.

"Well, it's been a long day," said the copilot. "But we delivered the plywood." It was quiet up in the cockpit, ahead of the noise. I looked back at the heart of Antarctica. It blazed white.

(3)

The storm lay in wait over gray hills when the *Hero* made its final stop in Antarctica. Every year this was the point of departure: Henryk Arctowski Station on King George Island, operated by Poland. Here Pieter Lenie would at last say good-bye to his continent.

All night in the Bransfield Strait the weather had been so still it was eerie. The moon had risen clear, flooding the sea with silver, but as the night passed, clouds had drifted slowly across it, smothering the shadows but not the light. Still the sails flapped and the cold sea lay smooth. But at Arctowski the wind came, and up on the hills around Admiralty Bay plumes of snow blew off the ridges.

Stu Willason made one last attempt to ward off the demons of the Drake.

"When it blows like this in here," he said with authority, "that means it's calm outside."

Wade Church looked at him with a good imitation of a stinkeye.

"That," he said, "makes about as much sense as other things you've said."

"Aw," Stu said with a grin. "I'm trying, I'm trying."

"This is one of the best anchorages in the South Shetlands," the captain said. "I've been in here in eighty-knot winds."

As we approached the long yellow buildings of the station a figure came out and ran the Polish and U.S. flags up the flag-poles. The captain, in a bright orange survival suit, led a group ashore. We landed through a growing surf, among washed-up brash that looked like frozen foam. We took a brief tour—a look at the greenhouse, where tomatoes grew year-round under lamps, and at the generator room, where men with short black hair and beards worked and long underwear hung drying over the engines. Then we sat with the captain in the wood-paneled room while he talked to an old friend here, Ryszard. During the time of the Polish conflict over the Solidarity labor union, the country's antarctic base had been almost forgotten, and the *Hero* had brought food to Arctowski. It was a ship they would miss.

Poland, like the Soviet Union, did not maintain diplomatic relations with Chile, but during the summer the Chilean priest came to Arctowski regularly by helicopter. Polish mail traveled with him.

"Politik is politik," Ryszard said. "But with Marsh Base we have very good relation."

At the end of the room was a portrait of Henryk Arctowski, the geologist who had been on the *Belgica* with de Gerlache, Amundsen, and Frederick Cook that hard winter in the ice. Arctowski was the one who had rung the rocks with his Wagnerian hammer. Near the portrait Ryszard and the captain talked quietly about the Antarctic Treaty, that surprising document that set aside the common conflicts of nations because at the root something else was more important. What were its chances of surviving, even of passing to other places that understanding of the value of our earth? While the rest of us drank homemade cherry wine the two men, two polarmen, sat together at the far end of the warm room and murmured of uncertainty and hope.

The captain was disposed to stay and reminisce, but he did not. He gathered his little group and we bucked the surf back out to the *Hero*. As the anchor came up, Ryszard called from Arctowski on the radio; someone had left a green coat behind.

"Never mind, Ryszard," the captain said. "Next time." He paused. "Well, anyway, someone can use it there. Okay, Ryszard, good-bye. Hope to see you again."

"Anchor's up," said Wade.

Latitude 62°9′ south; longitude 58°27′ west. Distance to land-fall: 492 nautical miles. Lenie reached up and pulled a rope handle. The *Hero*'s whistle blew three times.

Lights began to show in the yellow buildings on the shore. Then the buildings faded away. Big flakes of snow blew past. The crew put up the sails. The Polish flag came down. Three miles out of Arctowski, while still in the protection of Admiralty Bay, the *Hero* picked up the swell. With his hands deep in the pockets of his red vest, Captain Lenie paced back and forth in the pilothouse as the darkness came.

"I'm so used to it now," he said at last. "It's like my own back-yard. It's hard to believe that I'll never see it again."

The *Hero* came out of the mouth of Admiralty Bay and turned northeast into the storm. The sky ahead was black. But far out in the distance a single iceberg caught the sun. It glowed against the dark. It was the only light in the world. Like all Antarctica, it was strange; it was beautiful.

Epilogue

On the night of the winter solstice in the Northern Hemisphere, a young moon lies low in the night sky. The sun shines on a crescent edge and makes the moon just a bright curving blade. But the rest of the moon is not entirely black. It glows, its shape round and luminous. Why is the shadow so bright tonight, when in other months only the crescent can be seen against the night? It is not the quality of the air here in this city, or extra light from the sun. It is a promise, like the rainbow, to those who have been to the last new continent, that they have not entirely lost the place to which they may never return. This season, the south of our planet is turned into the sun. The dark of the moon shines with the light of Antarctica.

Index